GIANT

UNDER T

GIANT UNDER THE HILL

A HISTORY OF THE
SPINDLETOP OIL DISCOVERY
AT BEAUMONT, TEXAS, IN 1901

Judith Walker Linsley,
Ellen Walker Rienstra &
Jo Ann Stiles

TEXAS STATE HISTORICAL ASSOCIATION
AUSTIN

DEDICATED TO

Trey
Ruth Ann
David
Joseph
Judy
Allen
Shannon
Bonnie
Zachery
Dylan
Ken
Sam
L.Q.
B.A.
T.
And to the memory of Dan

Copyright © 2002 by the Texas State Historical Association, Austin, Texas. All rights reserved. Printed in the U.S.A.
First paperback printing, 2008

Library of Congress Cataloging-in-Publication Data

Linsley, Judith Walker
    Giant under the hill: a history of the Spindletop oil discovery at Beaumont, Texas, in 1901/ Judith Walker Linsley, Ellen Walker Rienstra, Jo Ann Stiles.

    p.cm. --
    Includes bibliographical references and index.
    ISBN 0-87611-182-7 (alk. paper)
    1. Petroleum industry and trade--Texas--Beaumont--History--20th century. 2. Gushers--Texas--Beaumont--History--20th century. I. Rienstra, Ellen Walker. II. Stiles, Jo Ann. III. Title.

TN872.T4 S75 2002
338.4'7622382'09764145--dc21   2001053026

Published by the Texas State Historical Association in Cooperation with the Center for Studies in Texas History at the University of Texas at Austin.

Design by Janice Pinney.

The paper used in this book meets the minimum requirements of the American National Standard for Permanence of Paper for Printed Library Materials, Z39.48-1984.

CONTENTS

ACKNOWLEDGMENTS

As we worked on this book, which grew daily in scope, we were exceptionally fortunate to have received the cooperation, assistance, and moral support of many individuals—and institutions—who unstintingly shared with us whatever resources they had to offer.

Rosine McFaddin Wilson, the granddaughter of W. P. H. "Perry" Mc-Faddin, one of the major players in the Spindletop drama, provided a generous financial gift to assist in publication as well as proofing our manuscript and offering us much moral support. Texas oilman Michel T. Halbouty, one of the last of the legendary wildcatters and coauthor of the landmark 1952 *Spindletop*, the first history of the oil field, gave his blessing to this history by graciously consenting to write a preface.

Bradley Brooks, currently director of Lilly House Operations and Programs at the Indianapolis Museum of Art and former director of the Mc-Faddin-Ward House Museum in Beaumont, lent many hours of his time and his considerable skills in editing our manuscript. Current director Matthew White, Sherri Birdsong, and the staff of the McFaddin-Ward House expended many and varied efforts on our behalf, especially Arlene Troutman, who willingly spent hours scanning our photographs, and Sam Daleo, who captured on film many old images we would not have been able to reproduce otherwise. Ryan Smith, director of the Texas Energy Museum in Beaumont, gave us an invaluable overview of the oil industry and offered us much food for thought, as well as furnishing us with many needed materials, as did Christy Gladden, his assistant.

David Montgomery and the staff of Tyrrell Historical Library, especially Penny Clark and John Swearingen, spent many hours helping us. The staff of the Center for American History at the University of Texas at Austin was also very helpful with photographs and research material.

Jo Ann's special thanks go to Dr. John Storey and the History Department at Lamar University for their cooperation with time required for research, and to Christy Marino, director of the Spindletop/Gladys City Boomtown Museum, for inviting Jo Ann to become academic director of the museum, thus paving the way for access to new resources. She also extends her thanks to leaseholders on the Spindletop Dome, especially Charlie Wilson and Terry Radley, who, through the years, allowed her to wander through the still-existing oil field, acquiring a "feel" for the area that so changed the industrial world; to Bill Stell of Houston, who provided invaluable information about oil well drilling, always freely and gladly given; and to his wife, Fannie Stell, who didn't mind Jo Ann calling with more questions in the middle of the night. Jo Ann is especially grateful for having had the opportunity in the late 1980s to interview the late Ethel Alice Shockley Slausen, whose family moved to the Spindletop field a month after the discovery, when "Miss Alice" was six years old. She made Spindletop real.

The late Allen W. Hamill Jr., the son of Lucas Gusher driller Al Hamill, opened his home to us and, with the assistance of Jan Kelley, made available his priceless collection of family photographs, letters, and memorabilia before his death in October of 2001. The Hamill Foundation of Houston, founded by the Curt Hamill family, was also generous with time and advice, especially through Charles Read.

Several fellow historians offered us their expertise. Beaumont author Robert Robertson proofed our manuscript and gave us much-needed general encouragement. Midcounty historian William D. Quick gave us historical leads, no matter how obscure, usually from his own infallible memory. Stellar Texas oil chroniclers Roger and Diana Olien and Joseph Pratt all offered us encouraging words. Dr. Shane K. Bernard helped with explaining the Louisiana salt domes.

The large number of people who graciously gave us photographs are listed on the individual images in the book. Special thanks go to Drew and Jennifer Patterson of Austin, who offered unfailing encouragement along with photographs. Robert Schaadt, director of the Sam Houston Regional Library and Research Center in Liberty, sent early pictures of Sour Lake. The staff and volunteers of the Alma Carpenter Public Library and the Bertha Cornwell Museum at Sour Lake offered a rare picture of the first Savage Brothers well, drilled there in 1895. Kevin Gaglianella of Telecon Productions and Dale Willson at Community Bank cheerfully lent us their technical expertise. Francis E. Abernethy passed along photographs of the early field at Nacogdoches. Vice President William Ennis of the Texas Oil and Gas Association and his assistant, Kelli Thornton; Robert McDaniel, Pattillo Higgins's great-nephew and biographer; Joel Draut at the Houston Metropolitan Research Center; area historian Michael Cate; and the Rockefeller Archives all contributed invaluable photographs. Photographer Brian Sattler of Lamar University photographed the Lucas Gusher site, and us as we now exist. Assistance with maps came from Polly and Dorcy Watler.

Many allowed us to use family photographs, some never before published, from the early days of the boom. Special thanks go to Charlotte Yust, who volunteered her numerous photos of her grandmother and great-grandmother, who owned a boarding house on Spindletop Hill. John Galey and the late Margaret "Peggy" Galey, descendants of John Galey, the old wildcatter who helped to bring in the Lucas Gusher, offered many rare photographs and informational sources we would never have accessed otherwise.

We also owe thanks to Terry Rioux, author of a newly published biography of George W. Carroll, for handing on information from her own research; Charlotte Holliman, Special Collections Librarian at Lamar University and compiler of the Spindletop Bibliography, for her willing assistance with sources; attorney Dale Dowell, for his legal expertise, freely offered, in sorting out the Lucas-Higgins lease tangle; Beaumont wildcatter Pete Cokinos; J. Lanier Yeates, who facilitated our meeting with Allen Hamill; local surveyor Joe Breaux and the organization of surveyors who located the site of the original Lucas Gusher; Frank Bonura, who shared with us his grandfather's recollections of Spindletop and Anthony Lucas; Scott Blain, who volunteered his grandmother's memoir; Evelyn Hackedorn of Houston, who placed Curt Hamill memorabilia in the Texas Energy Museum; Dale Ashmore, for sharing his collection of Spindletop stock certificates; James Craig Gentry, Petro Hunt, and Centennial Oil project manager Joe Lucas, who believe there is still oil and gas underneath Spindletop Hill; Doris Phelps; Margaret Suggs Whitaker; Walter Sutton; Mary Dale Carper; Rexine and Hez Aubey; James Lutzweiler; National Public Radio's John Burnett and Wayne Bell; and the late Edna Wherry Myers. If we have inadvertently omitted anyone, we nevertheless extend to them our lasting gratitude for all the assistance we have received.

Many friends helped with knowledge, logistics, and moral support, among them B. A. Coe, L. Q. Jones, and Thilo Steinschulte. Our children, David "Trey" and Ruth Ann Stiles, Judy and Allen Rienstra, Shannon and Bonnie Wilson, and Ken and Sam Linsley, endured our preoccupation and endless pronouncements that "we'll be finished by the end of the month."

And finally, our profound thanks go to our editors, George Ward and Janice Pinney, for their skill and, above all, their patience; and to Suzy Wilson, wherever she may be, whose long-ago middle-school project for Texas History Day furnished more primary information than any we historians had yet unearthed, and who taught us a thing or two about Spindletop.

The Authors

PREFACE

NUMEROUS articles and books on Spindletop have already been written, and I presume in the coming years there will be many more on that famous discovery which revolutionized industrialization and the standard of living worldwide. *Giant Under the Hill* is a history of the discovery told with inspiration and entrancement. Actually, the book is one big interesting story—built upon one story after another—a creative style that tells the complete tale of how and why Spindletop took place. The events leading to, during, and after the "gusher" are extraordinary and will keep the reader glued to the pages. The descriptions of the main principals of Spindletop are very human and warm. By the end of the book, the names of Pattillo Higgins, Anthony Lucas, and the Hamill brothers seem so familiar to you that you feel as if they are your next-door neighbors. The boom and the pandemonium that followed the discovery offer a perfect example of the disruption that can, overnight, change a small, tranquil community into a mercurial and unpredictable one.

There are many anecdotes that will put a smile on the reader's face. I compliment the authors for the manner in which much of the narrative reads like a novel, although the incidents are factual. This book should be considered as one of the best on the subject. It contains many heretofore unknown (or I might say previously unwritten) incidents not contained in prior publications—including *Spindletop*, written with my late friend, James A. Clark.

The last chapter is really an epilogue, and it alone is worth having the book. It not only reveals what happened to all involved, but how the event affected the community, the various industries, and the future of the area.

After reading *Giant Under the Hill*, I found myself reminiscing about the effect this one event, in the southeast corner of the state of Texas, in the dawn of a new century, has had on the world for the past one hundred years and will continue to have for long into the future. It represents the spirit of adventure and the determination to adhere to one's conviction, as Pattillo Higgins did—all so ably told in *Giant Under the Hill*, a truly warm chronicle of an event that will never be forgotten, and the like of which will never happen again.

Michel T. Halbouty
Houston, Texas

PROLOGUE

ON January 10, 1901, around 10:30 A.M. on a clearing wintry day near the small Southeast Texas town of Beaumont, the course of history veered sharply in a new direction.

Beneath the low hill just south of town, where a small wooden derrick housed the ongoing drilling operation of a single wildcat oil well, the ground began to shudder. Then, with an ear-shattering roar, the earth began to spew uncounted tons of mud, gas, rocks, and finally a towering column of heavy green crude oil, six inches around, erupting almost two hundred feet into the air.

The roaring geyser of oil hurled pipe skyward and scattered it over the prairie like discarded straws. It blasted away the crown block of the home-made derrick, knocked off the superstructure, and sent the terrified crew scrambling for safety before it blazoned the Southeast Texas sky with a soaring banner of oil. With the advent of this well—the Lucas Gusher, named for Captain Anthony F. Lucas, the Austrian mining engineer who brought it in—the Spindletop oil field was born.

For a time, euphoric madness reigned. Word of the gusher spread like a prairie fire, and by that evening, the world knew. Overnight, Beaumont became a boomtown. Oil men, sightseers, speculators, promoters, and charlatans of every stamp rushed into town to try their fortunes in oil. Every incoming train brought new throngs, some on standing-room-only flatcars. Hotels and private rooms overflowed, and even barber's chairs and seats in hotel lobbies were rented for months in advance. In a quantum leap, the town's population jumped from nine thousand to over fifty thousand. Fortunes were made and lost within hours, and tracts of land, some large, some minute, were often sold several times in one day, the price doubling with each sale.

For nine days the Lucas Gusher raged unchecked, spouting an estimated one hundred thousand barrels of oil a day before its drillers finally invented a valve assembly, the precursor of the modern "Christmas tree," to cap it. Then it rapidly descended from the realm of heroics into that of everyday mechanics. After it was caged, it never produced enough to pay for itself.[1] It was soon eclipsed by even bigger gushers in the same field, and its actual physical site was almost lost in the welter of wells that followed.

The oil boom engendered by the gusher came to an early end; production in the field peaked by 1903 and declined steadily thereafter. Wildcatters, speculators, fortune seekers, promoters, and young companies left for new locales and greener pastures, which were legion. But that moment in January 1901, when the colossal pressures from deep within the hill finally broke through the last few inches of caprock to unleash that roaring column of oil—that moment marked a watershed. The giant under the hill had awakened, and the world would never be the same again.

The actual event of the Lucas Gusher, divested of all panoply and accrued legend, stands stark, for good or ill, against the dawn of the twentieth century with that other Texan phenomenon of nature, the Great Galveston Storm of September 1900, whose hundred-mile-an-hour winds and gargantuan storm tides had leveled the island and taken over six thousand lives barely four months before.

But the Lucas Gusher boasts the singular characteristic of having been brought about by human ingenuity. The well was given life by a fortuitous conjunction of the right physical circumstances and the right cadre of personalities, as fine a crop of authentic American heroes as can be found anywhere: Pattillo Higgins, the catalyst, with his tenacious dreams. George W. Carroll, with his faith. George W. O'Brien, with his breadth of awareness and his capacious mind. John Galey, with his uncanny nose for oil. Al and Curt Hamill, with their everyday inventiveness and their determination. Anthony Lucas, with his knowledge, his capabilities, and his iron substantiality. Lacking any one of these men and their particular talents, the gusher surely would not have been brought in, at least not in that manner, at that time.

But the town of Beaumont—and the rest of the world—were as ill prepared for the gusher as if it had occurred without human assistance. In its immediate aftermath, there was no existing way even to cap the well, let alone store, transport, or market oil in that unimagined quantity. As for predicting any long-term implications of the discovery, no one on the face of the earth possessed that kind of vision. Such events can only be measured in retrospect.

What was so important about the Lucas Gusher itself, which, in those nine days it ran amok, spilled most of its almost million-barrel output onto the Southeast Texas prairie, to be burned in oil fires, borne in waterways toward the Gulf or simply reabsorbed into the earth, because no one knew what to do with it? What was so important about the Spindletop field, which dwindled into a pumper field less than three years later and whose gushers were soon outperformed by every neighboring oil field, and even by the old hill itself, when the second Spindletop field was brought in on its flanks in 1925?

Oil had, after all, already been found in Europe and Asia, notably in Russia, at the great Caucasian field at Baku. It had been found in this country, in Titusville, Pennsylvania, among other places, and even in Texas, in Corsicana. But it was the Lucas Gusher at Spindletop that produced twice as much oil *per day* as all the wells in Pennsylvania. What was more, the first six gushers in the Spindletop field produced more oil per day than all the rest of the fields in the world put together. The volume of oil found at Spindletop took the leadership in world production from Russia and gave it to America.

Therein lies the crux. It was the *sheer volume—the unexpected quantity—*of oil at Spindletop that forced human ingenuity to devise new ways and means to utilize it. After that watershed moment when the gusher blew in and oil began spewing high into the air, christening the prairie, pooling in ditches and bayous and hastily scraped-together earthen levees, staining the paintings on the wall in Mrs. Carroll's parlor or igniting into life-threatening infernos, there was nothing to do but use it. And from that point on, the only limit was human vision.

The implications—and the consequences—were global. Even though the American oil industry was already firmly established with existing production under the control of the Standard Oil Company, the field's immense size nevertheless drastically dropped the value of oil worldwide. New uses had to be found for the product.

Within a year, Spindletop oil was being shipped all over the world, as industry came to see the economic feasibility of converting coal-burning furnaces from solid to liquid fuel.[2] Train engines came first, then steamship engines, then much of the rest of the industry. And as the old show business saying goes, timing is everything; even as Edison's 1879 invention of the light bulb sounded the death knell of the late "new light," kerosene, more new markets were emerging for petroleum.[3]

One in particular. The infant automobile industry, waiting like a bride on the threshold of the new century, was claimed by the new internal-combustion engine. Its fuel of choice became the formerly unwanted by-product of the kerosene refining process: gasoline. The alternative sources, steam and electricity, were left in the dust. In 1900, there had been only eight thousand automobiles registered in the United States; by 1912, there were 902,000, the vast majority gasoline-powered.[4]

Another milestone loomed on the front edge of the new century. On December 17, 1903, in Kitty Hawk, North Carolina, with the first flight of a heavier-than-air, engine-powered craft, Wilbur and Orville Wright gave the world a brand-new industry that depended absolutely on petroleum products. In the words of wise old John Galey, whose luck (or was it a wildcatter's intuition?) had guided the stake that marked the Lucas Gusher's location, Spindletop signaled the birth of the liquid-fuel age.

All these changes spawned the potential for power—economic, political, social, military—on a global scale. Perhaps the first indication of the enormity of that power became apparent in 1911, only a decade after Spindletop, when, in the face of Imperial Germany's bid for world dominance, young British Home Secretary Winston Churchill committed Britain to converting the British Navy to the use of oil-based fuel. The impetus was plentiful Texas oil. And this was only the beginning. As contemporary oil historian Daniel Yergin has observed, oil has meant mastery throughout the twentieth century.[5]

And it was Spindletop that linked dream to reality. As James Clark, one of the chroniclers of the hill, observed, when Spindletop led the world to imagine that it had an unlimited supply of oil readily at hand, the world became a different place.

This effort is neither intended to perpetuate myth nor to catalogue exhaustive—and exhausting—lists of facts. The truth, as always, lies somewhere in between. It is instead an effort to place the Spindletop phenomenon solidly in its rightful spot in the history of the industry, to frame it in a centennial perspective, and to retell its story in the words of all the extraordinary human beings who lived it and brought it about.

After all is said and done, there remains the ongoing and yet ever-new drama of the interaction between the earth and its inhabitants. Perhaps therein lies the real story—and the historic significance—of Spindletop.

Chapter One

THE EARLY SEEKERS

"The greatest excitement of this age is oil—petroleum, as it is termed. . . .
This region of Texas will be wild upon the subject within a few months . . ."
—A. B. Trowell to George W. O'Brien, September 5, 1865[1]

IT all began with Titusville. *Or did it?*

In the spring of 1859, a retired railroad conductor named Edwin Drake drilled for oil near Titusville, Pennsylvania, with a wooden rig and steam-powered equipment. The following August, he struck an oil sand at sixty-nine and a half feet. The well, which produced a maximum of thirty-five barrels a day, launched large-scale exploration in the eastern United States. It is generally cited as the event that inaugurated the modern oil industry.[2]

But Titusville was far from mankind's first encounter with petroleum. For many centuries, isolated whispers of oil had echoed down the years until, in the last four decades of the nineteenth century, the voices joined to become a clamor, leading to a concerted search for oil—and ultimately, in the first few days of the twentieth century, to Spindletop.

Awareness of petroleum as a valuable substance is nearly as old as the beginning of civilization itself. In the ancient Mesopotamian city of Ur, dating to 3,000 B.C., asphalt was used as a building material. Greek and Roman writings abound with references to petroleum, asphalt, and natural gas. In the eighth century, the Byzantine Empire used the terrifying incendiary weapon of Greek fire, a petroleum-based compound, as a defense. Around the ninth century, the great oil and gas seeps and hand-dug wells at Baku, in Russia on the Caspian sea, were first commercially exploited, with the first record of oil export from Baku occurring in the tenth century.[3]

Hundreds of oil springs, gas seepages, and asphalt deposits existed throughout Europe, and the daily use of oil, primarily as medicine, was a matter of record from the Middle Ages. Primitive refining techniques came from the Arab lands, and in the nineteenth century, a small oil industry began to develop in parts of modern-day Poland, Austria, Russia, and Rumania, where oil was scooped from hand-dug shafts.[4]

In the New World, Native Americans, Spanish and French explorers, and Anglo-American immigrants alike caulked their boats, greased their axles, and doctored their wounds and diseases with oil from the territory's myriad springs and seeps. America's transplanted inhabitants brought with them knowledge of the commercial value of petroleum. They brought with them something else: the seeds of an ideology that would become synonymous with the American psyche—enterprise. Inquisitive, energetic, opportunistic— these Anglo-Americans were only too eager to exploit natural resources, and anything else that came to hand. By the 1830s, petroleum was being bottled and sold as patent medicine, a cure for everything ailing two-footed and four-footed creatures alike, from digestive troubles and rheumatism to worms.[5]

When, according to their natures, they pushed the boundaries of their horizons, some would come to Texas, whose name would become synonymous with the phrase "big oil" because of what they would find there in years to come.

Oil in Texas was first mentioned four centuries ago. In the wake of Columbus's discovery, as rumors of golden cities and other fabulous riches rang throughout the courts of Europe, the great sixteenth-century sea power of Spain began sending expedition after expedition in search of New World gold. In 1539, an expedition commanded by a hard-bitten Spanish conquistador named Hernando de Soto landed at Tampa Bay. Accompanied by six hundred men and armed with a mandate from Holy Roman Emperor Charles V, De Soto was charged with discovering riches, souls in need of conversion, and an overland route to Mexico.

The explorers traveled through much of the southeastern part of the future United States. When De Soto died of a fever en route, leadership of the expedition passed to a pleasure-loving native of Badajoz named Luis de Moscoso de Alvarado.[6]

Under Moscoso, the explorers penetrated westward into the eastern part of what would later become the state of Texas before the indolent commander, "who longed to be again where he could get his full measure of sleep, rather than govern and go conquering a country so beset for him with hardships," gave the order to retrace the route. When the expedition reached the Mississippi, they constructed makeshift caravels from native timber, intending to sail southwestward along the Gulf Coast until they reached New Spain.[7]

Some days out, the explorers encountered a storm, and the boats began to leak badly. Battling high winds and crashing surf, the men, "with the Creed upon their lips," kept the ships afloat as best they could. After the storm had spent itself, a party of the exhausted, mosquito-ravaged Spaniards went ashore for food. There, they found an unexpected answer to their prayers:

> . . . slabs of black bitumen almost like pitch, which the sea washed up among its refuse. It might have come from some fountain of that liquid that entered the sea or had its origin in it. The slabs weighed eight, ten, twelve, or fourteen pounds, and there were large numbers of them. . . .

They described the bitumen as "a scum the sea casts up, called copee, which is like pitch and is used instead on shipping where that is not to be had. . . ." Thanking *el Buen Dios* for the black, viscous stuff, they "payed [*sic*] the bottoms of their vessels with it," and the starved, filthy, half-clothed remnant of the De Soto-Moscoso expedition eventually straggled to the safety of New Spain.[8]

Historians have speculated that the explorers made landfall on the upper Southeast Texas coast somewhere between present-day High Island and Sabine Pass, because this "copee" was probably the residue of a peculiar natural phenomenon of the region: a large oil seepage from the ocean floor, lying just off the shore near the mouth of the Sabine River. The crude petroleum was washed ashore by the Gulf tides, and after the volatile elements had evaporated, it formed the slabs of bitumen that Moscoso's men had found—a natural asphalt-paraffin compound later dubbed "sea wax."[9]

This mysterious seepage boasted another attribute. Before the petroleum washed ashore, it formed a large pool on top of the water, which remained calm there even in the worst weather. In later centuries, ships took refuge in the pool, a bona fide testament to the biblical adage of oil's ability to calm troubled waters.

The Spanish empire eventually discovered that there was no ready gold to be had in the Gulf Coast lands and gradually lost interest in the area. However, from time to time the Spanish availed themselves of the region's manifestations of oil. Around 1790, the small company of Spanish militia near Nacogdoches, commanded by one Antonio Gil Ybarbo, collected oil from the surface of the local petroleum springs to use for medicine, and travelers along

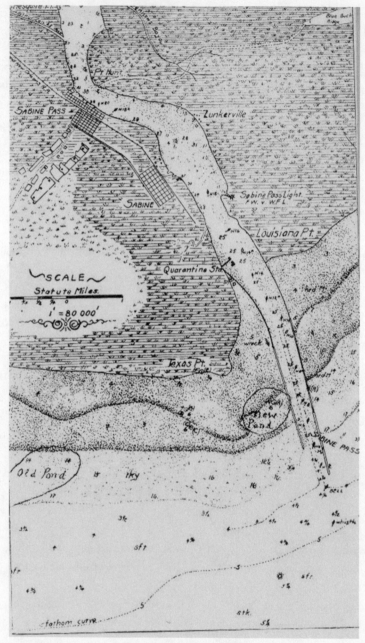

Sketch by William Battle Phillips showing location of ancient offshore oil seep, labeled "Old Pond." The "New Pond" was caused by overflow from the Spindletop oil field. *From William Battle Phillips*, Texas Petroleum *(1901); courtesy Mary and John Gray Library, Lamar University, Beaumont.*

El Camino Real used it for axle grease. Another Nacogdoches settler, a woman, heated a bucket of natural petroleum at her fireplace before dumping it on an unwelcome visitor: an Indian trying to break into her house.[10]

In 1821, in the twilight of Spanish naval dominance, a bloodless revolution established Mexico's independence, and Anglo-American settlers swept westward across the Sabine and Red Rivers into Mexican Texas like a strong, fresh wind. These new "Texians," as they became known, rapidly colonized the piney woods and coastal plains of eastern Texas.

Here they discovered something already known to the Native Americans. The woods and shorelands along the upper coast of the Gulf of Mexico were dotted with peculiar geological formations, mounds only a few feet higher than sea level but readily discernible as they rose abruptly above the surrounding prairies and marshes. These low hills were often flanked by clusters of varicolored and –flavored mineral springs and crude petroleum seepages similar to those that stood as the signs of oil in other parts of the world.[11]

The settlers were quick to avail themselves of the newly discovered resources. They drank and bathed in the mineral waters to cure a variety of ailments from skin rashes to rheumatism and intestinal complaints, dipped their animals to cure mange and repel fleas, and greased their wagon axles with the petroleum they collected from the seeps.[12]

Necessities, and the distances over which goods had to be transported, begat inventiveness. Given the growing interest in oil in the young republic to the north, commerce in petroleum was a foregone conclusion for an increasing number of American Texans whose opportunism was equalled only by their free-ranging curiosity.

One of the first of these to grace the Southeast Texas scene was transplanted Kentuckian John Allen Veatch, a soldier of fortune, physician, teacher, and surveyor by profession and a spare-time botanist, mineralogist, and geologist. A man of restless inquisitiveness and a wide spectrum of abilities, he sought to turn everything he saw to good account, including the distinctive geological features of East Texas. In 1833 Veatch moved with his wife and two children to Mexican Texas, settling in Bevil (later Jasper), where he surveyed for the Mexican government located at Nacogdoches and under the auspices of the local *empresario*, Lorenzo de Zavala.

The two land grants Veatch received as a Mexican colonist were both issued in 1835. The first, situated "in the prairie southeast of the ravine of Tevis" (Tevis Bluff, the early Neches River settlement that later became Beaumont), encompassed one of those geological anomalies common to the

Sour Lake Springs Bathhouses and Lake, circa 1877. *Courtesy Ray D. Edmonson Collection,*
Sam Houston Regional Library and Research Center, Liberty, Texas.

region, a low, sharply rounded hill twenty-six feet in elevation and about a
mile in diameter, protruding prominently from the surrounding flatlands.
The homesteaders had begun to call it Big Hill, or Sour Spring Mound, because of the five mineral springs located on its southeastern flank. Natural gas
bubbled up through the waters in a sulphurous rush, and in many places
seeped up through the earth itself.

The second of Veatch's two land grants covered a tiny portion of the Big
Thicket of East Texas, a three-million-acre tract of almost solid vegetation
that stretched in a huge southeast-to-northwest half-moon across the terrain
just north of Tevis Bluff. For centuries called Big Woods by the Native Americans, the Thicket harbored numerous oil seepages and mineral springs within its trackless green expanses, including two that would become well known
as health spas, near the present-day towns of Sour Lake and Saratoga.
Veatch's grant lay adjacent to the old Indian gathering place of Medicine
Lake, which would soon become the spa of Sour Lake.[13]

The specific nature of the value Veatch saw in those seeps and mineral
springs will probably always remain a mystery. But it is a matter of record
that, in conversations with his fellow soldiers during the Mexican War, he

indicated that he *deliberately* chose the tracts of land that contained the mineral springs. He declared that he

> had not investigated sufficiently to be able to decide as to the origin of the properties of the waters there—nor why oil rose and floated on them and . . . formed pools on the ground—nor as to what generated the gas which was continually escaping from the ground and through the water—but that [he] believed some mineral was the cause and underlaid the ground—and could be found by digging deep enough.

He went on to predict that Sour Lake would become an important health resort, and that his property would increase in value.[14]

As it happened, Veatch was right, in ways he could never have imagined. But he himself would not see the gain. After serving as a surgeon in the Mexican War, he succumbed to the siren call of California gold, where he distinguished himself by discovering the borax deposits in Lake County and by being divorced by his Texas wife on the grounds of "continued abandonment." His restless, inquisitive disposition finally drove him to Oregon, where he married a third time and taught "chemistry, toxicology, and *materia medica*" at the Willamette University Medical School at Portland until his death in 1870.[15]

Two decades after Veatch's pointedly expressed interest in Sour Lake, the site's oil signs were attracting new attention. Mention of mineral springs with their accompanying petroleum and natural gas seeps began showing up in contemporary Texas accounts with increasing frequency. Landscape architect Frederick Law Olmsted, an early Texas traveler, wrote in 1854 of "a fountain of lemonade" at the Sour Lake mineral springs in the Veatch survey, which had opened three years previously as a full-fledged, locally famous health spa. Olmsted described cool acid springs that boiled with an "inflammable gas" and gave out a slight odor of "sulpheretted hydrogen." He added that the surrounding marsh gave off a "strong bituminous odor, upon pools in which rises a dense brown, transparent liquid, described as having the properties of the Persian and Italian naphthas."[16]

Four years later, the state geologist of Texas, Dr. B. F. Shumard, stated in his report to the legislature that he believed Sour Lake in Hardin County to be the "most important locality [in the state] for the source of petroleum." He went on to write that a considerable quantity of oil could be collected from the surfaces of the springs, and that "the earth for some distance around these springs is also so highly charged with bitumen as to be employed for purposes of illumination and to some extent as fuel." Texas's awareness of petroleum's commercial potential was growing.[17]

Concurrently, in the rest of the country, the expanding industries and the exploding population were engendering two urgent new needs. The first was for a more efficient lubricant. With the increasing number of factories using high-friction, power-driven machinery, the traditional lubricant, lard, was no longer adequate.[18]

The other need was for more hours of light. A larger fuel supply would allow industry to operate twenty-four hours a day. But the abrupt decline in the whale population at the hands of East Coast whalers had actually created a scarcity of whale oil, the primary illuminant of the first half of the century.[19]

A variety of other illuminants derived from coal, generically called "coal oils," were available, but some were too expensive, some too explosive. None was ideal. Neither were the natural and artificial gas systems operating in some parts of the East. In the 1850s, a Canadian doctor-turned-geologist named Abraham Gesner finally developed a petroleum distillation process to produce a new illuminating oil he named "kerosene," from the Greek words for "wax" and "oil." It was cheaper, safer, cleaner to burn, and easier to transport than the existing illuminants. All that was needed was a more plentiful source of the raw material.[20]

In 1859 a New York lawyer named George Bissell determined to find one. Noting oil's annoying propensity to show up in fresh-water and salt drilling operations, Bissell, in a stroke of pure genius, conceived the idea of *drilling* for it instead of using the existing methods of harvesting it from surface seeps or digging for it by hand. He and a group of fellow investors then backed a drilling operation in northwestern Pennsylvania on land containing a small stream called Oil Creek, after the oil springs that bubbled up from the surrounding terrain. On August 27, 1859, their hired driller, Edwin Drake, struck oil.[21]

The Drake discovery well opened up a brand new horizon. With the technology of drilling, the world would have its ready supply of oil. Wells, then refineries, sprang up like new shoots after rain, and many of the coal-oil distilleries began converting to petroleum-refining capabilities. The Drake well created what was probably the first oil boom in the industry's history, sending land prices soaring and would-be oil men scrambling for leases.[22]

The national and the international market potential loomed limitless, and in 1861, the first shipment of oil left American shores for Europe. As his-

"Our Camp at Spindletop," 1862 sketch by a Confederate soldier of Spaight's Eleventh Battalion (Hood's Brigade), while camped at Spindletop Springs. Barely a mile due west lay Sour Spring Mound, the site of the landmark discovery that would assume the old tree's name. *Courtesy Sam Houston Regional Library and Research Center, Liberty, Texas.*

torian Daniel Yergin has noted, "Virtually from the beginning, petroleum was an international business." By 1865 American production showed a total of two and a half million barrels, most of it produced in Pennsylvania. Oil's time was coming.[23]

Back in Texas, during the Civil War, Confederate soldiers of Spaight's Eleventh Battalion camped near a place called Spindle Top, about four miles south of the small frontier town of Beaumont, near the west bank of the Neches River. The name, written in the old Spanish land grants as *cimas de boneteros* (literally translated as "tops of spindle-trees"), had originally referred to a tall cypress tree, shaped like a spindle, that had stood near the river, towering over the surrounding "island" of trees. Visible for miles in the flat terrain south of Beaumont, it had provided a landmark for early Neches River boatmen. Near the Spindle Top tree, close by the river marshes, flowed springs of sweet, clear water, which took the name of the old cypress to become Spindle Top Springs.[24]

Just west of Spindle Top Springs, less than a mile away, rose the sharply rounded knob of Sour Spring Mound, an eerie landmark in the middle of the flat Southeast Texas prairie. The knoll's crest, a barren "alkali scald" adorned only with patches of marsh grass and scattered pepperweeds, protruded prominently from the surrounding terrain, scoured by the prevailing Gulf winds. Whispers of old ghost stories now hung about the place, and horsemen sometimes saw balls of light hovering near the spot where, a half-century later, Anthony Lucas would drill for oil.[25]

The mound's mineral springs, sometimes known as Ingalls Springs after local farmer James Ingalls, then owner of the property, were already something of a local curiosity. A visiting reporter from the *Galveston Daily News* would observe that there were five or six wells, all deep, each with a different kind of water. The milky water of one well, he declared, was

> in a constant state of tumultuous ebullition, and so sour it puts the teeth on edge. It smells of gunpowder and the infernal regions, but it is very cool and pleasant to the mouth, and makes a fellow belch most furiously. . . . What the thunder gives it its exceedingly sour taste is more than I know, but they say it is sulphuric acid.[26]

Another spring tasted "like a pleasant drink of citric acid." Another was called the "Copperas Well," still another the "Iron Well." "The ebullition," the reporter continued, "is . . . the rushing forth of strong currents of gas from below." Prophetically, he noted also that

> if you will stick a hollow tube two or three feet into the ground and then apply a match to it, you will have a brilliant gas light. . . . Even the earth around these wells is very sour. You can put a tablespoon of it in a goblet of water and make good lemonade.[27]

(At least one attempt would be made to capitalize on the springs. In 1873, Beaumont merchant Mark Wiess would advertise that the "Celebrated Sour Springs near Beaumont, Texas," provided a cure for "dyspepsia, chronic diarrhoea, loss of appetite, general debility, and all cutaneous and eruptive diseases. . . ." and that they could be purchased through his sole agency. The water was put up in barrels, half-barrels, and ten-gallon kegs.[28])

The Confederate camp at Spindle Top, a collection of hastily erected tents and lean-tos, was used as a hospital during the yellow fever epidemic of 1862, when the mineral waters from the springs on Sour Spring Mound were administered to fever victims. Those patients who died were buried in unmarked graves on the top of the mound.[29]

One of the Confederate soldiers camping at Spindle Top was a young Beaumont lawyer named George Washington O'Brien, who had received his law license a bare three months before enlisting in the Confederate Army. O'Brien had opposed Texas's secession, but when the vote in early 1861 overwhelmingly favored it, he felt it his duty to support the decision.[30]

During his stint in the Confederate Army, O'Brien attained the rank of captain and the command of Company E of Likens's Battalion, Texas Volunteers, later part of Spaight's Battalion. Captain O'Brien's company trained in Beaumont and camped at Spindle Top, where he reportedly took interest in the unusual properties of Sour Springs Mound—an interest that would prove crucial to the development of subsequent events.[31]

With the cease-fire at Appomattox in 1865, the country embarked on a new era of explosive economic growth. Back East, there appeared an individual who would become the archetypal nineteenth-century robber baron, one who, "More than anyone else . . . incarnated the capitalist revolution that followed the Civil War and transformed American life." His character was a dichotomy: Baptist piety paired with ruthlessness, his genius for long-term vision coupled with a relentless thoroughness that focused fanatic attention on the smallest detail of his growing empire. His name was John D. Rockefeller.[32]

Always looking for new opportunities, Rockefeller created the Standard Oil Company in 1870, his goal being to control the infant oil industry. By 1879, he had achieved it. Standard Oil controlled 90 percent of the country's refining capacity. His long shadow would fall across the industry's farthest reaches for years to come.[33]

As Rockefeller consolidated his hold on Eastern oil, the search in Texas resumed in earnest. In September of 1865, after George W. O'Brien had returned to civilian life and resumed his Beaumont law practice, he received a letter. It was from one A. B. Trowell, a young attorney from the neighboring town of Liberty who had served with O'Brien in the Confederate Army. His letter proved that full awareness of the economic potential of oil had indeed penetrated the wilds of Texas. Trowell wrote that

> I heard . . . [somebody] . . . say that there was some *Sour* Springs . . .
> on the Ingalls tract. . . . Buy all the land in Jefferson County that
> has Sour Lake water or Sour Lake tar on it. If Ingalls' tract is worth
> one thousand dollars give two or three thousand. . . . The price you
> give makes no difference, provided . . . that you take a Bond of title
> to be made to you and me. . . . If you manage this thing judiciously

and get the Ingall[s] Springs, on the terms indicated, there is a larger sum of gold dollars in it for us, than we have seen or heard of in
our whole lives . . . must not breathe the subject of this letter to any
. . . being. . . . The greatest excitement of this age is *oil*—petroleum,
as it is termed. . . . This region of Texas will be wild upon the subject
within a few months. . . . It don't matter to us whether there is a
drop of oil, within a thousand miles of the Ingall[s] Springs, we will
make our fortune by selling before that fact is ascertained. . . .

Trowell added that he saw no use in "toiling and struggling with aching
brains and weary bones for bread when *gold* so temptingly invites you to reach
out and clutch it . . ." He further observed that he did "like occasionally during these hardtimes [*sic*] to trust my imagination to a few *millions in coin* . . ."[34]

Trowell's letter did something else. It bolstered the notion of the local
availability of oil in O'Brien's already receptive mind.

In the Big Thicket, lying just to the north of Beaumont, two settlers,
William Hart and J. F. Cotton, conceived the idea of searching for oil when
Thicket Indians offered to reveal the whereabouts of the petroleum seep at
Saratoga—for fifty dollars. Hart and Cotton refused to pay, but found the
seep by accident when their hogs, running loose in the woods, came home
sporting large brownish black smudges of oil on their hides.[35] In 1865, they
entered into a partnership to explore the seep and to "[obtain] Petroleum
by boring wells or otherwise. . . ." "Boring" a test well with a primitive rig
constructed of poles bound together to form a derrick, they found both gas
and oil in small quantities, but the equipment was too inefficient to bore
deeper.[36]

Nathan Gilbert, a newcomer to Jefferson County who served as the Confederate cotton agent at Sabine Pass during the Civil War, pursued oil interests in Southeast Texas as early as 1865. In that year, he made a twenty-year
lease of lands at Sour Lake in favor of "Nathan Gilbert agent and attorney for
G. W. Cochran of Jefferson County . . . for the purpose of boring, pumping,
excavating and otherwise working for oil or other mineral deposits in said
land . . ."[37] On October 6, 1865, Gilbert wrote from Beaumont to a fellow
businessman in Illinois, reporting that he had reached Beaumont and had
found "much excitement among speculators on the subject of petroleum."[38]

The next year, Confederate war hero Dick Dowling, a young Irish saloon
owner from Houston who in 1863 had led a successful defense of Sabine Pass
against Federal gunboats, leased land in the counties of Liberty, Hardin, Jef-

ferson, and Angelina to "commence exploring for oil salt water or minerals, on said premises by mining digging or drilling there on within two years. . . ." Dowling headquartered his oil company in his Bank of Bacchus Saloon in Houston, but did not live to see a return on his investments. He died of yellow fever on September 23 in the great epidemic of 1867, and the company was dissolved.[39]

Capt. George Washington O'Brien. His observations during the Civil War at Sour Spring Mound led him to assume a key role in the subsequent search for oil. *Courtesy Tyrrell Historical Library, Beaumont, Texas.*

In the meantime, in 1866, a Confederate veteran named Lynis Taliaferro Barrett drilled Texas's first producing oil well at Oil Spring, near the small settlement of Melrose, in Nacogdoches County. The Barrett well flowed ten barrels a day and even attracted outside backing from Pennsylvania, but because oil was already being produced in such quantity there, the project aroused no lasting interest. It was eventually abandoned.[40]

A telling item appeared in *Flake's Daily Galveston Bulletin* of July 11, 1866:

> Three reliable gentlemen visited our city this week, informing us of some facts concerning what they suppose to be the existence of petroleum in the section of country lying between the Angelina and Neches rivers. [They] say that there is a wide belt of country running east and west through Texas that will one day yield an immense amount of oil.[41]

It was natural for local attention to focus with increasing intensity on Sour Spring Mound. Its peculiarities attracted the notice of another of those multifaceted personalities: Dr. Benjamin Taylor Kavanaugh. Kavanaugh, like Veatch a Kentucky physician and teacher, was a colorful character whose other vocations included teaching obstetrics and gynecology, preaching, and editing a temperance periodical. He came to Texas in 1865, bringing a homemade divining device he called a "mineraloger," with which he explored much of East Texas.[42]

Kavanaugh arrived in Beaumont the next year and leased a tract of land in the Bullock Survey containing Spindle Top Springs, the freshwater springs a mile to the east of Sour Spring Mound. His purpose was, according to the lease, "mining for petroleum or rock oil."[43]

Not surprisingly, Kavanaugh's visit caused excitement in Beaumont. A retrospective *Beaumont Journal* article reported:

> Many people in Beaumont recall Kavanaugh's visit to this city. He was traveling by wagon and he had quite a number of men in his crew. He camped in South Park at what is now Elgie and Kenneth streets, and his presence there quickly attracted the attention of the few residents of that part of town. Kavanaugh pointed out the fine oil possibilities of the region.[44]

Years later, in a letter to the *Beaumont Lumberman* that appeared on January 18, 1878, Kavanaugh disclosed that he had found "some fine veins [of oil], one passing under the sour wells some mile or two southwest of Beaumont. . . ." But again, there was not sufficient quantity to make a commercial venture viable. Kavanaugh actually ended up drilling for oil near Sour Lake, reaching a depth of 142 feet before simultaneously hitting quicksand and running out of money.[45]

It seems likely that Kavanaugh's visit had another effect. According to one historian, George W. O'Brien was invited to meet with Kavanaugh during the latter's stay in Beaumont. Kavanaugh's opinions, following so closely on the heels of Trowell's letter, must have further piqued O'Brien's interest in oil.[46]

By this time, the race was on. The *Galveston Tri-Weekly News* reported on February 22, 1867, that "We have been aware for some months past that efforts were being made to bore for petroleum in several parts of our state." The paper further stated that a man by the name of Mulligan "bored" for oil twenty miles above Liberty and at Sour Lake, "from which a jet of gas and oil was thrown to a distance of 60 feet above the surface."[47]

An article in an 1878 issue of the *Beaumont Lumberman* reported that

> . . . it amounts . . . to a conviction with many that petroleum, or coal oil, will eventually be found here [Sour Lake]. So strong was this belief ten years ago that thousands of acres of land were located upon simply for its value in a coal oil point of view. Over a portion of [Hardin] county, 10 to 25 miles in extent, it is an every day [*sic*] affair to find a dark oil floating upon the surface of ponds and oozing out and standing in pools upon the ground.[48]

First oil storage tanks, constructed of wood, in Nacogdoches County, the "first oil field in the South." (The first steel tanks in Texas were also constructed at Nacogdoches.) *Courtesy Delbert Teutsch Collection, East Texas Research Center, Stephen F. Austin State University, Nacogdoches, Texas.*

Beginning in the 1880s, new discoveries were made in other parts of the state, including San Antonio and Waco, and renewed interest turned to the field at Nacogdoches. In 1886, a well was drilled with cable tools there, hitting oil at a depth of seventy feet. It flowed about 250 barrels of oil the first day, then was completed as a small pumper. This field, arguably the first in the state, set off a flurry of leasing and drilling and resulted in the formation of four small oil companies. A number of other Texas firsts resulted: the first steel tanks in the state (two of them), the first pipeline (a three-inch pipe fourteen and a half miles long), and the first primitive oil-refining facilities. As had always been the case with oil in Texas, however, production was small enough, compared to that of the Eastern oil regions, that the field was eventually abandoned.[49]

The year 1889 marked another first: Texas's premier appearance in reports of the United States Geological Survey and the *Census of Mineral Industries of the United States* as an oil- and gas-producing state. The reports credited Texas with "a total production of 48 barrels of oil and natural gas valued at $1,728." The 1890s saw minor development at Sour Lake, but again, the supply of oil, as in every other place in Texas, was insufficient to warrant

John H. Galey, one of petroleum's greatest pioneers and "the finest wildcatter in the business." *Courtesy Margaret Galey.*

wide interest, particularly in view of the fact that new fields in Ohio, West Virginia, and Indiana were being developed.[50]

Then, in 1894, an event occurred that served as a milestone in the history of Texas oil. The city fathers of Corsicana decided that, to ensure adequate economic development, the town needed a new water supply.

Accordingly, the city of Corsicana began to drill what they assumed would be a water well. Because there were no surface indications of petroleum, they were understandably surprised and annoyed when on June 9, 1894, at 1,027 feet, the drillers hit a good showing of oil. With some difficulty, because it was tricky to case off, the oil was kept at bay, and an artesian well was finally completed at 2,470 feet. For neither the first nor the last time, oil had been accidentally discovered in the search for water.[51]

The town leaders were happy with their fresh water, but all the rest of the populace could see was oil. Accompanied by an expert from Pennsylvania, several city residents organized the Corsicana Oil Development Company and began acquiring leases.[52]

On September 14, 1895, the company entered into an agreement with one John H. Galey, a first-generation Irish-American operating out of Pittsburgh who was fast acquiring a reputation as the finest wildcatter in the business. With his partner, James McClurg Guffey, Galey had prospected successfully for oil in Pennsylvania, West Virginia, Ohio, and Indiana, and had brought in a successful field in Neodesha, Kansas. Now, Galey agreed to drill five wells at no cost to the company in exchange for an undivided half-interest in them. He completed them before the end of the next year. The production from the Corsicana field did not compare favorably with that of the fields in the East, however, and Galey would soon begin to sell out his Corsicana holdings. But Texas oil had not seen the last of him.[53]

During that decade, a young Pennsylvanian named James Hamill came with his family to Corsicana from Waco, where he had worked for several years as a water-well driller. Jim Hamill brought his youngest brother, Allen,

An early Pennslyvania well, drilled by John Galey in the late 1860s or early 1870s. A blind mule provided the rotary power. Galey's brother Dan sits on the walking beam. *From the collection of Tom Galey and published in the* Kansas-Oklahoma Oil Reporter, *September 1960.*

to work with him in Corsicana, and they soon recruited their middle brother, Curtis, to move from Waco to join them. They formed the successful contracting firm of Hamill Brothers, drilling, cleaning out, and pulling casing from wells in the Corsicana oil fields, and soon acquired reputations for being the best drillers in the state.[54]

In 1897, the mayor of Corsicana, James E. Whitesell, invited another oil man to inspect the field and advise the town on future oil development: Joseph S. "Buckskin Joe" Cullinan. Cullinan, who had earned his nickname in Pennsylvania oil fields for being as rough and durable as the leather used for oil field gloves and shoes, was a former Standard Oil Company man who had lately formed his own oil-equipment company in Pennsylvania. Apparently liking what he saw in Corsicana, Cullinan stayed to become the "dominant oil figure" in the town. When the need for a refinery became apparent, he acquired Eastern financing, formed the J. S. Cullinan Company, and built a new refinery for Corsicana, firing its stills on Christmas Day, 1898.[55]

By the end of 1897, Corsicana boasted forty-seven wells with a total production of 65,975 barrels for the year and the distinction of being the first oil field of any size in the state. It also hosted the debut of rotary drilling, which employed rigs capable of drilling a bore hole with a bit attached to a rotating column of steel pipe. This method was destined to replace the standard cable-tool rig, which operated on the percussion principle of repeatedly smashing a weighted bit into a well to gouge its way down, then hauling it back up to repeat the process. By mid-1898, most drillers, including the Hamill Brothers, had converted from cable tools to the faster, cheaper rotary rigs.[56]

Notwithstanding the discoveries in the last half of the nineteenth century, Texas had not yet yielded oil in quantities to match those in the East. Nowhere in the state was there production sufficient to equal the established oil regions, which, in the last decades of the century, had expanded to include Kentucky, West Virginia, Ohio, Illinois, and Indiana, among others. Foreign crude was being produced, both at Baku and in the Dutch East Indies, but the state of Pennsylvania continued to supply the bulk of the world market. At the threshold of the new century, the oil industry was solidly established; refining techniques had been improved, pipelines had been tested and found effective, and ready markets for illuminating oil were waiting. The only element missing was an increased supply of raw crude.[57]

In the thriving little lumber town of Beaumont, Texas, on the west bank of the Neches River, a young man named Pattillo Higgins had read the signs and was looking for oil.

Chapter Two

THE HOMETOWN BOY

"There was a great cultural and technological gap between the world as conceived by Pattillo Higgins and the world in which most people of the area thought they lived."
Robert McDaniel, Pattillo Higgins's great-nephew and biographer[1]

ENTER the hometown boy.

Enter Pattillo Higgins, the prophet so completely without honor in his own land that finally, after the discovery he foresaw had vindicated him, thirty-two prominent Beaumonters who had once believed he was crazy agreed to issue a belated testament, signed, sealed, and duly delivered, to the significance of his vision.

Like most of the world's prophets, Higgins heard his own unmistakable cadence early in his life and marched to it all his days. The rub lay in his assumption that it was audible to everyone else. As his great-nephew and biographer Robert McDaniel has written, "There was a great cultural and technological gap between the world as conceived by Pattillo Higgins and the world in which most people of the area thought they lived." Both Higgins's virtues and his faults were larger than life. For good and ill, he simply was as he was—as it turned out, to enormous effect.[2]

In 1859, on the eve of the Civil War, Higgins's father, Robert, brought his wife, Sarah Ann Catherine Ray Higgins, and their children from Flovilla, Georgia, to Texas, settling first in Henderson, then migrating to the thriving deepwater seaport of Sabine Pass in Jefferson County, intending to sail from there to California. But Texas's secession from the Union on March 2, 1861, forced them to remain.[3]

Robert Higgins, a gunsmith by trade, took part in the sea battle fought at

Pattillo Higgins circa 1900. *Courtesy Tyrrell Historical Library, Beaumont, Texas.*

Fort Griffin, the small mud fort near the mouth of Sabine Pass, on September 8, 1863, when Confederate forces under the command of Irish saloon owner and future oil speculator Lieutenant Dick Dowling sank two Federal gunboats and successfully defended the pass against a Union coastal offensive.[4]

After the battle, Dowling sent Robert Higgins north to the town of Beaumont to warn local residents of possible Union escapees and to locate a place to house prisoners. Coming into Beaumont from the southeast, Higgins would naturally have passed Sour Spring Mound, rising abruptly from the surrounding grasslands on the way from Sabine Pass. He decided that the hummock, affording high visibility, would make a perfect prison for Union captives. In an eerie foreshadowing of his son's efforts forty years later, Robert Higgins shoved his marker squarely into the crest of the hill, and it was accordingly used as a temporary incarceration facility. On December 5, 1863, almost exactly three months after the Battle of Sabine Pass, Pattillo Higgins was born.[5]

In 1869, when Higgins was six years old, the family moved to Beaumont. The elder Higgins opened a gun shop near the south end of Pearl Street, and his family settled into a house just around the corner on Franklin Street. Young Pattillo Higgins would grow up in Beaumont.[6]

In the last quarter of the nineteenth century, the sawmill town of Beaumont still bore traces of the small frontier settlement it had been in the days of the Texas Revolution, when New Orleans merchant Henry Millard had laid it out in the grim Texian autumn of 1835. Located on the high western bank of the Neches River, it was sandwiched squarely between the Big Thicket to the north and the coastal prairies to the south. Streets kept the dense pine, hardwood, and underbrush at bay, but they became by turns dustbins in dry weather and seas of mud during the frequent Southeast Texas rains. One ingenious grocer built a mud sled, pulled by a mule, to navigate the almost impassable streets. And as the *Beaumont Enterprise* archly put it, "Sidewalks in

Texas Tram and Lumber Company, later owned and operated by the Kirby Lumber Company, on the Neches River at Beaumont. In the decades after the Civil War, Beaumont's lumber industry dominated its economy. *Courtesy Tyrrell Historical Library, Beaumont, Texas.*

Beaumont aren't a burning issue because there aren't any to burn." The paper complained of fleas "bad enough to make a statue lively."[7]

Although new homes—notably those of Beaumont lumber barons James M. Long and Francis Lafayette Carroll—were built of milled, painted lumber, their numbers were sparse compared to their older, log-built or hand-hewn counterparts. The town boasted a school, a courthouse, a newspaper, two churches, several stores and saloons, and a jail that, according to one early account, "was not stout enough to shut within it anyone with a real desire to be elsewhere."[8]

Like the rest of the South, the town in which Pattillo Higgins grew up was still raw and reeling from the effects of the Civil War, which had brought the economy to a standstill. Local railroads had lain in disuse and disrepair, the young lumber mills had been stilled, rice crops had been neglected, and many of the area's numerous cattle herds had been radically depleted to furnish beef and leather goods for the Confederate Army. Those were the contentious days of Reconstruction, when conservative white Democrats battled "radical" Republicans, both black and white, for local political control. For

Grocer C. B. Chenault making deliveries in the Beaumont mud. The house in the background belongs to Valentine Wiess, a partner in the Beaumont Pasture Company, on whose
land the Lucas Gusher would be drilled. After the Spindletop field came in, he built a more
palatial home. *Courtesy Tyrrell Historical Library, Beaumont, Texas.*

many years after the surrender at Appomattox, anti-Union sentiment in
Southeast Texas ran high, and Beaumont was no exception.[9]

In the postwar decades, Beaumont would regain its economic direction,
its citizens correctly perceiving its destiny to lie in the vast pine and hardwood
forests of East Texas. The railroads were rebuilt, providing transportation for
the developing lumber industry. The sawmills that had sprung up before the
Civil War grew into giants, transforming Beaumont from frontier village into
thriving sawmill town and creating a lumber barony, an increasing number of
elegant Victorian homes, and budding cultural aspirations. Local stores began
offering such amenities as fine colognes, French cognac, Havana "segars," and
celluloid cuffs; and in addition to subsistence goods, steamboats such as the
Van Buskirk and the *Laura* brought in the latest trinkets from Galveston, New
Orleans, and New York. Several small theaters and opera houses sprang up,
and a grand hotel—the Crosby House, long a city gathering place and local
landmark—was built in 1879, then rebuilt and enlarged to a dizzying three
stories in 1888.[10]

These glimmerings of gracious living notwithstanding, life was still

The sternwheeler *Laura*, surrounded by log rafts, at the conjunction of the Neches and Angelina Rivers, circa 1878. *Courtesy William Seale.*

frequently rough in Beaumont. A number of saloons flourished along the waterfront, and public drunkenness was a recurring problem. Lumbermen, railroad workers, and riverboat men frequently used firearms to punctuate their revels and settle their squabbles. As one old settler put it, "in those days, if you heard what sounded like shots from a gun, that's what it was."[11]

Young Pattillo Higgins was very much a product—and a survivor—of this rough-and-tumble environment. Between 1869 and 1873, he received his only four years of formal schooling. He early exhibited the contentious nonconformity that would mark his personality for life; according to his own report, he "graduated" one day when, disgusted with the whole scenario of formal education, he jumped out of the schoolhouse window and never went back.[12]

Fortunately for posterity, curiosity and enterprise were two words custom-made to define Pattillo Higgins's character. Unfortunately for some individuals, so were fractiousness and bellicosity. From his early youth, Higgins, nicknamed "Bud," began acquiring a reputation as a rowdy and a bully. Rawboned, rangy, and big for his age, he learned to fight early and continued to hone his skills on whomever was hapless enough to cross his path. When he was seventeen, he went to work at one of Beaumont's sawmills, doing his best along the way to further his reputation as a fighter. He frequented Beaumont's bars and loved to gamble for petty stakes. He also began to run with a gang of dangerous young toughs; although he later described their activities as "harmless, rowdy fun," they frequently crossed the line into arson and racist terrorism. After Beaumont's volunteer fire department was organized in 1880, Higgins and his gang specialized in such tricks as setting fire to empty buildings, alerting the fire department, then stringing ropes across the street to trip the volunteers as they rushed to answer the call. He and his sidekicks also freed prisoners from the town jail and regularly raided the black community in Beaumont to pick fights with the residents.[13]

One September night in 1881, Higgins got himself into real trouble. He and two of his friends went on one of their customary destructive raids. Taking slingshots and homemade torpedoes with them, they began to terrorize occupants of an African-American church holding services that night. As reported in the *Beaumont Enterprise* of October 1, 1881, Deputy Marshal William E. Patterson, on duty, heard one of the torpedoes explode and went hastily for help. On the orders of the town marshal, J. H. Bolton, he deputized local resident George White and placed him "in ambush," then returned to the church alone to try to apprehend the culprits.

As he rounded the corner of the church, Patterson heard the pop of the slingshots' bands, the "ping" of buckshot striking the buildings, and the shattering of glass as church windows fell in. He sprinted out into the open and nabbed one of the miscreants, Briant Platt, but released him to go after Higgins. Platt and the third man escaped, racing in the opposite direction from the post where the newly deputized White lay waiting.

Patterson yelled for them to halt, then pulled his pistol and fired over their heads. Taking due advantage of Patterson's distraction, Higgins pulled his pistol and shot Patterson in the groin. As he fell, Patterson fired back, his bullet striking Higgins in the left arm between the wrist and elbow. Higgins shot again, hitting Patterson in the "bowels," according to the newspaper, and Patterson wildly returned the fire. A total of six shots were exchanged, four from Patterson and two from Higgins.

After Higgins fired his second shot, he escaped at a run. White, who had left his lookout post to rush to the scene as quickly as he heard the gunfire, was too late to apprehend him. It was left to White to collect the fatally wounded Patterson and put him to bed at his own house.

After the justice of the peace heard the particulars of the case, he issued a warrant for Higgins's arrest. Since Higgins himself was "not in a fit state, from his wound, for removal to jail," he was placed under guard at his father's house. The newspaper reported:

> By morning the doctors had made a careful examination of Patterson's wounds and considered them mortal, and at about 11 A.M. on Sunday Justice Lamb took the dying declaration. About 3 P.M. Patterson breathed his last. A coroner's jury was empanneled [sic] by the justice, and who after viewing the body, and hearing the evidence of Dr. Tyree, who made a post mortem examination, rendered a verdict to the following effect: "That W. E. Patterson came to his death from two gunshot wounds at the hands of Pattillo Higgins."
>
> The funeral was fixed to take place at Magnolia Hill Cemetery on Monday at 4 P.M., but as decomposition set in so rapidly it was necessary to bury the body much earlier. . . . Had it been possible to have waited till [sic] the time first fixed, a very large procession would have been formed, in which the mayor and aldermen would have joined.

The newspaper went on to note that an inscription at the head of Patterson's grave proclaimed that he had "died from wounds received while in the discharge of duty." [14]

Higgins's wounded left arm became infected, and doctors amputated it above the elbow. Resilient as always, he recovered quickly. Bolton came under a storm of criticism from local townspeople for dispatching two deputies to make the arrest instead of doing it himself, and the whispers went round that he was afraid either of Higgins's father's stature in the community—and the fact that the elder Higgins was a very good shot—or of Higgins himself. At any rate, several weeks after the incident, the city council impeached Bolton and removed him from office. [15]

Higgins was charged with murder. In November of 1881, he was brought to trial before the local district court. He pleaded self-defense and, after the jury had deliberated only a short time, he was found not guilty. A few days after he was acquitted, he observed his eighteenth birthday.

Higgins, barely grown, emerged from the scrape perhaps a little more streetwise, but not discernibly chastened—a tall, rawboned young man with chilly blue eyes and lean, aquiline features. Supercharged with an abundance of physical and mental energy, he was never still. Although he seemed to be fairly popular, especially with the town's younger set, he still kept rough

Pattillo Higgins with guns and a friend. *Courtesy Robert McDaniel.*

company, frequented bars, and displayed a definite penchant for saloon girls. His reputation as a fighter acquired a new dimension; it quickly became known around town that he was as brutally effective with his lone right fist as most men were with both. He was the despair of his respectable father and "a constant embarrassment to his sisters and mother."[16]

He continued to sport not only guns, but other weaponry as well. A picture of him as a young man taken soon after the shooting incident shows him staring cold-eyed and defiant into the camera, holstered pistol mounted on a cartridge belt at his waist. Another, smaller pistol is thrust into his vest pocket, a knife is stuck into the cartridge belt, and the fingers of his right hand are curled knowingly around the barrel of a rifle. His empty left sleeve is pinned decently behind him.[17]

The next year Higgins went back to the sawmill world, Beaumont's all-pervading economic engine. The town was by this time full in the throes of its lumber boom; mammoth mills hugged the banks of the Neches, their stacks belching smoke, their saws whining, turning out millions of board feet of lumber per year. Great piles of lumber lay everywhere, sometimes in random piles, sometimes in neat stacks in the mill yards or in readiness to be loaded onto railroad cars, ready for transport. Sawdust blanketed everything, and the air was split at regular intervals by the governing scream of the steam whistle.[18]

Higgins took a job with the Beaumont Lumber Company, one of Beaumont's largest mills, located on the river just east of the foot of Main Street. He worked first as a cutter, manning one end of a two-man saw in the boundless piney woods stretching many miles to the north of town, but eventually he became boss of a crew working on the Neches just above the mill. The crew's job was to cull the harvested and branded logs from those of the other companies, send them safely down the river to their final destination, and guard against the piracy rampant along the river's large, wooded expanses.[19]

Armed with hooked spikes called peavies and wearing "corked," or waterproofed, boots, the men literally had to walk on water, traversing the surface of the river across the tops of thousands of floating logs, manhandling them to break up the massive, grinding pileups and constantly driving them downstream. This was difficult, dangerous work, and injury—and mortality—were high. Higgins became proficient at this hazardous job, in spite of the fact that he couldn't swim. He could leap across a jam, find the offending key log, and, with his powerful right arm, break it loose with one deft twist of

A lone horse and buggy navigating Pearl Street, one of Beaumont's muddy thoroughfares, circa 1890. *Courtesy Tyrrell Historical Library, Beaumont, Texas.*

the peavy. Around this time, he also began sending his own logs downriver for sale, his particular brand a dollar sign. He seemed set on a predictable course of business in Beaumont, even if his behavior could arguably have stood some improvement in a few areas.[20]

But in late August of 1885, the unthinkable happened. Higgins's life was abruptly jerked out of its less-than-reputable status by the onslaught of a force as unexpected and, for Higgins, as unlikely as a blast of summer lightning—the Holy Ghost.

There was a revival being held in town, and Higgins's boss, George Washington Carroll, a son of Beaumont Lumber Company owner Francis Lafayette Carroll and an executive with the company, was helping to host it. Carroll, a promising young civic leader, was already known for his bedrock religious views and his generous philanthropy. Slight in build, mild-mannered, kindly, and soft-spoken except in defense of his faith, he was a devout Baptist who never hesitated to attack the Devil head-on in any situation. Many times he took it upon himself to raid local bars and gambling houses, accompanied by a band of fellow believers. Word had it that Pattillo Higgins had on more than one occasion dived out the back door as Carroll and his fellow vigilantes were charging in the front.[21]

The revival was to be held at the Crosby Opera House, a two-story wooden theater next door to the Crosby House Hotel. Carroll had staked the First Baptist Church of Beaumont to the fifty dollars requested by celebrated preacher William E. Penn. (The Reverend Major Penn, a lawyer from Jefferson, Texas, who was sometimes called "[Texas's] great evangelist," had consented to come to Beaumont to preach on sin and judgment to the local flock only after being promised the money—in advance.)[22]

The revival, Beaumont's first except for the numerous camp meetings held throughout the early years, drew a crowd. Penn's name was enough. In the hot August twilight, people came into town on saddled horses and mules, in wagons and buggies, and on foot. Tying their animals among the trees across the road, the devout and the curious stepped onto the boardwalk in front of the theatre (by now, Beaumont boasted a limited expanse of wooden walkways) and filed inside to sit on plain wooden seats by the flickering light of kerosene lamps—farmers, ranchers, and town folk alike, all come to hear the miraculous Reverend Major Penn.

Penn more than met everybody's dramatic expectations. A hush fell; then, at the appointed time, the evangelist, tall, weighing approximately 250 pounds, "long hair lying on the shoulders of his frock coat and rippling gray beard streaming to his waist," strode down the aisle to the platform to sing "Bringing in the Sheaves" in his "roaring bass" and to deliver himself of his glorious word, "so convincingly that men and women hear[d] in his ringing voice the trumpet of the last day."[23]

Penn must have been convincing. The reasons a man of Higgins's disposition and habits attended such an event in the first place can only be wondered at, but the fact remains that he did. (Some doubting souls have suggested that he came to impress his boss, George Carroll.) When the call to salvation came, Pattillo Higgins walked the aisle, slapped his lone right hand into that of the preacher, and made his profession of faith in an act that would remain Beaumont's most talked-of topic since the shooting scrape. His father was not present, but his mother was, and family tradition holds that she almost "passed out" when her renegade son came forward to repent of his countless sins. After the revival service, Carroll waited at the back of the theatre to congratulate Higgins on his conversion and to offer him help if he ever needed it.[24]

Several days later, Higgins, along with several other converts, was baptized in the Neches near the site of an old cattle crossing not so very far from the spot where he had wrestled logs for his employer, Beaumont Lumber Company, and his boss, George Washington Carroll.

Soon after Higgins's conversion, he wrote the Reverend Major Penn:

> I am getting along splendidly. I have been reading the Bible a great deal, and am so much interested in it. . . . I read 5 or 6 [chapters] before I can stop. . . . There is a great change in me. I do not keep late hours as I did before, and now I shun all bad company. I have disposed of my two six-shooters that I used to carry with me at all times. . . . Now I go unarmed without the least uneasiness. . . . I used to put my trust in pistols . . . now my trust is in God and I feel much safer. I love Christians and I love their company. The boys don't try to get me back with them, but most of them say they are glad to see the great change in me . . .

The letter was signed, "Your brother, Pattillo Higgins."[25]

Whatever Higgins's original reasons had been for setting his feet on this particular path, his conversion stuck. Always a man of extremes, he embraced his new religion with the same fervor as he had his previous misadventures. It soon became apparent that his wild streak was permanently in abeyance; he set his feet on the path to respectability, even going so far as to write a religious treatise called "Little Sins," propounding his own religious views, which, predictably, did not coincide with those of his fellow Christians. Characteristically, he lost no opportunity to throw stones at those whose beliefs did not match his own. He himself described his own conversion as the "silent, supernatural working of the Holy Spirit."[26]

He would remain outspoken, fractious, and opinionated; that was his nature. And thankfully for history, his energy, his tenacity, his soon-to-be-manifested intellectual curiosity, and above all, his sovereign individualism, he would retain all his life. His unique qualities, directed by his newfound religion into positive channels, metamorphosed into a force to be reckoned with.

Inevitably realizing that his rough-and-ready life as a log man was inconsistent with his new direction, Higgins took what cash he had saved from the work at the lumber camps and moved into real estate, probably at the suggestion of George Carroll. He specialized in appraising timber and real property and brokering cutover timberlands, a real challenge to sell. With his intimate knowledge of the woods and waterways of Southeast Texas, he thrived in the real estate business, here and there acquiring tracts of property for himself.[27]

While riding horseback one day on a tract of land in Orange County, east of Beaumont just across the Neches, he noticed that his horse's hooves were turning up a reddish clay that lay just underneath the black topsoil. His curiosity aroused, he dug up a sample with the small shovel he always carried on his saddle and took it home. Scorning such considerations as education and experience and relying on his own autonomous methods, he set about analyzing the clay, devouring all he could find on the subject, including government reports on the properties of various soils.

Quickly concluding that the clay he had found was perfect for the manufacture of brick, he forged ahead to launch himself on a new career: brickmaking. There were no local brickyards between Houston and New Orleans at the time, making brick an expensive building medium in the Beaumont area, and Higgins's aim was to manufacture affordable brick.

With money he had saved from his real estate ventures, he purchased a part of the tract where he had found the clay and laid out his brickyard. Then he probed every aspect of the brick-making business from the design and operation of kilns to the finances, forming his first company, the Higgins Manufacturing Company, in 1886 for the production and marketing of bricks. He located the brickyard on the Southern Pacific railroad tracks at a place that came to be known as Higgins Junction, near present-day Vidor.[28]

Higgins's homework paid off; the bricks were of good quality, and the company grew rapidly. An increasing number of buildings made of "Diana" brick (after Diana, the small settlement on the railroad track where the loading ramp was located, about three miles from Higgins Junction) began to appear in Beaumont. Eventually, the new Jefferson County Courthouse would be built of Diana brick. The complete metamorphosis of Pattillo Higgins had been effected. The shooting scrape—and Higgins's less-than-savory past—were subsumed into his new, respectable—and respected—image as a pillar of the Beaumont community.[29]

As if to underscore his turnaround, Higgins became a deacon in the First Baptist Church in Beaumont. And in a final gesture perfectly suited to confound anyone unwise enough to typecast him, the former despair of polite society accepted a position as a Sunday School teacher. But even more astonishingly, it so happened that the Sunday School class at the First Baptist Church was composed mainly of *adolescent girls*. A century later, a man with his history would never have been considered for the position.[30]

With this development, the individualistic and always surprising Mr. Pattillo "Bud" Higgins silenced his detractors for good, because he took his duties seriously and excelled as a teacher. He embarked on the instruction of his "scholars," as he called them, with the same intensity that he brought to all his ventures.

In the meantime, Higgins went East by train in the fall of 1889 to scout for new ideas to improve his brick-manufacturing business. In Indiana, he learned that the quality of the clay used in brick manufacture was no better than it was in Texas, but that equipment and manufacturing techniques were far superior. Characteristically, he set himself to find out why. He discovered that the fuel used to fire the kilns was oil and gas, which burned with a constant temperature and made the kilns more efficient to operate.[31]

His next port of call was Dayton, Ohio, where he encountered the petroleum industry firsthand, and from there, his final stop was Pennsylvania. The entire scene must have been a revelation to him. Higgins, never anyone's fool, would have already been aware, of course, of the 1859 Drake discovery well at Titusville and the subsequent development of the oil regions in the East. And he would have been equally aware of the oil-related events in Texas, particularly the small oil field discovered in Nacogdoches in 1886, with its corresponding boom. In terms of money to be made, people were already talking millions, and Higgins would have heard that, too.

Whatever he knew, or had heard, an eyewitness experience such as he had in the East was all it took to fire his imagination. He was still interested in liquid fuel as a means to enhance his brick production, but his omnivorous interest soon veered like a shark after fresh blood to the science of petroleum itself. The signs—oil and gas seeps, mineral springs, and soil type—that had lured the wildcatters in the North were the very same surface indications that he had seen in his home territory of Beaumont, Texas, just south of town, on Sour Spring Mound.

He remembered the family tales: his father, flagging the mound as a temporary Confederate prisoner-of-war camp; the stories of the soldiers using the springs as medicine. In his early youth, those springs had caught his own imagination. According to Higgins family lore, he had bathed in them regularly for a time, then had attracted local attention by announcing that they had medicinal qualities, notably "improv[ing] the bowels." The hill was as familiar to him as the streets of his hometown. He put these memories together with his new knowledge and jumped to the reasonable conclusion.[32]

There was oil in Beaumont, under Sour Spring Mound, and he was going to find it.

Chapter Three

GLADYS CITY

"I have come to the conclusion that those geologists and other learned
men know but little or nothing about the origin and location of oil . . .
                                                            Pattillo Higgins[1]

WHEN Pattillo Higgins returned to Beaumont, he put to use the information
he had gathered in the East. He implemented measures to improve his brick
business, redesigning the kilns, bringing in steam-powered machinery, and
hiring an expert from the North to run the plant. He relinquished management of the brickyard to the stockholders and went back to real estate. But
Higgins had turned another corner. His energy was now largely focused on a
new obsession: finding petroleum under the hill just south of Beaumont.[2]

Even before he left the East, he obtained from the United States Geological Survey in Washington all their information, such as it existed, on anything related to the new science of petroleum geology. Back home, he rode
out to Sour Spring Mound. He reexamined the familiar ground in the light of
his new *idée fixe* with the thoroughness peculiarly his own. He paced off the
hill, scrutinizing for the thousandth time the sulphurous bubbling of the
springs, listening again to the constant hiss and chuckle of the gases as they
seeped from the myriad tiny fissures in the earth, sifting the waxy soil between
his fingers. Gases, mineral waters, soil texture—he had seen the same signs in
the Pennsylvania oil fields. To satisfy himself completely that what he remembered from Pennsylvania corresponded with what he now contemplated, he
dug post holes six to ten feet deep all over the mound.[3]

As he looked over the familiar terrain with new eyes, the businessman in
him was bound to have considered the Sabine and East Texas Railroad, running
just west of the mound from Beaumont to Sabine Pass; the Neches River, only

a mile to the east; Sabine Lake, less than fifteen miles to the south, and thence to the Gulf of Mexico; and the sizeable town of Beaumont, four miles to the north. In all directions lay the components of a transportation network to move the oil he was already sure he would find.

Higgins, never dealing in small dreams, saw more than that. He envisioned a city, not a rough-and-tumble place like Beaumont that had grown according to the vagaries of fortune, but a perfectly conceived, perfectly executed industrial utopia, "an inland manufacturing and commercial city," as he would later term it, complete with refineries, pipelines, and a salt-water harbor. The city would be powered by the oil he would find underneath this hill. That he might fail to find it simply never entered his mind, then or ever.[4]

After his father's death in 1891, Higgins built a brick home next door to the old family homestead on the corner of Pearl and Franklin Streets. Every morning he walked to the downtown barber shop for a shave, where he picked up the latest news and gave his fellow townsmen an earful of the latest thoughts on his pet visions. As time went on, he showed an increasing tendency to hold forth on the vast quantities of oil and gas just south of Beaumont. Few took him seriously.[5]

He did not confine his studies to geology. Still pursuing his religious bent with customary fervor, he studied the Bible incessantly, freely criticizing his fellow church members for their sins. He also continued to teach his Sunday School class of "young ladies" at the First Baptist Church.

With them, he demonstrated a side of his character that, in all probability, no one else (with the possible exceptions of his mother and sisters) had ever seen. His journals show that the thirtyish bachelor Higgins, the former terrorist, the veteran of a hundred street fights, had a soft side, after all. He seemed to cherish feelings of genuine affection for his girls, apparently untainted by any hint of prurience, borne out by the simple fact that, in that era of summary justice, the slightest hint of an inappropriate act toward any one of the town's cherished daughters would have resulted in instant and terrible retribution. It is to Higgins's credit that no accusation of anything resembling sexual misconduct was ever leveled at him.[6]

Higgins's girls loved him in return. One, Kittie Ogden by name, wrote him to "Always remember and never forget, the black-eyed girl who loves you yet." He saved the letter for over fifty years. Two others in his class, both named Gladys, were particular favorites. When busybody matrons chided him about his bachelor state, he always answered that he was waiting for Kittie Ogden's younger sister Gladys to grow up. He apparently developed genuine

Pattillo Higgins and his Sunday School class, circa 1895. Though Higgins taught some boys, his classes were composed predominantly of girls. *Courtesy Robert McDaniel.*

romantic feelings for Gladys Ogden; after her death from a ruptured appendix in 1895, he saved a lock of her hair in a gold lavaliere as long as he lived. The accompanying note, in his hand, reads:

> This little locket was given to me by Mr. Lew P. Ogden as a keepsake to remember Gladys his little daughter, 12 years and 8 months old. Gladys was a scholar in my class at the Baptist Sunday School. Gladys was a good-hearted girl. She was kind to me. . . . Gladys was my pet and the reason was she treated me better than the rest. Her nobleness and goodness caused me to love her more than anybody in this world. Her death was great grief to me and there is only one hope that comforts me. That is, I know that Gladys went to heaven to live with Jesus and some day I will meet Gladys in heaven and rejoice there with her. Pattillo Higgins[7]

Higgins's cronies from the early days would probably never have believed it.

Although there is no evidence that he cherished similar feelings about his other favorite, a dark-haired, dark-eyed charmer named Gladys Bingham, he would eventually accord her a much more public honor. Although it as yet existed only on paper, he would name his dream city after her.

On balmy days Higgins often took his "scholars" out to Spindle Top Springs, the local picnic spot south of town near the west bank of the Neches, where the old Spindle Top cypress tree had grown. There the springs bubbled cool, sweet water under the shade of huge old oaks, to the delight and refreshment of the local populace. It is a further testament to the general trust Higgins enjoyed that he was allowed to take the girls on field trips, for, as he put it, their "everyday application of religion." (These forays apparently "raised a few eyebrows, but [Higgins's] clear religious commitment and dedication seemed to override overt objections.")[8]

It was natural that, on the way home, Higgins would circle around to end the excursions at Sour Spring Mound, about a mile to the west. There he entertained the girls with the strange physical properties of the hill, showing them the sour springs with their old cypress curbing (possibly put in by Kavanaugh thirty years earlier) and giving his own explanation of the geology of the hill when they wrinkled their noses at the rotten-egg stench of the hydrogen sulfide gas on the humid Gulf air. He loved to shove a hollowed-out bamboo cane into the gas-saturated earth, ignite the gas coming out the other end, then enjoy the childrens' gasps of surprise as the blue flame caught and burned.[9]

Every night Higgins fell asleep over his books until the mill whistle blew at four A.M., waking him to retire for the night. He devoured the booklet from the United States Geological Survey and everything else he could find even remotely related to petroleum geology.[10]

The infant science, at that time suffering from what one historian has called "deficient data, inadequate working hypotheses, few professional practitioners, and lack of managerial support," held that the geologically youthful Gulf Coast region hosted no petroleum deposits because it contained no oil-bearing rock formations. Geologists were not the only ones who believed there was no oil on the Gulf Coast; no less a personage than Standard Oil Company executive John D. Archbold had once promised to drink every gallon of oil produced west of the Mississippi.[11]

A paper Higgins read in the summer of 1892 convinced him that Sour Spring Mound was an anticline, or dome-shaped arch of stratified rock, where oil, lighter than water, floated upward through layers of water-bearing sands to become trapped just underneath the crest of the dome. This theory seemed to him to fit the hill perfectly. There was no wonder that, after reading all the available material, he felt he knew better than the experts; after all, he'd seen the surface indications on Sour Spring Mound with his own eyes. On that subject, his personal drummer beat loud and clear.[12]

On one of his Sunday School excursions, Higgins happened to see a posted notice on the north edge of the hill. It stood in the old pre–Texas Revolution survey originally belonging to John Allen Veatch, that other amateur geologist for whom the mound and the sour springs had held such fascination. The notice offered 1,077 acres, approximately half the mound, for sale at six dollars an acre. Although Higgins was financially secure because of his brick company and his real estate efforts, the total price was a large sum of money. Even so, he must have regarded the sign as an omen that the time had come to act on his plans. He inquired of the agent in Beaumont and discovered that a multimonth option on the property could be bought for a thousand dollars. He then proceeded to develop a final plan for the city of his dreams.[13]

Raising the money to buy the land on the hill remained a problem. Higgins set about solving it with characteristic confidence, but when he approached one town leader after another, each turned him down. The more rejections he received, the harder he tried. He became the town gadfly; his barbershop pronouncements grew in scope until he was speaking in terms of thousands of barrels of oil and millions of dollars in returns for stockholders in his industrial city. People began to point to their heads when they heard his name and to cross the street when they saw him coming. Derisively, they called him "the millionaire." His hard-won respect was fast eroding.[14]

Undeterred, he recalled the summer night in the Crosby Opera House, when his life had been wrested into its radical new direction by the Lord and the Reverend Major Penn. He remembered the man who had shaken his hand years before and had offered him help if ever he needed it: his erstwhile boss, George Washington Carroll.

Despite his relatively young age of thirty-six, Carroll had become one of Beaumont's most venerated town leaders. Since Higgins's conversion, he and Carroll had remained close friends, the older man (by only eight years) serving, in Higgins's words, as his "pastor," or shepherd, in the religious sense and his mentor in secular matters. It was probably Carroll who had encouraged Higgins in his real estate and brick-making ventures and who had facilitated Higgins's acceptance by the people of Beaumont.[15]

Higgins now took his plan to Carroll, who informed him at the outset that he already knew about it. (By this time, there was probably not a man, woman, or child in town or the surrounding countryside who didn't.) What may have been a surprise to Higgins was that Carroll believed the plan had merit, in fact thought it was a "magnificent" idea.[16]

Higgins made his pitch to Carroll, counting off the telltale signs that they both knew so well, arguing point by point why each one indicated the

Beaumont lumberman George Washington Carroll. Carroll was the first to show faith in Higgins's theories of oil under Sour Spring Mound. *Courtesy Tyrrell Historical Library, Beaumont, Texas.*

presence of oil. He presented Carroll with waters from the sour springs, an improvised soil analysis, a study of the area's adaptability to industrial use, and a detailed plat of the proposed industrial city that he had drawn on an old county map.[17]

"Mr. Carroll," Higgins told him, "if you will furnish me a thousand dollars [to buy the option on the land], I will make millions for both of us."[18]

Carroll, the man of faith, agreed. He put his faith in Pattillo Higgins—and his money into Higgins's venture. On September 17, 1892, the two men cosigned a note for five thousand dollars to buy the tract in the Veatch survey on Sour Spring Mound. The two men already saw eye-to-eye on one aspect of the proposed complex: it would boast an atmosphere of "purity," an essential element as far as they were concerned, and would offer opportunities for families to lead wholesome Christian lives. There would exist no opportunity to sin in the new city.[19]

After concluding the purchase, Higgins and Carroll decided that they would try to acquire the rest of the Veatch survey, which, according to the old surveyor's intention, covered most of the rest of the hill. When Higgins investigated the ownership, he found that, except for fifty acres frozen in an estate wrangle under the name of the Cleveland Heirs and another 273 acres belonging to Beaumont lawyer J. Fisher Lanier, the balance of the acreage in the survey belonged to that other prominent Beaumont namesake of the country's first president, George Washington O'Brien, and to his daughter, Emma O'Brien John.

O'Brien was by this time nearing sixty and one of Beaumont's premier citizens. An attorney of distinction, the tall, bearded, hazel-eyed Irishman had made his influence felt in many spheres of Beaumont's town life, serving stints as county clerk, district attorney, and town alderman as well as publisher of two early Beaumont newspapers. A founder of the First Methodist Church in Beaumont, he was also a grand master of Beaumont's Masonic lodge. If Higgins could win O'Brien's support, he could count himself well on the way to succeeding in his venture.[20]

Higgins might not have known it, but when he talked to O'Brien about oil, he was preaching to the choir. O'Brien already knew Sour Spring Mound and its peculiar properties from his days at the Confederate Army camp. And undoubtedly he recalled B. T. Kavanaugh's predictions about the "fine veins" of oil that lay under the sour springs, as well as his army friend Trowell's mandate to buy the land containing the springs at any cost, because they indicated the presence of oil. O'Brien already had a good idea of what was under Sour Spring Mound.

He had, after all, taken Trowell's advice. In 1877, the heirs of John Allen Veatch had hired O'Brien's firm to assist with litigation involving the estate. O'Brien and his son-in-law and law partner, Alfred Scott John, were paid for their legal services in 1888 with a one-half interest in the Veatch properties, including the tract on Sour Spring Mound, presumably at O'Brien's request.[21]

O'Brien informed Higgins that his property in the Veatch survey on Sour Spring Mound was not for sale. He would, however, be willing to deed it in for the purpose of forming a company to explore for oil.[22]

On August 10, 1892, Higgins, Carroll, and Lanier met O'Brien in his office. Higgins made his pitch, showing the others a sketch of his anticline theory and explaining how the layers of stratified rock tilted up to form the dome-like structure of the hill. He also explained how he believed the oil lay trapped under the caprock of the dome and how it could be reached by drilling down about a thousand feet. He touted his industrial city, spinning his favorite dreams of what the region could become—if his guidelines were followed, of course. The men agreed to form a partnership for the purpose of building the city and finding and producing oil and gas on Sour Spring Mound. Since O'Brien was already predisposed to believe there was oil under the hill, he was much more enthusiastic about prospecting for oil than he was about developing the city, but when he committed to the project, Lanier did too.[23]

Higgins, remembering little Gladys Bingham from his Sunday School class, asked that the brand new company—and the city—be named for her. It was christened accordingly, and on August 16, 1892, the Gladys City Oil, Gas, and Manufacturing Company was incorporated. Eight days later, on August 24, 1892, it was chartered by the state of Texas.[24]

A story is told that Higgins, Carroll, O'Brien, and Lanier called on Miss Bingham at her home to inform her of the honor they wanted to bestow on her. A few days previously, her mother had threatened Gladys that if she did

not behave herself, she would send for policemen to arrest her. When Gladys
was called to the parlor to greet Higgins and company, she was afraid they
were the ones who had come to take her to jail. Relieved when they asked instead if they might name their new city for her, she graciously consented. As
proof of the occasion, they presented her with a framed certificate for two
shares of stock in the company.[25]

On September 17, 1892, the partners deeded their land to the company
in return for prorated shares of stock. Higgins and Carroll deeded in their
jointly owned 1,077 acres and were issued 216 shares of stock, with two going
to Gladys Bingham; O'Brien and daughter Emma John deeded in 1,350 acres
and were issued 270 shares; and J. F. Lanier deeded in 273 acres for 54 shares.
The company's acreage now totaled 2,700, valued at $20 per acre to equal
$54,000, or 540 shares of issued stock with a par value of $100 per share. With
the exception of the fifty-acre Cleveland tract, under title dispute, the Gladys
City Oil, Gas, and Manufacturing Company now owned the lion's share of the
land on and immediately north of Sour Spring Mound.[26]

The young company proceeded with the business of turning dreams into
reality. Carroll was named president, O'Brien vice president, J. F. Lanier, secretary, and Pattillo Higgins, treasurer and general manager. O'Brien was authorized to try to buy the excluded fifty acres and Higgins was commissioned
to retain city engineer L. F. Daniell to survey the area and to draw a plat of the
proposed Gladys City.[27]

Daniell's resulting plat reflected Higgins's vision; oil and gas wells, neatly
relegated to their own "manufacturing squares," as he called them, would fuel
the various iron smelters, brickyards, and other industries. Squares were also
designated for industrial, commercial, and residential areas, schools, churches, hotels, city parks, a fire department, a glass works, and a town hall. The offices of the Gladys City Oil, Gas, and Manufacturing Company would occupy
a central spot.[28]

Since the assets of the company lay in real estate, Higgins asked for and
was given permission to market Gladys City land as a source of revenue to finance drilling operations. Accordingly, the holdings of the company were
subdivided into lots and Gladys City was officially christened as a townsite.
Several lots along Florida Avenue, the north line of the survey, were located
the farthest distance from Sour Spring Mound and therefore were the least
desirable for drilling operations, but were the most desirable as residential lots
since they were nearer the town of Beaumont. Eventually, sales from this land
financed the drilling of the first well.[29]

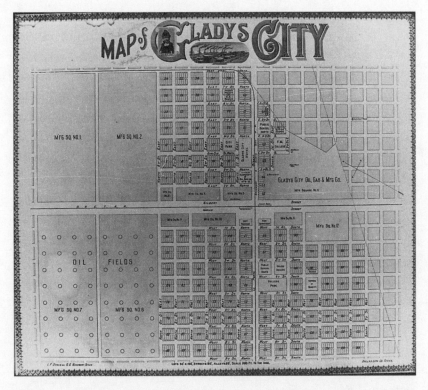

Beaumont City Engineer L. F. Daniell's *Map of Gladys City*. Note squares designated for oil fields and industrial, commercial, residential, and manufacturing areas. The offices of the Gladys City Company occupy a central location. *Courtesy Texas Energy Museum, Beaumont, Texas.*

Higgins was also commissioned to design a letterhead for the company. Since he had already decided how it should look, he was only too happy to oblige. His finished design showed a picture of Gladys Bingham with an expansive view of the proposed city, complete with oil tanks, smokestacks, railroads, and city buildings. The words "Gladys City Oil, Gas, and Manufacturing Company" were prominently displayed across the top in eye-catching lettering, the officers of the company and the $200,000 capitalization amount in smaller lettering.

The whole product was splashy, geared for effect, obviously aimed at sales promotion. Some of the directors objected to the marketing slant on the grounds that the city didn't yet exist, but Higgins, the former real estate jockey and perennial salesman, assured them that the scene would attract potential buyers.[30]

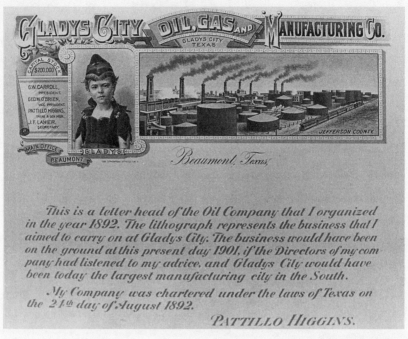

Pattillo Higgins's design of the Gladys City Oil, Gas, and Manufacturing Company letter-head, with Gladys Bingham occupying a place of honor. *Courtesy Texas Energy Museum, Beaumont, Texas.*

The company gave Carroll the authority to deed four blocks of the town-site to Higgins to compensate him for his work. (A story goes that Higgins used the land as collateral to borrow money from the bank in order to buy a fine quarter horse and a handsome gig from the local druggist, because he needed the transportation.)[31]

From the moment of the Gladys City Company's birth, Higgins stayed at loggerheads with the other directors. Never a patient man, he had long since been ready to drill for oil with all possible speed. His more conservative fellow directors wanted to proceed with caution, which Higgins interpreted as dithering and procrastination. As far as he was concerned, any fool could plainly see the riches that lay in store; the danger lay in hesitation.

His impatience grew by the hour. He likened his fellow directors to the sea captain who waited for a fair wind to sail, then, when it came along, wait-ed to see if it would hold; then, when the wind died, he had to wait for it to turn fair again. He confided to his personal journal that if the directors of his company were asked to choose the best method of transportation between

New York and San Francisco, "we would have to ride there on the bare backs of long-eared jackasses without bridles." As one historian has observed, "It was a difficult period for friendship and the Golden Rule."[32]

Higgins's attempts to attract local investors to the company's venture met with increased incredulity, if that were possible, and his boasts grew more strident and grandiose. He was now earning his derisive "millionaire" nickname. People who had thought him crazy before were now convinced of it. To complicate matters, he had personally bought options on several tracts of land that hinged on the development at Gladys City, thus overextending his credit. Something had to happen soon.

Perhaps at Higgins's urging, perhaps in spite of it, the directors of the Gladys City Company finally decided it was time to proceed. In early 1893, they authorized Higgins to begin drilling operations on Sour Spring Mound. He recruited a sewage contractor from Dallas named M. B. Looney, whom he had met when the latter was installing sewer lines and drilling a water well for the town of Beaumont. On February 17 the Gladys City Company contracted with Looney to drill a well on Sour Spring Mound at a price of $3.50 per foot for the first 1,000 feet and $4.00 a foot for the next 500 feet, not to exceed 1,500 feet, the purpose being to find "oil, gas, sulphur or other valuable minerals in that vicinity, and if not, artesian water." Drilling was to commence on March 1 (it actually began on March 22) and to be completed in 180 days. In a shrewd move, Higgins required Looney to post a performance bond, not a common practice in those days.[33]

Looney in turn subcontracted the job to an aspiring young water-well man from Corsicana named Walter B. Sharp. Higgins chose the location for the well, driving a stake near Copperas Pond, a large pool of copper-tasting water on the east side of the hill.[34]

When the drilling rig arrived, however, he took one look at it, declared it to be little better than a "coffee grinder," a "rattletrap outfit . . . used in drilling water wells," and ordered the work to halt. It was a rotary rig, which was more desirable than the old-fashioned cable tool variety, but Higgins knew that it would be too lightweight. The hill would defeat it. He tried to cancel the contract—but without the consent of the other directors of the company.[35]

The others were understandably chagrined at Higgins's arbitrary interference. If the drilling stopped, the Gladys City Company would still be liable for the full fee stipulated in the contract. They refused to halt the drilling, then reprimanded Higgins, even stating in an official company resolution that his authority did not include interfering with the contractor's operations, and that he had acted without sanction. Higgins had no choice but to yield.[36]

He was right, of course. In the first sixty feet, Sharp hit a promising pocket of gas, then ran into quicksand, that treacherous substance that was thereafter to prove the nemesis of any who tried to penetrate Sour Spring Mound. Because of the "heaving sand," as the quicksand was called, the drill hole repeatedly closed, necessitating continual redrilling. This was the first hint of what future drillers on this hill would learn the hard way: everything about it lay outside prior knowledge or experience. External disasters occurred, too; spring rains flooded the drilling site, and once a high wind blew down the derrick. The drilling was progressing at only about fifty feet a month.[37]

After one extension of time, Looney and Sharp were forced to abandon the well at a depth of only 418 feet. The company recovered $683.00, or most of its investment, by suing under the performance bond. In the meantime, Higgins, encouraged by the showing of gas from the aborted well, individually contracted to bring in a small "gasser" on adjoining property. It produced "enough gas to fire a boiler." (He later set the well afire and it burned for a couple of years, a lone beacon to his persistence.)[38]

By this time, Higgins was in sore financial straits. To satisfy his creditors, he sold off some of his own land, but he also continued trying to sell Gladys City stock to potential investors. Because of his gas well, he now touted a new fuel: natural gas. He took prospective investors out to the hill to see the flare and brought a sample of the gas into Carroll's office in a wooden keg. To demonstrate his find to Carroll, he turned on the spigot and ignited the gas, but fortunately, the flame went out before it could mix with the requisite amount of oxygen and blow the office, Higgins, and Carroll to Kingdom Come.[39]

To compound Higgins's—and the Gladys City Company's—problems, a nationwide depression hit in 1893. The goal of finding gas and oil on the hill seemed even more remote since the recent failure of Looney and Sharp; no investors would have bought into the company, even if there had been any around. Times were hard all over; the price of lumber had plummeted, adversely affecting the economy of Beaumont. Both Carroll and O'Brien were financially secure enough to survive, but Carroll, a lumber man, was hard hit. O'Brien had never been excited about the prospect of the "dream city," and at this particular time, neither man was in a position to dream big at all. Lanier, less affluent than either of the other two men, sold his stock in the Gladys City Company to Carroll on September 20, 1894.[40]

Higgins remained undaunted, pressing on with his efforts to enlist investors, but by now, his credibility was nil. Thinking professional endorsement might improve public relations, he invited no less than the geologist for the state of Texas, E. T. Dumble, to come to Beaumont for a tour of Sour Spring Mound, or, as Higgins was now calling it, the Gladys City Mound. Dumble sent William Kennedy, his assistant and the author of a recent article on the geology of Jefferson County, to Beaumont to evaluate geological features and conditions. Higgins looked forward to Kennedy's inspection; the thought that the geologist might fail to vindicate him apparently never entered his mind.[41]

When Kennedy arrived, Higgins gave him a tour of the hill, showing him its topography, the oil deposits, the gas, and the ill-fated Looney-Sharp well. He offered a thorough explanation of his own theory that the hill bore the earmarks of an anticline.

Higgins was in for a rude shock. Kennedy categorically disagreed with him, reiterating the prevailing theory that the Gulf Coast prairies were too recent in origin to harbor oil-bearing rock. As proof, he cited a well drilled for artesian water at the Jefferson County Courthouse a few years previously that had reached fourteen hundred feet without hitting rock of any kind.[42]

Not only did Kennedy disagree with Higgins, he wrote an article, printed in the *Beaumont Journal* on March 23, 1895, publicly refuting all Higgins's theories. But he didn't stop there. Calling the Looney-Sharp project "a piece of extravagance only equalled by the foolishness of the advice under which it was undertaken," he went on to advise the town of Beaumont to look for a good supply of water instead of "frittering her money away upon the idle dreams or insane notions of irresponsible parties in the vain outlook for either oil or useful gas."[43]

Higgins was thunderstruck. Added to all the previous ill luck, this newest blow struck especially hard and deep. Kennedy's article reinforced what most already believed about Higgins's pronouncements and convinced the few who didn't that he really was irresponsible, if not outright crazy. Prospects for further oil exploration looked grim, indeed.

It is probably fortunate that Higgins's reaction was lost to posterity. It was probably also fortunate that he had undergone his religious conversion. As his biographer has observed, "had it [happened] a decade or so earlier, another killing might have occurred in Beaumont." Even so, the incident deepened Higgins's already existing mistrust for professional geologists and academicians.[44]

Higgins never forgot, nor ever really forgave, Kennedy's attack on him, remembering into his old age "that young squirt who came down from the state geological bureau in Austin." Higgins would have his revenge; in just a few years, he was to prove Kennedy wrong in as public and spectacular a way as anyone could ever wish.[45]

In the meantime, Providence, in the form of a new epidemic of oil fever, intervened. In 1893 a few exploratory wells had been drilled around the old spa community of Sour Lake, and the following year had marked the Corsicana oil discovery. The Corsicana field attracted the notice of the Savage Brothers, a drilling firm from West Virginia also known as the West Virginia Minerals Company. While the Savage Brothers were in the neighborhood, so to speak, they also began to drill around Sour Lake, bringing in three shallow wells in 1895. Local awareness was greatly heightened by all the new production, and the Savage Brothers firm had naturally heard about Sour Spring Mound. They approached the Gladys City Company about leasing its holdings, offering 10 percent royalty and an acceptable bonus.[46]

Carroll and O'Brien, astonished and delighted with this unexpected stroke of good luck, were very much in favor of the lease. In what must have seemed to them the ultimate act of perversity, however, Higgins opposed it. As always, he had his own reasons. In the first place, he was afraid control of the venture would pass out of the Gladys City Company's hands, and with it would disappear his dreams for Gladys City itself.[47]

When Higgins voiced his opposition, the directors angrily voted him down. Over his objections, the lease between Savage Brothers and the Gladys City Company was signed May 27, 1895. He had no choice but to go along, but he did manage to convince them to include a clause stating that the well had to be completed to the required depth within six months, or the drilling company would lose its lease.[48]

In the second place, he took one look at the equipment the Savage Brothers were going to use and realized the project was doomed from the start. Characteristically, he said so, adding for good measure that the Savages' equipment was not even as good as Sharp's. It was a cable-tool rig; its modus operandi of literally chopping its way into the earth by repeated blows from a weighted bit simply would not work, not in Southeast Texas, not on this particular hill, and Higgins knew it. The project would fail.[49]

And fail it did. After six months, Savage Brothers had penetrated only 350 feet. Higgins lobbied for refusal to grant an extension, and this time, the other directors agreed with him. Savage Brothers packed up their cable-tool rig and

The first of three shallow wells drilled at Sour Lake in 1895 by Savage Brothers. Note the stream of oil in the foreground, flowing from the well. *Courtesy Bertha Terry Cromwell Museum, Alma M. Carpenter Library, Sour Lake, Texas.*

left. When the newspaper reported that the well was a dry hole, Higgins took issue with the reporter, declaring that the well was merely incomplete, not having reached the stratum that held the oil. He reiterated his belief that oil would be found at around one thousand feet.[50]

But in the eyes of the public, this latest aborted attempt reinforced the prevailing opinion of Higgins as a wild man and a dreamer, not to be believed or trusted with anyone's money. His partners, too, were probably beginning to wonder why they had ever gone into business with a contentious, bullheaded man like him in the first place.

In the meantime, however, O'Brien and Carroll were still convinced that there was oil on Sour Spring Mound, especially given the limited success at Sour Lake and since the surface indications there were nearly identical. They began negotiations with Savage Brothers to try their luck again.

Higgins remained adamantly opposed to the idea, but he was again outvoted by his fellow directors. This time, he resigned his directorship. Carroll, who had originally furnished all the cash, would sue Higgins for his undivided half in the twenty-seven-hundred-acre Gladys City tract. Higgins "compromised" (his word), and the case would settle out of court. Carroll bought his stock, and as of September 28, 1898, Higgins was no longer a part of the

Gladys City Oil, Gas, and Manufacturing Company. From that point on, he would witness events from the sidelines. But he didn't relinquish his dream. With the proceeds he received from the sale of his stock, he bought a thirty-three-acre tract on the summit of Sour Spring Mound, near the Gladys City Company land. This tract would eventually serve him very well, indeed.[51]

In the meantime, on June 4, 1896, the Gladys City Company made a new lease with Savage Brothers, operating under the name of the Texas Oil and Mineral Company. But this last drilling attempt, another cable-tool operation, failed, too, as Higgins had known it would. The well was abandoned at an even earlier stage than the first two wells on the hill. Afterward, the gas escaping from the three abandoned holes constituted a danger to local families living around the mound, and the wells were set on fire to remove the hazard of airborne natural gas. At night, the flames could be seen for many miles, mute testimony to their unfulfilled promise.[52]

The Gladys City Company languished, the directors at one point so eager to rid themselves of the financial burden that they offered to sell Higgins the company and its assets for fifty-four thousand dollars, but he lacked the money to buy it back.[53] He himself retreated into his real estate ventures, but he never lost sight of, or even questioned, his initial goal: to find oil on the hill. He resolved to raise enough money to drill for oil himself. Local towns-people refused to discuss the matter with him at all, and his efforts at raising northern capital were squelched from the outset. In May of 1896, he wrote to the Standard Oil Company, requesting that they purchase the Gladys City Company stock, giving an interest to Higgins. He received the following reply from Cleveland, Ohio, dated July 9, 1896, from Frank Rockefeller, John D. Rockefeller's brother and a vice president of the company:

> Dear Sir:
> Again after a long absence I have returned and find yours of May 20th awaiting me. On careful reflection I do not think that I care to undertake the proposition that you submit. There is too much guesswork about it. I am however very greatly obliged to you for your kindness. Truly yours, F. Rockefeller[54]

Higgins had to find a backer. And in his efforts, he would encounter the one man who would combine knowledge, training, and experience in precisely the right areas with an immense creative capability—and the force of character needed to conquer Sour Spring Mound.

Chapter Four

THE OUTSIDER

"I can say right now that you will have good cause to be pleased of having met me."

Anthony Lucas to Pattillo Higgins, June 7, 1899[1]

ENTER the outsider.

Higgins's quest for oil was about to acquire a new dimension—a cosmopolitan dimension—in the person of Captain Anthony Francis Lucas, who would bring a worldly perspective to Southeast Texas via Austria, Saginaw, Michigan, Washington, D.C., South Louisiana, and points in between.

Lucas was born on September 9, 1855, in the ancient and beautiful Roman city of Spalato on the Dalmatian coast, at that time a part of the Austrian empire. Christened Antonio Francesco Luchich, he was the son of Francis Stephen Luchich, a prosperous Montenegrin shipbuilder and shipowner from the island of Lesina, and his wife, Giovanna Giovanizio, a woman of "unusual learning and piety."[2] According to Lucas himself, who was proud of his heritage, the Luchich family was pure Montenegrin by blood, descended from ancient Illyrian nobility.[3] After the discovery at Spindletop, a reporter once asked Lucas if he were indeed a count by family right, as rumor had it.

> Lucas laughed. "Who told you about it?" he asked. "You couldn't repeat my real name if I were to tell you."
>
> "Then write it," suggested the reporter. Here is what was transcribed: Count [Anthony] François Maria Vincent Giovanizio de Bertuchevich Lucas.[4]

Young Antonio Luchich's early childhood was spent in Spalato, at the foot of the Dinaric Alps, where the Slavic and Italian cultures commingled freely, although Antonio probably grew up speaking the region's native Serbo-

Captain Anthony Lucas, circa 1900.
Courtesy Texas Energy Museum, Beaumont, Texas.

Croatian. At the age of six, his parents enrolled him in the local schools, but at some point the Luchich family moved to Trieste, then also a part of Austria, while his father served in the Austro-Hungarian navy. Here Antonio became fluent in Italian.[5]

At that time, an autocratic Austrian government was attempting to "Germanize" the city of Trieste. In a 1917 interview, the adult Anthony Lucas commented on the difficulty of his childhood years and on a young adulthood in educational and military institutions that discriminated against Slavs. To illustrate, he told a chilling tale of an annual fight held at the end of each school year in Trieste, when the Italian and Slavic boys of the school met the German youths on a hill in the suburbs and "settled accumulated grudges with clubs, stones, and fists."[6]

Young Antonio apparently distinguished himself early in the field of engineering. In 1875, at the age of twenty, he graduated from the Polytechnic Institute at Graz, Austria, and followed his father's profession by entering the Naval Academy of Fiume and Pola as a midshipman. He received his commission as a lieutenant in 1878. (His rank was never higher than second lieutenant. He was later dubbed "Captain," a rank his father had held, probably as a courtesy title; he accepted the designation, but when people attempted to give him an even higher rank, he corrected them.)[7]

In the same interview, without giving details, he alluded to an unpleasant incident that occurred during his stint in the navy, which he attributed to his Slavic origin. It was with gratitude and relief that he accepted an offer from his father's brother to visit him at his home in Saginaw, Michigan. In 1879, the twenty-four-year-old Antonio Luchich received permission to make a six-month trip to the United States. It would eventually stretch into a ten-year sojourn. He would not see his homeland again until he was a married man, on his honeymoon.[8]

When he arrived in Saginaw, he found that, because of the difficulty Americans had in spelling and pronouncing "Luchich," his uncle had Americanized his name to Lucas. The young visitor did the same. When he decided to stay, he retained the modification.[9]

Michigan was timber country, and Saginaw was a lumber center. During his stay in Michigan, Lucas worked in a sawmill. At one point he was charged by the management with improving the design of a gang-saw currently in use there. Accepting "with pleasure," as he later reported, he completed the project successfully and supervised its installation. Other opportunities followed, and at the end of his six-month stay, his employers offered him a "flattering engagement," with a salary that was more than three times what his pay as an Austrian navy lieutenant had been. He requested and received another six-month leave, at the end of which time he simply stayed on in the United States—without benefit of another leave.[10]

At some point during his visit, he decided to become an American citizen. In his words, he made "proper application" and effected the "change of allegiance," filing the necessary papers at the Circuit Court in Saginaw. Four years later at Norfolk, Virginia, on May 9, 1885, he became Anthony Francis Lucas, American citizen.[11]

Lucas stayed with the lumber mill for three more years, then began traveling, looking for ways to make his fortune. He went West in 1883 to enter the gold, copper, and silver mining businesses in Colorado and California and was for a time employed by a railroad in California.[12]

Returning to the East, he designed grain elevators at Newport News, Virginia, and at one point worked with the Havemeyer sugar refinery in Brooklyn. He mined in North Carolina for iron, finding one of the richest deposits in the state, then continued to work his way south through South Carolina, Georgia, Alabama, Mississippi, and into Louisiana.[13]

In North Carolina, his search for minerals awarded him riches of a different kind. He met "a gifted and charming Southern girl," Miss Caroline Weed FitzGerald, the beautiful, dark-haired daughter of the recently deceased Dr. Edmond T. FitzGerald, a prominent, well-connected physician in Macon, Georgia. "Casting his present fortunes and his future at the feet of one of Georgia's fair and most accomplished and highly connected ladies," he proposed—and was accepted. Lucas himself, in an interview after the Spindletop discovery, told a reporter:

. . . You want to know how I found my wife? Well, it is a very pretty little story . . . I made up my mind I wanted her as soon as I saw her, and I kept trying till I captured the prize. She was a beautiful girl visiting in North Carolina. It was soon after her father's death. I saw her, and was struck by her beauty and manner . . . I sought an introduction to Miss Fitzgerald [sic], and gradually let her know I was in earnest. I was satisfied that she had not been without splendid opportunities in the matrimonial market, but that did not deter me. I kept on until I won.[14]

Lucas married Carrie FitzGerald in 1887, and the young couple honeymooned for an entire year in Europe. Lucas took his bride back to his childhood haunts; the nuptial couple visited Spalato, Trieste, and Pola, where he had attended the naval academy. Even though he was by then a naturalized American citizen, Lucas later confessed to some trepidation regarding "the rigor of Austrian law," as he put it, because of his "informal" departure from the Austrian navy. To his surprise, he was royally entertained by the officers. He attributed his immunity to Mrs. Lucas's "charm of manner" and to the fact that she was an American.[15]

The couple arrived back in the States in 1888 and made their home in Washington, D.C., where Lucas entered the profession of mechanical and mining engineering. On July 21, 1889, their only child, Anthony FitzGerald Lucas, was born.

Taking Carrie and young Tony with him, Lucas prospected for gold for two years in the San Juan region of Colorado and also in California, but with little success. On his return to Washington, he began to look around for other opportunities in the mining industry.[16]

In 1893, Lucas, then aged thirty-eight, turned his attention to the peculiar geological formations of the Louisiana Gulf Coast, finding employment with Myles and Company of New Orleans superintending operations at a salt mine owned by the Avery family at Petit Anse, Louisiana, now known as Avery Island. This "island" was not an island at all, but a piercement-type salt dome, a particular kind of anticline formed by a narrow finger, or plug, of salt that thrusts upward from deep salt beds (the residue of ancient oceans), piercing the overlying sedimentary rock to form a dome. There were many such salt domes protruding from Louisiana's swampy coastal prairies, including the group that came to be known as Louisiana's famous "Five Islands." Avery Island was one of them.[17]

At Avery Island Lucas found an antiquated mill and a mine damaged by water that had seeped in and dissolved the salt, forming a large cave. (The salt deposit, originally discovered before the Civil War by a slave digging a water well, had been worked by the Confederacy until a Union attack destroyed the facility. The salt had been used by Indians and other early settlers but not commerically mined until the Civil War. After 1879, it had been poorly managed.) Lucas worked at Avery Island for three years, mastering problems with cave-ins and encroaching water and developing an intricate method of "overhead" mining. His skill restored the mine to safety and profitability. The salt from this mine was used in the manufacture of the Tabasco Brand hot pepper sauce, for which the McIlhenny family of Avery Island is still known today.[18]

Caroline Weed FitzGerald "Carrie" Lucas, wife of Anthony Lucas. *Courtesy Tyrrell Historical Library, Beaumnont, Texas.*

During his work at Avery Island, Lucas encountered the actor and comedian Joseph Jefferson. One of the most beloved figures in the American theater, Jefferson had played the role of Rip Van Winkle, Washington Irving's famous character, on the stage for forty years. He had retired to Louisiana, purchasing a piece of property a few miles from Avery Island that included Côte Carline, another of the Five Islands, but eventually renamed Jefferson Island after him.[19]

In 1896, Jefferson employed a crew to drill for water, but when sand and boulders threatened to halt the operation, the actor asked Lucas if he was willing to bring his engineering skills to bear on the problem. "Eager" was the word Lucas later used to describe his reaction, and in a short time he had worked out a way to drive the casing through the sand and gravel, a bit of acquired knowledge that would later prove invaluable. In the process of drilling, Lucas discovered a vast bed of salt, and Jefferson then employed him to continue exploration of the salt bed.[20]

While Lucas was drilling at Jefferson Island, he was accused by local gossips of tricking Jefferson, "salting" the mine (a particularly apt expression in this instance) by hauling in and planting carloads of salt to make the mine appear more productive. Lucas, proud of his accomplishments and his reputa-

Lucas (center) examining core sample while drilling at Jefferson Island (also known as Côte
Carline). He came to Louisiana in 1893 to mine its salt domes, becoming an expert on those
geological formations and the sulphur and oil often associated with them. *Courtesy Tyrrell
Historical Library, Beaumont, Texas.*

tion, was still explaining over twenty years later that he had used salt to make
brine with which to bore the shaft. "You will understand," he explained in a
subsequent interview, "that if I [had] used fresh water I would have dissolved
the walls of the bore." He went on:

> Owing to this malicious gossip, Mr. Jefferson asked me if I had
> found enough salt, as he wanted to stop. I replied that I had salt
> enough to salt the earth; I was proceeding nicely, and was anxious
> to find the floor of the salt, when he stopped me at 2,100 feet, thus
> balking a possible study in geology, for I wanted to learn on which
> geological formation this salt was resting.

In spite of Lucas's wishes, Jefferson stopped operations and ultimately left the
property to his grandchildren.[21]

A year later, of his own volition, Lucas explored Belle Isle, Louisiana, the
legendary rendezvous of Gulf Coast pirate Jean Lafitte and the only one of the
salt domes that was actually an island. There he made a pivotal discovery, the
magnitude of which can be judged only in hindsight. He discovered salt, as he
had expected, but with it sulphur, petroleum gas, and an oil sand. Speaking
later of his find, he said simply,

Lucas (left) in Louisiana, pictured with William Rittan and a Colonel Knapp. *Courtesy Tyrrell Historical Library, Beaumont, Texas.*

This led me to study the accumulation of oil around salt masses, and I formed additional plans for prospecting other localities. *Thus I began my investigations into the occurrence of oil on the Coastal Plain* [italics added].

The year was 1897.[22]

Lucas proceeded to acquire title to one-half the mineral resources of Belle Isle, which he later sold to the American Salt Company for thirty thousand dollars in bonds and five thousand in cash. He continued operations in Louisiana, mining salt at Grand Côte, then at Weeks Island in 1898. Then, at Anse la Butte, just north of Lafayette, he again found salt and petroleum together. (There is also substantial evidence that Lucas had made investigative forays into Jefferson County at this point. In March of 1898 he entered into an agreement with members of the McFaddin family to explore for "oil, gases and other minerals" in lands belonging to the estate of William McFaddin.)[23]

In 1898, Anthony Lucas, perhaps knowing more about salt domes than any other engineer in the world, stood uniquely qualified in every way to make his greatest discovery. By virtue of his background and training, he had behind him all the mining lore of Central Europe and the entire European geological tradition, where it had been established since the eighteenth century that the relationship between salt, sulphur, natural gas, and petroleum found together was not coincidental. He had verified his Old World knowledge with practical New World experience. Finally, he possessed the intellectual capacity and the imagination to know what could be done and the iron determination to accomplish it.[24]

He was about to cross paths with a man who, as unlike him in every other way as it was possible to be, boasted a strength of will as durable as his own, and who would provide the setting for his achievement: Pattillo Higgins.

Amazingly, Anthony Lucas and Pattillo Higgins had each come separately to the same conclusions from diametrically opposite directions, each by his own methods, each bypassing the prevailing current of American geological theory. Neither Lucas, the product of the European system, nor Higgins, the self-taught geologist, had ever been formally taught that oil-bearing rock did not exist on the Gulf Coastal plains. From his experiences at Belle Isle and Anse La Butte in Louisiana, Lucas already knew that oil, salt, and sulphur *could* coexist—and frequently did, and Higgins was convinced that oil, gas, and sulphur existed on Sour Spring Mound because he had observed the surface signs. In a prescient letter, Lucas once wrote to Higgins, "I can say right now that you will have good cause to be pleased of having met me." That proved to be true, but the path was neither straight nor smooth.[25]

Just how Higgins and Lucas connected has long been a mystery. Most accounts hold that Higgins placed an advertisement in either a trade journal or a newspaper, prompting a reply from Lucas. To date, no ad has ever been found. When questioned after the discovery by a reporter from the *Kansas City Star*, however, Higgins explained:

> The government asked me for a report on sulphur. This report fell
> into the hands of Captain Lucan [*sic*], who wrote me about it. . . .
> We corresponded and he came to Beaumont. Together we visited
> the ground and the result was that we entered into partnership.

Lucas was also interviewed by the same reporter. In the same article, he stated that he "knew from the reports of the United States Geological Survey [presumably Higgins's report] that there were indications of oil near Beaumont..."[26]

It wasn't quite that simple, but fortunately, surviving letters from Lucas to Higgins during this initial period shed some light on what actually happened. In a group of twelve letters, four from Washington, D.C., two from New Orleans, and the last six from Lafayette, Louisiana, covering a three-month period from May 4 to August 4, 1899, the two men explored the possibility of a joint venture and learned a great deal about each other. Higgins's answers have not survived, but Lucas's letters to him suggest their content.

Lucas's first letter to Higgins, dated May 4, 1899, bears out Higgins's explanation of how they established contact. "Pardon me for writing you direct," Lucas began,

> yet would say that as I have practically done all the explorations of
> salt deposits in La [*sic*], I am naturally much interested to learn con-
> ditions of things of the Sulphur deposit you are interested [*sic*] near
> Beaumont . . . therefore I beg leave to ask you for a copy of a report
> if it was made one [*sic*], if not, to please let me know condition of
> things in which your deposit occurs.[27]

Early in their correspondence, Lucas began firing specific questions about every aspect of the previous drilling attempts. How many holes were drilled, and when? Were the layers composed of sand? Was it impregnated with water? To what extent? Was there a nearby stream to furnish water for the drilling? And significantly, did the "ground" yield "oil of a black nature like in Calcasieu?"[28]

Apparently, Higgins was not forthcoming enough with information. In subsequent letters, Lucas's mounting impatience at the Beaumont man's equivocal replies became increasingly evident. In his letter of May 29, 1899, Lucas voiced his frustration, saying that "while I was desirous of investigating [the mound] and am so still, the vagueness of the report has somewhat dampened my ardour." Compounding his sins in Lucas's eyes, Higgins failed to send a requested sulphur sample from one of the earlier drilling attempts on Sour Spring Mound, and when Lucas assumed in his second letter that Higgins owned the land in question outright, Higgins did not correct his error.[29]

From Higgins's viewpoint, Lucas committed sins of his own. Lucas sent a sulphur sample in his letter from Washington dated May 21, 1899, claiming that it came from a dry lake in East Texas. "Can you say anything about it, and do you know where it came from?" Lucas asked Higgins. "If you do not, would suggest that you try to find out, as it may be very important."[30]

Higgins apparently challenged the assumption, for Lucas corrected himself in his letter of May 29, 1899, saying that it was probably from "the [dry] lake of sulphur in Western Tex. and of which I am surprised you did not hear anything about it," he added, a little acerbically. Whether he made a genuine error or whether he was simply testing Higgins's knowledge is an interesting question.[31]

Lucas's first letter to Pattillo Higgins, dated May 4, 1899, in which he inquired about the "sulphur deposit" Higgins was interested in near Beaumont. *Courtesy Jackson Broocks Osborne Collection, Tyrrell Historical Library, Beaumont, Texas.*

At first, both men spoke ostensibly of sulphur in the letters, but Lucas's up-front question about oil showed that it was prominent in his mind. From the one-sided correspondence, it is not clear when the emphasis switched from sulphur to oil, but by the end of the exchange, there was no more talk of sulphur. Both men, after all, had already committed themselves to finding oil before they had ever made contact with each other. It is tempting to speculate that, all along, Lucas had been aware of Higgins's real object, and that, in talking initially of sulphur, they were simply jockeying for negotiating positions.[32]

The exact date of their physical meeting is not known; it probably took place somewhere in early to mid-June of 1899. On June 7, Lucas wrote Higgins from New Orleans that "as soon as I can I will come to meet you, and go over the field with you. . . ." His excitement showed; in a burst of exuberance, he told Higgins that he felt "highly gratified to note that you are evidently a broad gage [*sic*] man, and meet fully with my views . . ."[33]

The individual to whom Pattillo Higgins would have extended his hand at the train station in Beaumont that hot day in June was a big man. There are few physical descriptions of Anthony Lucas from those early months, but his size is mentioned in all of them. About six feet two inches in height, he weighed around 225 pounds, with a massive chest and an erect, military bearing, "almost a giant," as one contemporary source reported, "but who carries [his weight] easily in muscle and heavy frame." One of the Hamill brothers commented that he was "heavy." Another source commented on his slight accent, and yet another on the fact that he spoke five languages. According to most sources, he did not smoke, chew tobacco, swear, or drink alcohol. (Others mention that he enjoyed cigars, and that he accepted an occasional "cordial.") His photographs show him as mustachioed, balding, and light-eyed, with the strong, handsome features that bespoke his Slavic heritage. Captain Anthony Francis Lucas, aged forty-four, at the height of his considerable abilities, presented a powerful figure and a formidable presence when he stepped upon the stage at Beaumont that summer day in 1899.[34]

When Higgins took Lucas out to examine Sour Spring Mound, the Captain instantly recognized it as an incipient, or piercement-type, salt dome, of the same kind he had mined those years in Louisiana. To analyze the gas seepage, he inserted a clear glass bottle in one of the natural vents, or fumaroles, with the result that a few days later a light film of yellow sulphur had formed on the glass, suggesting sulphur dioxide. In his words,

> This mound attracted my attention on account of the contour,
> which indicated possibilities for an incipient dome below, and be-
> cause at the apex of it there were exudations of sulphuretted hydro-

gen gas. This gas suggested to me, in the light of my experience at Belle Isle [where, for the first time, he had found deposits of oil and sulphur together], that it might prove a source of either sulphur or oil, or both."[35]

Until this point, Higgins, still holding to his anticline theory, had known nothing about salt domes at all. (The hill was, in fact, an anticline, but of a particular type: a salt dome.) All that was important, however, was that he and Lucas agreed on the basic premise: salt, sulphur and oil, or some combination thereof, could be found beneath the surface of Sour Spring Mound.[36]

On June 20, 1899, Lucas signed a one-year lease with option to buy with the Gladys City Oil, Gas, and Manufacturing Company for a 663-acre tract on the mound, with options to extend for up to three months or for the duration of the lease to buy the land for $31,150, to be paid in three installments. Lucas was to pay $11,050 down and sign promissory notes at 7 percent interest for the rest.[37]

No sooner was the agreement with the Gladys City Company signed, however, than he and Higgins began haggling over a separate agreement between themselves—an arrangement that Lucas was actually under no obligation to enter except by the dictates of his own conscience. The letters show that Lucas remained unfailingly polite throughout, even when he received a draft of a contract from Higgins in which the Beaumont man tried to retain 20 percent of the net profits from any gas, oil, and minerals as well as 20 percent of the profits from a sale of the land, while still requiring Lucas to "[bind] himself in good faith to develope [sic] said lands as aforesaid at his own expense." Even though Higgins did not own the land, he was asking a percentage that would have been fair only if he had already invested money.[38]

Understandably, Lucas rejected the proposed contract, striking the offending clauses and inserting others of his own. He wrote:

> I cannot sign [the contracts] as drawn for the reason that I never
> made any promises to give 20 percent of the net profits to be de-
> rived from said gases, oil, etc. I . . . have agreed to allow you 20 per-
> cent interest in the option or the profits that may be derived out of
> said purchase or sale.

In this draft, Lucas even offered Higgins a one-fourth interest in the option, but that would have required Higgins to put up 20 to 25 percent of the money to buy the land, money he was not likely to have.[39]

In the following letter to Higgins, Lucas generously reiterated his origi-

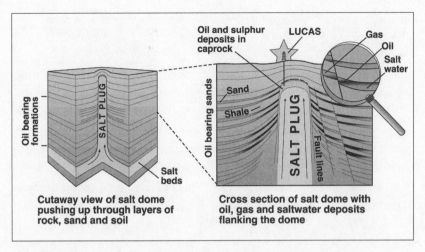

Illustration of salt dome formation and oil deposits. *Drawing by Drew Patterson.*

nal offer of 20 percent of the option, even promising to forego his own commission in order to "help the trade go through." He refused to sign the second draft of the contract, however, because he claimed that unnamed northern "capitalists" he had approached to fund the operation did not want to deal with Higgins at all, preferring instead to deal directly with the Gladys City Company. (Lucas could not resist gibing Higgins that he, Lucas, "had originally instructed them that you owned the land," because that was what Higgins had led him to believe.) In effect, he told Higgins that, if the latter was not willing to accept those terms, he, Lucas, had plenty of "inducements in other directions." At one point, Higgins apparently accused Lucas of acting in bad faith, for in Lucas's next letter, dated June 28, the Captain protested that he had "no desposition [*sic*] personally to go back on the spirit of our conversation, although there was no promise on my side." At the end of the letter, with what appeared to be a touch of exasperation, he suggested that Higgins show the letter to George W. Carroll, "a gentleman and a friend of yours whom I esteem," to suggest "some way out to mutual satisfaction." Lucas was probably hoping that Carroll would point out to Higgins that his, Lucas's, requests were reasonable.[40]

After a period of negotiation during which the deal almost collapsed, Lucas finally signed a contract with Higgins dated July 24, 1899, in which, because of the Beaumont man's efforts in putting the deal together, the Captain gave him a 10 percent interest in his own option to lease or buy. If Lucas sold out, he would pay 10 percent of the profits to Higgins; in turn, if Higgins sold out, he would give Lucas a thirty-day sole option to buy him out. Higgins, whose negotiating position was not strong, agreed. The grateful directors of the Gladys City Company, probably at Carroll's instigation, also offered Higgins a gentleman's agreement of a 10 percent interest in royalty income from any minerals found on the property.[41]

Lucas pushed ahead swiftly with his plans for exploration. In his letter to Higgins of July 23, 1899, he wrote that he would be in Beaumont on July 25 with "the papers" (presumably the signed agreement) and would go to work at once on the dam to provide water for steam for the drilling operation, set to begin shortly on Gladys City Company land. He hired road contractor Tom Sugg, Higgins's brother-in-law, to clear the well site, and in the last of the letters, dated August 4, he wrote that he had not heard from him regarding progress. Lucas also mentioned that he had written a letter to prominent landowner and cattleman William Perry Herring McFaddin, who owned land on Sour Spring Mound immediately adjacent to the Gladys City property, asking permission to flood some of his land in the process of building the levees. (By the date of the letter, McFaddin had not replied.)[42]

In the late summer of 1899, Anthony Lucas moved his operations to Beaumont—and Sour Spring Mound. He made periodic trips to town, staying at the Crosby House while the press pursued him, already hot on the trail of this stranger who had appeared so suddenly in the very heart of Southeast Texas. (He also boarded for a time at the Park House, a boarding house situated just behind City Hall and said to be "the best place in town." Sally Blain, a young matron who had recently moved to Beaumont and was boarding there with her husband, remembered coming down to breakfast the first morning and being seated next to Captain Lucas, whom she pronounced to be "very pleasant."[43])

Lucas had initially asked Pattillo Higgins to keep quiet about their negotiations and to buy up as many leases in the general area of Sour Spring Mound as possible. Lucas, too, was quiet about his early coming and going. On a visit to Beaumont in July of 1899 he told a reporter briefly and emphatically that he had nothing to give out that would interest the public, and persuasion or questioning would not induce him to release even enough for an imaginary story. When he returned in September, a reporter for the *Journal* pressed him for information. This time he replied with more diplomacy:

> Just say that the development of Gladys City will be undertaken by
> private parties with their individual funds. If they succeed Beau-

Beaumont rancher and businessman W. P. H. "Perry" McFaddin, part owner of the Lucas Gusher site, in Beaumont, circa 1894. The McFaddin holdings were developed in Southeast Texas as early as the 1830s. *Courtesy of McFaddin-Ward House Museum, Beaumont, Texas.*

mont will be benefited beyond the expectation of any of its most enthusiastic citizens. If they fail, only their money will be lost, and Beaumont will be no worse than when the development was undertaken.[44]

As Lucas prepared to drill on the mound, he brought his family to Beaumont. He, Carrie, and Tony found a house in the Iowa Colony subdivision on the Beaumont-Gladys City road (now Highland Avenue), about a mile from the hill. The house stood on a flat plain, with no trees to obscure the view of the dome. The Lucases lived there with a cook, a nineteen-year-old African American woman named "Philis" Benard, who evidently came with them from Louisiana. Not unexpectedly, Lucas filled the two-story frame dwelling with his library and his collection of minerals and curiosities.[45]

The Lucas family moved into community life in Beaumont. On an October Saturday afternoon in 1899, the three of them—Anthony, Carrie, and Tony—joined an excursion of some forty to fifty people on the *H. A. Harvey, Jr.*, down the Neches River to the Port Arthur ship channel. The day-long excursion included a stop at the Pleasure Pier in Port Arthur and was enjoyed by a number of prominent Beaumont families, including J. Fisher Lanier, one of the original members of the board of the Gladys City Company, and his children.[46]

In addition to his own work, Lucas often gave advice on various mineral matters to others in the community, including Leon Levy, owner of the Union Market on Crockett Street and Levy's General Merchandise Store, and several others who took soil to him for analysis. Lucas, styled by the *Beaumont Enterprise* as "an expert in such matters," analyzed the samples and coyly advised the businessmen to investigate for salt, commenting that a salt mine was as good as a silver mine.[47]

All the while, Lucas was setting about the business of drilling for oil. Already knowing of the quicksand problem and the failure of the earlier cable-tool operations, he decided to employ a rotary rig, importing the rig and a contractor he had used in Louisiana. According to one source, Higgins told Lucas at the outset that the rig was too light; as it happened, he was right. Lucas did take his suggestion, however, to locate the drill site on Lot 44 of the Gladys City development, just east of the Texas and New Orleans (Southern Pacific) railroad tracks, spudding the well in August or September of 1899.[48]

He had not drilled very far before encountering the "heaving sands." The rotary rig managed to penetrate the quicksand, but as the autumn wore on, the work was difficult, and the progress was painfully slow.

By late December the drilling had reached a depth of 250 feet. Lucas continued his policy of secrecy in the face of local rumors, but persistent newspaper reports proclaimed that favorable soil formations had been found, suggesting natural gas flows. Bemoaning the paucity of information, the *Semi-Weekly Journal* of December 29, 1899, complained that signs had been posted around the "drill," warning visitors to keep away, and that the workers had suddenly assumed a "know-nothing" demeanor. As the depth of the well reached four hundred feet, this "secrecy," as the paper termed it, bred rumors of an eminent oil strike.[49]

Over the next few days the rumors grew, and reports began to circulate of "illumination" seen on the mound, leading to talk of burning gas or house-fires. The newspaper speculated that Lucas had discovered gas deposits and was testing their force, while keeping the experiments secret and instructing his men to give no information.[50]

Lucas responded to the rumors with wry humor in a letter published in the *Journal* of January 2, 1900. "All of the above is news to me," he wrote. "I decided to become a good subscriber to your newsy *Journal*," he went on, "so that I, at least, may be '*en courant*' of what I am doing on Gladys City hill, or rather under it." He attributed the light to a large prairie fire just south of the hill, and not to gas, except, perhaps, to the St. Elmo's fire that was often seen playing eerily about the crest of the hill.

Responding to the charges of secrecy, he suggested that the newspaper's informant was frightened off "by some fetching signs conspicuously placed around the works stating, "Keep Off the Grass," "Move On," and "Ask No Questions and We Will Tell You No Lies," etc. The signs, he confessed, were placed there in fair weather when idlers were in search of some exciting novelty. Now the visitors were scarce in the "chilly blast" of the northers, the rain, and the "genuine Texas mud spattered all over." He continued:

> Gas? Yes, bless you, we have it in plenty. Enough to stock a book agent or, shall I say, a land agent, or light up a Beaumont crossing. Besides gas, we have lots of hard work and are dealing with nature's agencies, which, I am sorry to say, are even worse than the most persistent book agent that ever lived. We are harnessing it up, however, and may in time reach a point where we could write a history of how it was done and who did it. When such time does come, if ever it will, I would be most happy to invite the whole city of Beaumont and neighborhood to come and see the new gas works on tap. I have no secrecy in the matter and would be happy to be the means of establishing a new and prosperous industry in this growing city . . . I am glad to have visitors of the right kind and such that can appreciate my efforts.
>
> Respectfully yours,
A. F. Lucas

The letter reflects Lucas's sense of the ridiculous, but it also hints at the frustration he must have frequently felt at the town full of wary local folk who watched and criticized and probably caused multiple problems for his drilling crew.[51]

Lucas reached a depth of only 575 feet before disaster struck, as it had with the three earlier attempts to drill on the hill. Extreme gas pressure collapsed the casing, destroying the well and taking with it most of his money—but not before he had found an oil sand and recovered several demijohns of crude oil.[52] And that was enough. Lucas now became as zealous as Higgins had ever been about the oil that he now knew beyond any doubt was under Sour Spring Mound.

Chapter Five

THE BROTHERS

"So in October, early in October, we loaded our rotary on at Corsicana and I went down and met with Captain Lucas [in Beaumont], and he met me at the train . . ."

Al Hamill[1]

THERE was one problem, and it was a major one. Anthony Lucas was now out of money. In an improbable reprise of Pattillo Higgins's travails, the Captain now found himself in a position almost identical to that which Higgins had occupied earlier. He had spent all his available resources drilling for oil on the unique and formidable Sour Spring Mound. Now in the clutches of an obsession as full-blown as any that ever had gripped Higgins, Lucas himself had become the one faced with recruiting the capital to finance the assault on it.

In following Higgins's financial footsteps, Lucas faced two considerations that had not concerned Higgins: his wife, Caroline, and his son, Tony. A passionate and dedicated family man, he harbored grave reservations about laying on them so heavy a burden. He discussed the matter with Carrie, offering to resume "the legitimate practice of [his] mining engineering," but she, from all accounts a loyal, independent-thinking woman with a great deal of residual strength, insisted that it would make her very unhappy if he gave up.[2]

In the days to come, Caroline Lucas would be called upon to back up her words. When money became scarce for the Lucas family, she would sell the expensive furniture they had brought with them from Washington, devising makeshift pieces from drygoods boxes and covering them with calico.

In fact, Lucas later confessed that Carrie at one point had kept him from abandoning the entire project. As the months passed and he began to doubt his own geological calculations, he was on the point of giving up, but Caroline intervened. According to Lucas, she "stamped down her foot and would not allow any such action," cheering him up and making him ashamed of himself for wanting to quit.[3]

With his wife's strong support, Lucas followed Higgins's example by approaching Beaumont capitalists to fund another drilling operation. Because of the Captain's more extensive formal training, wider experience, and outside contacts, he should have had the advantage over Higgins, but local investors, made wary by four dry holes on the hill, understandably refused to respond with cash. Lucas met with as little success as Higgins had, and local townspeople began to regard him with the same good-natured contempt. In the end, Lucas was forced to take his proposition outside Southeast Texas.[4]

It didn't help his case when experts decried him with public statements that undercut his theories. A mutual friend took him to see Congressman Joseph Crocker Sibley of Pennsylvania, where Lucas laid out his project. Sibley, apparently not in the most conciliatory of moods that day, read Lucas a lecture on the "consequences of unsubstantiated enthusiasm." He told him further that he could not be a party to "such a wild scheme," and that unless Lucas could guarantee a well of several thousand barrels a day, he would be obliged to decline financial assistance. "If I had such a production," Lucas retorted, "I would not have come to see [you]."[5]

In February of 1900, Lucas gained an interview with Henry Clay Folger Jr., an executive with America's favorite bugaboo, the Standard Oil Company. Texans, in particular, were wary of the giant company; its marketing subsidiary, the Waters-Pierce Company, would be ousted the very next month from the state for violating antitrust laws. But at this point, Folger received Lucas graciously enough in his New York City offices and listened while the Captain propounded his theories and showed him a bottle of the oil he had recovered during his first drilling attempt on the hill. The night before the meeting had been bitterly cold, Lucas explained, and he had seized the opportunity to conduct a practical test. He had left the oil, which was of 17 percent Baumé gravity, outside his hotel window all night, in subzero temperatures. In the morning, he had been delighted to find that the oil had not congealed at all, demonstrating that it could be shipped or stored in the coldest of temperatures.[6]

Lucas explained further that he wanted no money for himself, only assistance in proving the field. Folger politely but firmly declined to join him, but granted him one small concession. He sent Standard's expert from Titusville, Calvin N. Payne, to Beaumont to examine the field firsthand. With Payne came his old friend and protégé from Standard Oil days, J. S. "Buckskin Joe" Cullinan, the new head of the J. S. Cullinan Company, which had opened the refinery in Corsicana on Christmas Day, 1898.[7]

Just as Higgins had done before him, Lucas was about to run head-on into the brick wall of American geological theory. When Payne and Cullinan arrived in Beaumont in late February, Lucas walked the hill with them, showing them the location of the first shallow well and explaining his nascent-salt-dome theory. After appearing to consider the project carefully, however, the two men still declined to join him. Payne told him flatly that he had been in Russia, Borneo, Sumatra, and Rumania and in every oil field in the United States and that the signs Lucas had shown him had no analogy to any oil field known to him. "There [is] no indication whatever," he concluded, "to warrant the expectation of an oilfield on the prairies of south-eastern [*sic*] Texas. . ."[8]

Lucas showed him a demijohn of the oil recovered from the first attempt, but Payne declared it to be of such poor quality as to be worthless, and readily available almost anywhere. He concluded by kindly advising Lucas to go back to his profession of mining engineering.[9]

Not surprisingly, the very sincerity of Payne's advice shook Lucas's confidence, but not for long. In the words of the Captain's biographer, "It was necessary for him to take several deep breaths before deciding not to capitulate."[10] In that brief moment, Lucas must have caught himself. The Standard Oil man was simply wrong. After all, every oil sign that both Higgins and Lucas had seen in other places in the country was present on Sour Spring Mound. What ailed the "experts," that they couldn't see the connection? Now the Captain must have understood Higgins's frustration in full measure. But in spite of the adverse opinions, he determined to continue.[11]

That April of 1900, however, Lucas suffered yet another blow from two more "experts." Dr. Charles Willard Hayes, chief of the United States Geological Survey, and Edward W. Parker, a former head statistician of the Survey, "dropped in on me," as Lucas later reported, "to see what I was doing." He again recited his litany of "possible oil accumulations around great masses of salt."[12]

By this time, he could probably have written the script for Hayes's response. The geologist reeled off the standard American geological creed that "there were no precedents for expecting to find oil on the great unconsolidated sands and clays of the Coastal Plain." And just as William Kennedy, in his rejection of Higgins's theories, had cited the water well at the Jefferson County Courthouse as proof positive that there was no oil in Southeast Texas, so

Hayes now used the example of a large water well, over three thousand feet in depth and costing nearly a million dollars, that the nearby city of Galveston had recently drilled in search of a fresh-water supply, without ever encountering rock of any kind, much less oil.[13]

Lucas countered that the city of Galveston had not drilled on a salt dome. Hayes and Parker ignored the argument. Furthermore, Hayes went on, there were no oil seepages on Sour Spring Mound. Lucas riposted that, if salt domes were present, surface indications were not necessary for the presence of oil. He also pointed out to Hayes that a limited supply of oil—a heavy grade, it was true—was being produced along with sulphur at the great dome at Sulphur, Louisiana.[14]

All to no avail. None of Lucas's arguments budged the two geologists from their convictions. This incident shook the Captain's confidence even more, because he considered Hayes to be one of the best geologists in the country. And by his own admission, Lucas himself lacked the final measure of confidence he would have had if he had been a certified geologist. "The plain fact of the matter," he once conceded, "is that I am not a trained geologist[,] hence do not see my way to give the proper and necessary interpretation to my—well, visions."[15]

Such was the magnitude of Lucas's obsession and his absolute conviction that he was right that he never even considered abandoning the project. But that final rejection was to have its consequences. In order to obtain funding for further exploration, he would be forced to give up most of his control—and his profit. In light of later events, he was to remark with a touch of pardonable bitterness that Payne and Hayes were the cause of his "selling [his] birthright for a mess of pottage."[16]

Help, as unexpected as it was welcome, came in the person of another "expert," Dr. William Battle Phillips, a field geologist at the University of Texas who headed the Texas State Mineral Survey. After visiting the site, Phillips expressed some confidence in Lucas's "nascent dome" theory and encouraged him to plunge forward with the project. This unanticipated moral support must have meant the world to Lucas, who at this point was understandably discouraged. But Phillips did the Captain another favor, without which his present attempt to find oil on Sour Spring Mound might have ended in another failure. He introduced him by letter to John Galey.[17]

Galey, already a wildcatting legend, was operating at that time out of Pittsburgh with his partner James McClurg Guffey in the firm of Guffey and Galey. Although they had recently sold their interests in Corsicana because of

Tintype of oil men James M. Guffey (left) and John H. Galey (right), in California on business in the 1890s. Note San Francisco's Cliff House on the studio backdrop. This is the earliest known photograph of the two together. *Courtesy Margaret Galey.*

disappointingly low production, Galey was still there much of the time, tending to what business remained. Lucas went to see him in Corsicana.

Galey, the field man of the Guffey and Galey operation, was a quiet, self-effacing man, slight in build, with lean features, a strong chin, and a large white handlebar mustache. Even in the oil fields, Galey always dressed formally in three-piece dark suits tailor-made for him in London.[18]

It was Galey who paced off the land and found the oil reserves, then, when oil was struck, went on to wildcat elsewhere. For him, the joy was in the finding. Those who worked with him were convinced that he could actually smell the presence of oil. When he spoke, they listened. "Behind those bright eyes of his," wrote William Larimer Mellon, a family friend and a member of Pittsburgh's Mellon banking family, "there went on incessantly an almost feverish thinking about the hiding-places of petroleum."[19] More than one photograph of Galey shows him, head ducked, looking modestly down toward the earth whose secrets he already knew.

Lucas's arguments piqued Galey's interest. That September he came to Beaumont to inspect the mound, then invited the Captain to come to Pittsburgh to meet Guffey and to discuss the possibilities of making another drilling effort.

Guffey was the diametric opposite of Galey in every way. Flamboyant, self-promoting, a bit of a dandy, he wore his hair in longish waves and was known to favor Prince Albert coats, showy waistcoats, and Windsor ties. A politician by nature, he served at one time as chairman of the National Democratic Committee. Guffey was as brilliant at raising money as Galey was at finding oil, and his role in the company was to garner funds to finance Galey's discoveries.[20]

Whether it was Lucas's presentation that convinced Guffey or whether the Pittsburgh oil man simply had faith in his partner's abilities is an interesting question. Whatever the answer, Guffey agreed to participate in the venture.[21] Again, Lucas found himself walking in Higgins's shoes; in his own prior effort, he had been the one to put up the money, and the ideas and the contacts had been Higgins's. Now the situation was reversed.

Since Guffey and Galey were themselves currently short on capital, they had to sell the deal to larger investors. Taking Lucas with them, they approached financier Andrew Mellon, who as a representative of his family's banking interests in Pittsburgh was well on the way to becoming one of the wealthiest men in the country. Galey's connections with Mellon went back a long way; their fathers had come from Ireland to America on the same boat. Although at least one member of the Mellon family, William, disliked and distrusted Guffey, he entertained a huge respect for Galey's wildcatting skills, as did all the Mellon family.[22]

In a move that would prove to have global significance, Mellon agreed to finance the venture. He, Guffey, and Galey cut a deal with Lucas, but they drove a hard bargain. Mellon would fund the operation to the tune of three hundred thousand dollars. Under the terms of the contract between Guffey and Galey on the one hand and Lucas on the other, they would drill three wells, at least twelve hundred feet deep, under Lucas's direction. If the first hole showed disappointing results, they would not be required to continue. It was so critically important to Anthony Lucas that the first well be successful that, in spite of looming financial difficulties, he affirmed his confidence in the venture by proudly refusing a salary or any other reimbursement for his own investment. Reportedly, this gesture impressed James Guffey.[23]

As Lucas had given Higgins 10 percent of the first venture, he was himself now cut into the deal for 12½ percent. In return, he was given strict instructions to go back to Beaumont, lease all the available land on or around Sour Spring Mound, and keep the entire operation secret; if it became common knowledge, prices would escalate. He was also ordered to leave Higgins out of the deal completely, unless he gave the Beaumont man a share of his own portion.[24]

Lucas had no bargaining power at all. He was fresh out of money. Moreover, four previous attempts on the hill had failed, and several eminent geologists had stated publicly, one in print, that no oil would ever be found in Southeast Texas. If Lucas wanted any part of this venture, he would have to follow orders.

He made his decision. He would make the deal and leave Higgins out. Even if he had given him a part of his own share (after all, something he, Lucas, had offered to do in their previous negotiations), he would have had to go against the order of secrecy to make the offer. He had no choice but to keep Higgins in the dark. Two days before the three-month extension of the original lease was to expire, and without telling Higgins, he renewed his lease with the Gladys City Company. The lease was signed on September 18, 1900.[25]

When Higgins learned of his exclusion, as he inevitably did, he naturally felt misused, and from that time on, Lucas and Higgins had no further association, either personal or professional. According to some sources, Carrie Lucas, who supposedly admired Higgins, made some effort to patch up the relationship between the two men, even telling Higgins about the reasons for his exclusion from the Lucas-Guffey-Galey deal, but neither man ever confirmed or denied it. After the discovery, Higgins was interviewed by a reporter from the *Kansas City Star*. When questioned about his association with Lucas, he replied tersely that "[their partnership] was dissolved, but not by mutual consent."[26]

By June of 1900, Lucas had leased approximately fifteen thousand acres of mineral rights on and around Sour Spring Mound. (As it happened, most of the acreage was useless for oil production; during the early years of drilling, no well was brought in at any distance off the mound.) Among the land parcels he acquired was a 3,850-acre tract he leased from three prominent Beaumont cattlemen, Perry McFaddin, Valentine Wiess, and Wesley W. Kyle, who grazed cattle on the land held by their partnership, the Beaumont Pasture Company. This large acreage of marsh grass near the top of the mound would very soon prove to be the most vital lease Lucas made.[27]

It remained for Lucas to drill the well, and his work was cut out for him. Both he and Galey were aware of the problems unique to drilling on Sour Spring Mound; no attempt had penetrated the hill beyond his 575-foot try, and all efforts had been defeated by the treacherous quicksands. Both men knew that, to reach the desired twelve-hundred-foot depth, they would need to employ the best drilling contractors available.

From his experience in Corsicana, Galey was in a perfect position to know whom to hire to drill the well. He told Lucas that he had worked with a drilling crew in Corsicana who could do it if anyone could—the Hamill brothers, Al, Curt, and Jim.[28]

When Galey cast his vote for the Hamills, he guaranteed the result. Theirs was the genius of the practical, the everyday, the improvised miracle. In the days to come, they would face a set of conditions, all difficult, some dangerous, that were as yet unknown in the infant oil industry, all soon to be encountered in one place. Without fanfare, they would invent a solution for each new challenge, whether they employed a piece of canvas as a check valve or ran a neighbor's cattle through a slush pit to churn up mud to stabilize a drill hole.

Many years later, both Al and Curt Hamill gave extensive interviews on the drilling of the Lucas Gusher. Conducted fifty years after the fact, they are sometimes contradictory on details, but a general agreement between Al and Curt emerges on the importance of the pioneer drilling process. And their work ethic rings through, trumpet-clear. As Curt explained it,

> We was all farmers and we'd been used to crude machinery. . . . And when we went into the oil fields, we found everything was crude there, and we started . . . from the grass roots with crude machinery. . . . Everything was hard to do. . . . We had to use perseverance and we had to use regular old horse sense.[29]

The Hamill boys learned hard work—and horse sense—early. Their parents, Anna and Graham Hamill, had come to Waco by rail from the coal country of Westmoreland County, Pennsylvania, in 1876, when Al, the

Expert drillers from Corsicana. From left: Al Hamill, Curt Hamill, and Jim Hamill. *Photographs courtesy Tyrrell Historical Library, Beaumont, Texas.*

youngest of the family, was six months old. They had hoped that the dry climate would improve Anna's health, but she died in childbirth when Al was three. He later described himself as a "little old runt," a sickly child, with constant chills and fever.

Graham Hamill remarried when Al was five, and an aunt in Pennsylvania insisted the boy be sent to live with her. His "ague," as it was then called, disappeared with his return to the East, where he lived with various relatives until he was fifteen. The other two boys, Jim and Curt, remained in Waco with their father and stepmother.

Jim, the oldest of the brothers, first found success with the water-well drilling firm of Fowler and McGilvery in Waco. At some point Jim realized that his baby brother Al was working "pretty hard" in Pennsylvania without much chance of an education. (In Al's words, he "got up to the fifth reader.") Jim sent for him, and Al, by that time largely recovered from his earlier ill health, returned to Waco to work with Jim as a tool dresser, drilling artesian water wells.[30]

After the Corsicana oil field came in, Jim saw his opportunity, bought a cable-tool rig of his own, and began drilling for oil in that area. Al went with him, working a twelve-hour day for the princely sum of a dollar and a quarter. "It was a good task," said Al modestly of his work as a tool dresser. "Give you strong muscle if you could stay with it." In the fall of 1898, he and Jim went into business for themselves, forming the Hamill Brothers Drilling Company. They also began trying to recruit their middle brother, Curtis (Curt), to come to work with them.[31]

In the meantime, Curt, who had attended Baylor University in Waco but had dropped out because of illness, had become a farmer and dairyman. By this time, he and his wife, the former Eva Smith, had four children. Curt related that one day a letter arrived from Jim with thirty-five dollars for traveling expenses. Curt could no longer resist; in the face of opposition from both his wife and his elderly father, he went to Corsicana to join his brothers, working for fifty-five dollars a month.[32]

Curt worked on the cable rigs as a tool dresser, sharpening drill bits, but also on the new rotary outfits as a roughneck. Quickly realizing which way the wind was blowing, he advised Jim to abandon the old cable-tool method. Jim agreed. In that same year of 1898 Hamill Brothers invested in a new rotary rig, and during the next two years the brothers quickly acquired their stellar reputation. When John Galey and Anthony Lucas sought drillers in 1900, the Hamills were unquestionably the drillers of choice.[33]

In August of 1900, Galey wrote a short letter to Jim Hamill in Corsicana, informing him that "their man, A. F. Lucas," would soon call on Hamill Brothers to inquire about the possibility of moving equipment to a spot near Beaumont and to take their bid for drilling a well there. Galey also told Jim that any trade they made would be financed by Guffey and Galey.[34]

According to Al, Lucas arrived in Corsicana "on a Sunday," while Jim, the business manager of the firm, was away. Al picked Lucas up at his hotel in the company buckboard and showed him around the Corsicana oil field. When Jim returned to meet with Lucas the next day, they discussed a plan to move a rotary rig down to Beaumont. The two parties agreed that Hamill Brothers would drill for two dollars a foot for a twelve-hundred-foot test, with Guffey and Galey furnishing the pipe. Hamill Brothers would furnish the derrick, drilling equipment, fuel, and everything else. Jim would stay in Corsicana to manage the business there, and Al and Curt would go to Beaumont to start the new venture, with Al serving as general contractor.[35]

John Galey himself chose the location for the new well. The old wildcatter made an unexpected trip to Beaumont while Lucas was out of town. As Lucas later related the story to Al, Carrie Lucas took Galey out to Sour Spring Mound, to

> this place where those springs were, you might say—or it wasn't
> springs. It was just a rough box in this little lake there. It had been
> put in by somebody. We never knew who. There was about five of

Perry McFaddin (left), Valentine Wiess (center), and Wesley W. Kyle (right), partners in the Beaumont Pasture Company, who leased Lucas the 3,850 acres on which the gusher was drilled. *Photographs courtesy Tyrrell Historical Library, Beaumont, Texas.*

them there, that the rainwater would collect there and this gas would boil up through . . . the sulphur gas coming up through was stronger in some than the other ones and discolored them more.[36]

Curt later recalled that Galey drove a stake into the ground, setting a precise spot at "the gas seepage in this old seepage box" for the location of the well. Rather than on the Gladys City property, the site lay on the McFaddin, Wiess, and Kyle partnership's Beaumont Pasture Company lease, a little over nine hundred feet to the southeast of the earlier hole and only fifty feet from one of Higgins's earlier efforts. The location lay only one hundred feet from the boundary line of Higgins's thirty-three-acre tract.[37]

In early October, the Hamills loaded their rotary rig onto the train at Corsicana, and young Al, aged twenty-five, came with it. He stepped off in Beaumont, ready for action. The Hamill boys were a strong, rugged, good-looking lot, and photographs of Al reflect a handsome face, the honest, engaging modesty for which the brothers were noted, and the latent sense of humor that emerges in their later interviews.

Captain Lucas met Al Hamill at the station. They stopped first at the Beaumont Lumber Company's yard to order lumber to build the derrick, and who should come riding up on his fine horse but Higgins's former employer and mentor, George Washington Carroll, the part owner and manager of the Beaumont Lumber Company. He dismounted, and Lucas introduced them. Al later gave this account of the meeting:

"Mr. Carroll," Lucas said, "I want you to meet the young fellow who's going to drill a well for us out here." And Mr. Carroll smiled, of course. . . . Something came up about Higgins, and [Carroll] said, "You know Higgins, his prediction out there, if we drill deep enough, we'll get a well of [5,000-barrel capacity] . . . I'll tell you one thing. If you get a well equal to that, this bill of lumber won't cost you anything."[38]

"He was a fine man, Mr. Carroll was," Al added.[39] On the subject of George Washington Carroll, Al Hamill, Anthony Lucas, and almost everyone else in town agreed completely. Everybody loved Carroll. And Carroll would keep the promise he made—Hamill Brothers never had to pay a penny for the lumber they bought for the derrick.

On the subject of Higgins, Al allowed that he never knew Higgins well. "He was a—a rather peculiar man, I think," he said in a later interview. "He had his own way of looking at things." He went on:

I asked Mr. Higgins one time if that was a dream or how he [came] to arrive at that opinion [that there was oil under the mound]. Well, he never gave me a direct answer. . . . But I think the Beaumont people thought the same of us when we were going in there. And I think the way Mr. Carroll laughed, I think he thought we were just about the same character [that] the people thought Higgins was.[40]

The next step toward beginning the well was buying fuel for the rig's boiler. The clerks at the lumber company referred Al and Lucas to Bain Price, a young man who handled the slabs of pine used to burn in the fireboxes. (Young Price would become the husband of Gladys Bingham, Pattillo Higgins's erstwhile Sunday School–class favorite.) Lucas already knew Price, so he and Al looked him up, and the deal was made later that day.[41]

As the preliminaries got under way, Lucas discovered just how wisely Galey had chosen his drilling crew. A railroad gondola full of pipe for the well was sitting on a Southern Pacific spur line near Sour Spring Mound, waiting to be unloaded. Lucas needed the pipe that very afternoon, and the railroad company needed its car. The bids to unload it were high, and the techniques were cumbersome. No one in town could devise a simple way to do the job.

After driving out with Lucas to take a look, Al climbed onto the car, took off his coat, wrestled down two pieces of pipe, and leaned them against

J. C. Ward's Waverly electric car, the first automobile in Beaumont, pictured in 1900. *Courtesy Tyrrell Historical Library, Beaumont, Texas.*

the side of the car as an improvised ramp. Then he rolled all the four-, six-, eight-, and ten-inch joints of pipe down from the flatcar

> so fast that Captain Lucas was kept busy to roll them out of the way
> to make place for the avalanche of pipe rolling down the skids, so
> that in less than an hour the whole car was unloaded.[42]

On the way back to town, Lucas and Hamill encountered a house-moving contractor on his way to give Lucas an estimate for unloading the pipe. When Lucas informed him that the car had already been unloaded by the man sitting next to him in the buggy, the contractor went straight to the railroad switch to see for himself before he believed it.[43]

When Al and Lucas got back to town, Al rented a hotel room, then wired Jim to send the rest of the crew: brother Curt, who would serve as driller and all-around helper; Will "Peck" Byrd, the fireman; and Henry McLeod, the derrick-builder.[44]

Curt Hamill and Peck Byrd came by train to Beaumont the next day, bringing with them a young African American man to cook for the crew. McLeod would arrive a few days later. When they stepped off the train, they

Gladys Bingham as a young lady, circa 1901. *Courtesy Tyrell Historical Library, Beaumont, Texas.*

were given a foretaste of the conditions they would be facing; there had been a heavy rain in town, and the ditches on either side of the railroad track were full of water. Someone had laid a twelve-inch board across one of the ditches for passengers to cross to Beaumont's infamous muddy streets. Lucas had sent a four-mule team and wagon to haul baggage as well as grain and hay for the mules to the drilling site. Curt and Peck Byrd drove the wagon. Going out Pearl Street, one of the lead mules "got down" in a mud hole, and they were forced to cut the harness from the mule to keep it from drowning.[45]

Out on the hill, Al, Curt, and Peck Byrd set up housekeeping about a half mile from the well site in a warehouse, "a little sharpshooter affair, a kind of boxcar" that Captain Lucas had constructed during the drilling of his earlier well. The cook operated at one end, which housed a homemade table, and the men slept in the other end on four bunks, one over the other. "Not a very desirable residence," Al commented, "but it made out."[46]

Southeast Texas pests added an unwelcome dimension to their lives on the hill. The cabin was full of old bedding, used tools, and other refuse, and when the men cleaned it out in order to move in, they found it alive with roaches, other insects of all kinds, and frogs. During meals, these small frogs, of every imaginable shape and color, adopted the unfortunate practice of jumping on the table and landing in the butter, which was melting in the Southeast Texas heat.

The grass around the little shack was "as high as the fences," and the voracious hordes of mosquitoes were terrible beyond description. The building had two board windows, but no screens. The men installed mosquito netting over the windows and draped it over their bunks, but the netting was not very effective, so they found some ancient, spoiled hay and burned it around the building. As Curt put it, "The smoke annoyed the bugs and mosquitoes, but it was pretty uncomfortable for us, too. We took our medicine, and did the best we could. . . . Well," he concluded, "we had a lot of fun even at that."[47]

The morning after they set up camp, Peck and the cook began cleanup operations, and Al, Curt, and McLeod drove the buckboard the half mile over to the drilling location, where the derrick sills Al had ordered in Beaumont had already arrived. Al and McLeod went into Beaumont for supplies, and at Al's direction, Curt went to the small bayou nearby to investigate the water supply.

Curt had just finished and was sitting on the derrick sills at the location, waiting to be picked up, when a tall, one-armed man drove up to the fence in a buggy, got out, and walked over to him.

Driller Will "Peck" Byrd (second from left, back row) on the derrick floor of the Mc-
Faddin #10 well, Spindletop, 1902. This is the first photograph found of Byrd, who is
identified on the back of the original, along with Scott "Cap" Forney (third from left,
back row), who worked with Guffey and Galey in the early days of the Spindletop field.
*Courtesy Energy Museum of Southeast Texas, Beaumont, Texas, and Center for American His-
tory, University of Texas at Austin.*

"Young fellow," he asked, "are you going to work on this well?"

"Yes, sir," Curt said.

The man introduced himself as Pattillo Higgins. "If you get this well
down," Higgins said, "you're going to bring in an oil well.[48]

Pattillo Higgins had never yet been wrong about the hill, and this time
would be no exception. Curt commented later that, as far as he was concerned, Higgins was the man who found the Spindletop oil field, although he
gave Lucas credit for developing it.[49]

The day after Curt's visit with Higgins, the rest of the lumber for the derrick arrived. Following Galey's instructions, the crew located the derrick next
to the boxes housing the sulphur springs. When they began building it, however, the Hamills made the sobering discovery that their derrick builder,
Henry McLeod, didn't know what he was doing. The Hamills themselves had

never built a derrick before; in Corsicana, contractors employed their own "in-house" derrick builders or hired experts to build them. Kindhearted Al never accused McLeod directly of incompetence, at least not then, but the more plainspoken Curt declared bluntly that McLeod didn't know any more about building the derrick than they did.[50]

The Hamills didn't ask questions, complain, or quit. They simply figured out how to do the job; then, without ceremony, they did it. As Curt said, "We made us a pattern, and laid it right out on the ground . . . just like a woman pattern[s] an apron." They built the derrick in sections, first laying down the twenty-foot-square base and nailing up the "girts" (the braces between the legs of the derrick), then sawing the green, poorly cured lumber, straight from the Neches River, for the next section, until they reached the top of the sixty-four-foot derrick.[51]

"When we got it up," Al commented proudly, "it was a mighty good-looking job." Then, lest any think he was bragging, he added modestly, "Anyway, it did the job . . ."[52]

While they were building the derrick, Perry McFaddin, one of the cattlemen on whose land the well would be drilled, drove up in a buckboard with his African American driver. Two hound dogs were chained in the back. Captain Lucas was on the derrick floor, and McFaddin joined him. While they were visiting, Lucas looked out toward one of the spring boxes, just in time to see the driver, who had the dogs by their collars, dousing them up and down in the spring.

"Don't do that!" Captain Lucas shouted. "My wife drinks that water!"

"Captain," McFaddin said, "I have been bathing my dogs in those springs for more than a year, to keep the fleas off them."

"My wife has been drinking it all the time," Captain Lucas said with some chagrin. "She thinks it is healthy mineral water."[53]

The derrick took between ten and twelve days to build. In the meantime, the crew began moving their machinery in and setting it up. After they were finished, Curt commented that the rig "was possibly as good a machine as there was at that time." They tried pumping water for the boiler and the slush pit from the little bayou around seven hundred feet from the well site, but there was just enough water to fire the boiler, and they soon pumped the bayou dry. They drilled a twenty-foot water well just beside the floor of the derrick. The ever-present gas spit a small amount of water out of the pipe, but they still had to install a steam jet to force the water out.[54]

All the while, mule teams were digging the slush pit, located beside the derrick and measuring about fifteen by thirty feet, "finished," as Curt said, "in red Beaumont clay at the bottom." After the derrick was finished, the crew dug the boiler pit by hand.[55]

The stage was set. It was time.

Chapter Six

THE WELL

"It roared, I'm tellin' you, it roared . . ."
—*Beaumont resident Dillard Singleton[1]*

IN the early morning hours of October 27, 1900, they spudded the well.

With no fanfare but the whistling of the Gulf wind in the marsh grass, the Hamills' new twelve-inch steel bit sliced into the top layer of paraffin dirt on Sour Spring Mound. They drilled where John Galey had indicated, near the old cypress-boxed springs on the south slope of the hill just below the crest, about a half mile south of the site of Lucas's first attempt. A "surprise party" for the oil industry had begun, and these men would bring it about.[2]

The actual event went unreported by the Beaumont newspapers, although the day before, the *Beaumont Journal* had carried an article praising the new equipment Anthony Lucas had obtained, more substantial than that used on his previous attempt on the hill, and noting the new site he had selected for drilling. In the interview, Lucas denied the latest rumor that "a large flow of oil" had been recently discovered. He observed drily that, since he was the only one known to be looking for oil close to Beaumont, the talk must be referring to his own efforts. He dismissed the rumor as "humorous to a degree easily appreciated," since the old hole had been abandoned and he had not yet "started his drill into the earth" in the new location.[3]

(Lucas was probably right about his being the only one drilling for oil at that moment; however, his effort was soon to be followed by at least two other exploration efforts in Jefferson County: in the coming months local operator W. R. J. Stratford would drill for the Sabine Oil and Pipeline Company, and Chicago civil engineer-turned-oil prospector J. A. Paulhamus would

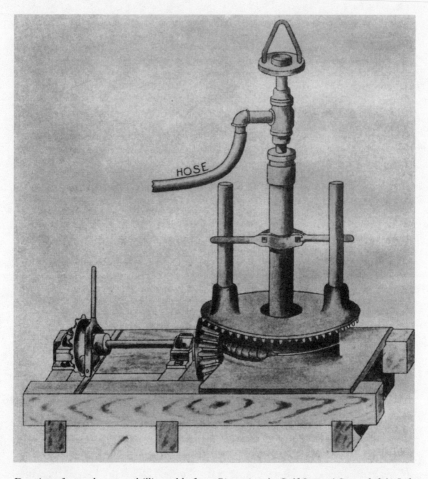

Drawing of an early rotary drilling table from *Pioneering the Gulf Coast: A Story of of the Life and Accomplishments of Captain Anthony F. Lucas*, Lucas's sanctioned biography by Reid Sayers McBeth. *Courtesy Tyrrell Historical Library, Beaumont, Texas.*

start a well for the Forward Reduction Company, evidence that some others, if not the geologists, believed oil existed on the Gulf Coast.[4])

Instead of noting the actual beginning of the Captain's latest attempt, the October 27 papers were filled with news about the area's developing rice industry, the long-distance phone service that now reached all the way to Nacogdoches, and the visit to Beaumont four days before of Buffalo Bill Cody's Wild West Show.

The show's parade on the morning of October 23 had been viewed by thousands of people. Colonel William F. Cody led the parade down the dirt streets of Beaumont to wild cheering, which did not abate with the passing of the U.S. Army Fife and Drum Corps, a detachment of Teddy Roosevelt's Rough Riders, assorted Native Americans, and a band playing "There'll Be a Hot Time in the Old Town Tonight." After four dry holes, how could the drillers on Sour Spring Mound compete with Russian Cossacks, a detachment from the Queen's Own Lancers, Japanese soldiers, and a squad of cavalrymen from Germany?[5]

Besides, there was something else still riveting local attention. Some weeks before, on September 8, 1900, nature had roused itself to remind humankind of its ultimate sway over their puny affairs. After one of the hottest Augusts on record, a monster hurricane had savaged the Texas coast, smashing with fearsome force squarely into the island city of Galveston.

With winds estimated at up to two hundred miles an hour and a tidal surge of over fifteen feet, the storm splintered buildings, hurled great steamships far inland, and took over six thousand lives, the number forever uncertain because many bodies were never found. In the wake of the gargantuan storm, what was left of Galveston lay behind a three-story serpentine wall of shattered buildings, human remains, and stinking debris. That day in September, the once-glittering city of Galveston lost its future, and a century later, the Great Storm of 1900 would remain the deadliest natural disaster in the country's history.[6]

The enormity of the disaster captured worldwide attention. Contributions poured into the Red Cross from all over the country. Seventy-eight-year-old Clara Barton rushed to Galveston with a trainload of carbolic acid and other disinfectants, then later sent in one and a half million young strawberry plants to give coastal residents an industry that would quickly produce both crop and profit. More immediately, Texas towns, including Beaumont, organized relief efforts. Houston sent a thousand loaves of bread, and Beaumont sent a boat carrying ice and water (it was reputed to be the first to arrive). When Curt Hamill and Peck Byrd had readied their drilling equipment in Corsicana to send by train to Beaumont, they had loaded it in a station through which relief supplies were being routed to Galveston.[7]

Just ten days into the new century, barely four months after the Great Storm blew ashore, another natural event of great significance would occur. This time, nature's forces would be unleashed deliberately.

The Hamill brothers, the final human component in the sequence of events leading to the discovery, set about to effect it. In the uncertain weather

Great Galveston Storm of 1900, which transformed the face of Texas in September of that year. *Courtesy Rosenberg Library, Galveston, Texas.*

of the Texas October, their bit chewed steadily through the successive layers of earth on Sour Spring Mound, then deeper into the unplumbed viscera of the hill. It waited, its formidable weaponry ready at hand.[8]

Later, both Al and Curt Hamill would give detailed accounts of drilling the well, not always agreeing. Al recalled that they made good time for the first 160 feet before they plunged into the "heaving sands," the treacherous quicksand that had fouled all previous drilling operations, but Curt remembered great difficulty from the very beginning. By either account, the sand threatened to defeat them. But they would conquer it with a series of innovations that would set new benchmarks in the history of the oil industry.[9]

Quicksand lay outside the Hamills' drilling experience, or, for that matter, anyone else's, prior to drilling on Sour Spring Mound. During the drilling process, water was normally circulated through the hole in order to flush the bit's cuttings to the surface, into the slush pit, and thus out of the way. In quicksand, the water dissipated into the sand formation at the bottom of the drill hole before it could return the cuttings to the surface. The walls of the hole would then collapse, and the quicksand, under tremendous gas pressure from underneath, would "heave up" into the pipe, clogging it and making further progress impossible. As Curt Hamill put it, drilling through quicksand was like "trying to drill a hole in a pile of wheat, using a brace and bit."[10]

"We fought this sand[,] losing our water and everything . . . ," Curt remembered. "This was very difficult for us as we had never drilled in loose sand prior to this time. And we had to . . . get our own experience, and fight the sand the best way we could . . . we was [*sic*] determined to make this hole [to] 1,200 feet," he added, "as that was our contract."[11]

To honor that contract, they kept drilling, encountering layer after layer of quicksand, pulling one bit after another, trying various sizes of pipe, inventing new solutions as they went. At 160 feet, they hit an especially thick bed of quicksand, which kept heaving up into the well. In Al's words, it "run us out of the hole . . ."[12]

Taking an idea from his cable-tool drilling days in Corsicana, Al decided to try driving eight-inch pipe down by hand. The crew removed the drill bit and attached a hollow "drive shoe" onto the bottom of the pipe, strong enough to batter through the formation. They also attached a heavy forged drive head onto the protruding top of the eight-inch pipe, to absorb the blows.[13] They ran the eight-inch pipe down into the hole as far as possible, then inserted four-inch drill pipe inside it. The eight-inch pipe would form a casing to keep the walls of the hole from caving in, and the four-inch would serve as "wash pipe," the conduit for circulating water to flush the sand out from the bottom of the hole.[14]

With nothing to consult but their own ingenuity, they constructed a heavy wooden drive block from eight-foot timbers, bolted together to form a sort of shallow trough, open on one side. When upended, it would fit around the four-inch pipe with the capability of sliding up and down it. After they fitted the drive block around the pipe, they tied heavy Manila rope on its upper end, wrapped the rope onto the cathead of the draw works, then hoisted the drive block high into the derrick. When it was as high as they could get it, they dropped it by slipping the rope loose from the cathead. With the force of a pile driver, the block slid back down the four-inch pipe to smash into the heavy steel drive head attached to the top of the eight-inch, ramming it into the ground "by main force and awkwardness," as Al observed, to make a few more painful feet. Over and over, the sweating, straining crew then hauled the drive block back up for the next blow.[15]

It was a man-killing job. According to Curt, they spent approximately twenty days penetrating the sand formation, burning up several thousand feet of rope in the process. Some days they made only a few feet; nevertheless, it was progress. Both the ditch and the slush pit filled up with sand washed from the drill hole, and periodically, they had to stop to clean them both out.

At that point, Henry McLeod quit, saying he didn't come to Beaumont to shovel sand. His departure left only Al, Curt, and Peck Byrd to do the work. (Al's comment was that McLeod wasn't any too good a worker, anyway.) There was no division of labor; they all did whatever needed to be done, for as many hours as it took. Since Al, as the boss, had to be gone occasionally, sometimes overnight, often it fell to Curt and Peck Byrd to keep the rig going as best they could in his absence.[16]

While they were assaulting the recalcitrant hill with drive block and brute force, it threw another blockade into their path. The deeper they drilled, the greater grew the gas pressure from the interior of the mound. The quicksand alone was trouble enough; combined with the increasing gas pressure, it created a nearly insurmountable obstacle. When the men had battered the pipe down to a depth of somewhere between 250 and 300 feet, they hit yet another layer of coarse gray quicksand, and every time they stopped the pump to place another length of pipe into the hole, the immense gas pressure from below would choke the line with sand.[17]

One day in late autumn, while they were struggling to pound the pipe through these soft formations, the pipe stuck, the line clogged with a hundred feet or more of sand, and the drilling stopped cold. The crew tried to relieve the six-inch pipe by going over it with an eight-inch, but it became stuck as well. When Lucas arrived on the scene later in the day, he and Al struggled to find a solution to the problem. None was forthcoming. The drilling effort stood at an impasse, and Lucas was terrified that the operation would fail.[18]

Lucas, "in great distress to proceed with the work," tried to imagine a way to keep sand out of the pipe. The problem left him sleepless. He wrestled with it, weighing alternatives, nearly all that night. Toward sunrise, it suddenly hit him. A boiler with a hundred pounds of water pressure could be pumped full without any water escaping because it was equipped with a check, or back-pressure, valve. If he could apply the same principle to the well, he could prevent sand from fouling the pipe.[19]

Lucas flung on his clothes, grabbed an old pine packing box from his back yard, hitched his buggy, and raced out to the well, where Al was working his shift. Between them, they constructed a check, or back-pressure, valve by cutting a round from one of the pine boards to fit inside the joint of the four-inch pipe, then cutting a slightly smaller round from a piece of balata-impregnated canvas belting. Boring a two-inch hole in the center of the wooden round, they attached the edge of the canvas round to one side of the piece of wood. The device was placed between the couplings of the pipe at the bottom of the hole. When water was pumped down the pipe, it would push aside the canvas flap to flow down into the hole, but when sand heaved up into the pipe from the bottom of the well, it would push the flap closed, preventing the sand from rising any higher. The homemade valve kept the casing clear of sand until they reached a depth where the gas pressure was too great for it to work. But temporarily, it helped. Lucas thought about patenting the invention, but forgot "in the frenzy of progress that the check valve made possible."[20]

After the check valve was installed, the crew kept on pounding the eight-inch pipe down into the resisting earth and finally landed the pipe safely in a solid formation at about 445 feet. With cathead line and drive block, they had mauled the pipe down through the lethal quicksand formation, almost 285 feet in depth, that had foiled all of the earlier attempts to drill on Sour Spring Mound.[21]

In the harder formation, drilling went more easily. By this time, the intermittent Texas northers were periodically blowing through, bringing heavy rain and dropping temperatures by as much as twenty degrees in an hour before vanishing in a few days' time to leave the men once again with mild temperatures, humidity, and mosquitoes. The pine-slab firewood was so wet at times that it would put out the fire in the boiler, and Peck Byrd, the fireman, had his hands full coaxing it to burn so he could keep up steam. The Hamills wrestled the lengths of pipe, sweated, and fought the hill. The bit gnawed its way farther into the core, sometimes by feet, sometimes inch by laborious inch. Through it all, Lucas hovered, worried, and prayed.[22]

At 645 feet the hill sprang another little surprise. Water began to flow backward out of the hole, up through the rotary table. Then water and gas blew halfway up the derrick, permeating the air with the sharp, unmistakable odor of hydrogen sulfide gas. The "little gas blowout," as Al called it, was of short duration, but it cut the collar on the drill pipe and slightly damaged the rotary by cutting its grip rings off, the sharp sand coming out "just like a blast furnace." The incident served as a wakeup call. The same thing could happen again, at any time, with greater force.[23]

They reasoned that, if they hit another gas pocket, they could reduce damage by keeping the well clear of sand. To prevent the drill pipe from sticking and filling with sand and the gas from accumulating, they would drill during the day but keep the circulating pumps going at night and the pipe rotating in the hole. Because there were just three of them, the only way to accomplish this was to institute eighteen-hour shifts, or "towers," as they were—and still are—known in the oil fields. Heretofore, the men had worked only during the day. Under the new regimen, all three men continued working during the day, but every third shift, one man would work all night to maintain steam, keeping the pumps working and the drill pipe rotating slowly, "making hole" only if possible.[24]

Besides the backbreaking labor of drilling the well, the men were plagued by boredom and isolation. Al, young, handsome, and single, lamented that they had few visitors at the well that fall, in particular none of the young ladies of Beaumont.

> . . . the women of Beaumont didn't seem to pay so much attention
> to the Spindletop boom. . . . In fact, all the time we was [sic] drilling
> the old Lucas well, we boys felt kinda badly that none of the girls
> ever showed up out there. When we was on wildcats out on other
> places, why, the whole country'd turn out and come to see us, espe-
> cially on Sundays. . . .

Even Perry McFaddin, on whose land the well was being drilled, visited the site only once, in the company of his business partner, Valentine Wiess. The only company the lonely drillers had on a regular basis was the occasional schoolboy out for a rabbit hunt. "We didn't have any visitors," Al complained. "They just thought we were crazy."[25]

In the solid formation, they set an eight-inch pipe, then sent a seven-and-seven-eighths–inch bit through it to the bottom of the hole. The drilling process made them "a little muddy water." At that moment, the seed of one of their most successful innovations was sown. Would "heavier" water, i.e., water with mud mixed into it, dissipate less quickly in the sand formation? Curt tucked the idea away in his mind.[26]

By early December, they had penetrated deeper than any had ever gone. But the hill wasn't through with them; more nasty surprises lay in store. They hit another pocket of sand—a coarse water sand, the worst they had yet encountered. All the returns from the bottom of the well were lost, seeping out into the sand. The bit plugged up, and they had to pull out of the hole. When they took the bit off the pipe, anywhere from two to six feet of sand were packed inside. Every time they started back down with the pipe and flushed up the first load of sand, it would sink down again when the water dissipated into the sand layer. Then the sand would clog the drill stem (at that point, they were using four-inch pipe). They would have to pull it again. It happened over and over.[27]

To add to their troubles, they ran low on water because they had lost so much in the sand formation. The jet that forced water down the hole and back up again, keeping the pipe clear and maintaining pressure in the hole, went out of commission, a casualty of the sand's abrading action.[28]

They had just taken off another plugged bit when the wood wagon drove up with the few pine slabs remaining from the last load that had been dropped off at the railroad switch. They would soon run out of wood to fire the boiler. They had already ordered another carload of slab for fuel, but about that time, their wood man came up the hill to tell them that it had not been sent. This was probably Willie Henry, a young African American who worked for the Reverend John Chaney, an area rice farmer and sometime preacher who hired out labor to the drilling crew. Henry hauled wood for the Hamill brothers on the Lucas well. As he later told it, he

> hauled hardwood, four-foot cord wood, and . . . pine slabs from the railroad and also from a sawmill that was in the vicinity of Spindle-top . . . I had to haul these slabs . . . across the pastures where there were no roads, so I always had four mules to my wagon. I did this work myself.[29]

Sand, a broken water jet, a wood shortage, no water. In Curt's words, "We really were a disgusted crew of men." Before they could drill a foot farther, they had to find more wood.[30]

"Things are pretty rough," Al said. "I'll take the dull bits to town and . . . see if I can get some wood. You boys clean out the [slush] pit while I'm gone, and be ready to run as soon as I get back." He also instructed them to wash the sand out of the water well and, if they had time, to chip (clean) the rotary table. He left about ten that morning.[31]

There remained their biggest problem—the sand. If they were to go on, it had to be conquered. But first, room had to be made for it in the slush pit. Curt and Peck asked Willie Henry to go back to Chaney's place to secure mule teams and equipment to clean out the pit.

Early that December afternoon, four black workers, including Henry and another of Chaney's employees, Earl Green, came driving up to the well in a wagon drawn by four mules. Two more mules plodded along behind, tied to the back of the wagon, which carried a heavy walking plow and a Fresno scraper. With the mules hitched to the Fresno, they cleared the pit of sand.[32]

Toward sundown, Chaney rode up. He eyed the large pile of sand they had removed from the pit. "Where in the world," he asked, "did you get all this sand?"

Curt explained that they were losing all the water they pumped into the well because it was flowing out into the sand layer at the bottom, and the sand was jamming the well.

"I believe that if we could get some muddy water," Curt told him, "we could . . . keep our pump running and get through the sand."[33]

"I can furnish you all the muddy water you want," Chaney offered. His corral, he explained, was of the same red clay as that of the slush pit, and when it rained, his livestock churned up plenty of mud. Why not try the same thing here? Curt and Peck had nothing to lose. They agreed to try it.[34]

Early the next morning, Chaney's men arrived at the well. They plowed the clay bottom of the pit to a depth of ten inches, then began pumping water in from the bayou. It was slow work. They improvised a makeshift fence around the slush pit, and Chaney and two of the workers brought cattle belonging to Perry McFaddin from the nearby pasture, some four or five hundred yards away. Some of them got away, but enough were detained to do the job. The unhappy cattle were given a few minutes to settle down; then, for four hours, the workers drove them around and around the pit, poking stragglers with long whips to keep them moving. As it happened, the cattle did a good job, producing a fine pit of red muck.[35]

Around three o'clock the next afternoon, Al came back. He had solved the wood problem, arranging for fuel to be delivered that night: dry cork wood, several wagonloads of pine knots, and a car of slabs that had been sent to the railroad switch. When he arrived, Peck was firing the boiler and watching the pump, and Curt was holding the one-inch joint of pipe, circulating muddy water. The mud was ready.

"What are you boys doing?" Al asked, understandably puzzled. Peck told him. "That will do no good," Al said. He shut the steam off the pump. "I've bought a new water jet," he announced. "Let's get this jet in[to] the [water] well so we can fill the pit with water and start drilling."

He had brought his own solution to the sand problem: a new drill bit. Made to his specifications, it consisted of a steel blade laid across the width of a four-inch collar, with a rod inserted through the center of the blade. "The sand won't rush up into this pipe so bad [sic] [that we can't] jar it out," he said.

Curt and Peck were sold on the mud idea, and Al was sold on his new drill

McFaddin-Wiess-Kyle irrigation canal headquarters near Sour Spring Mound, later Spindle-top Hill. *Courtesy Tyrrell Historical Library, Beaumont, Texas.*

bit. It remained for Curt and Peck to convince Al that the mud would work. That night, over their supper, they discussed it. Curt and Peck told Al the story of how Chaney had implemented Curt's original idea. Reluctantly, Al agreed to try it, but decided not to put any more water into the slush pit until the mud proved its value.

The next morning, the men stirred the mud in the slush pit until it was red and thick. Then they moved into the hole with the drill stem. At first, it seemed that the mud would not work. When they reached the sand layer, they immediately lost almost half the muddy water, and the heavier mud gave them a great deal of trouble because of the roots and chunks of earth it contained. But they persisted, sending the heavy mud directly through the pump and into the well.

Although they continued to have trouble with the pump, by the end of the day they had drilled through the sand into a very welcome layer of gumbo. That night, Peck ran the pump until midnight, then Al went out to relieve him, and ran it until morning. By the time Curt and Peck got back on the job with him, he had made about four feet of hole in the gumbo. *And while he had been drilling in the sand formation, he had not lost any more water.* The hole had stabilized, and the mud had done the trick.[36]

Such an innovative solution to a problem, with such prosaic ingredients as the hill's own red clay. But they had just accomplished something no one else had—they had manufactured drilling mud and had intentionally pumped it into an oil well, with a positive result. From that time on, mud became an essential part of the drilling process.[37]

One idea had worked; the other, Al's blade bit, did not. Unable to make any headway with it, they replaced it with a tried-and-true fishtail bit, and the drilling went easier for awhile. At somewhere beyond eight hundred feet, the men pulled the pipe to sharpen the bit, and Lucas noticed that a lump of clay was sticking to it. When they washed it down, they found a rock the size of a small egg. When Lucas examined it, he determined that it was limestone with calcite intercalations and fragments of dolomite and sulphur. Excitedly, he told the crew that this was a very encouraging sign. The men couldn't understand the Captain's interest, but to him the portent was huge, the best news yet. It meant that the drill had entered the dome structure proper, and it proved that they were drilling in the right place. As he later told a reporter, "I knew then that I had won the day."[38]

The night of December 9 they had "a little excitement," as Curt understated it. When Al got up at midnight for his eighteen-hour shift, he tried as usual to make all the hole he could. About three o'clock in the morning, he noticed that the pump was working freely and the rotary was turning "as easy as could be."

The evening before, they had put up an additional twenty-foot joint of drill pipe, ready to go into the well. Now, Al began to let the pipe down. Both pump and rotary were still going easily. Disbelieving, he kept going. Soon he was able to let all the pipe down, "as if there was nothing down there at all." About an hour later, he detected a gassy odor. He tried to investigate, but the lights were too dim.

As the sun rose over the hill, he saw on the surface of the slush pit the rainbow sheen of oil. "[It] had come out in bubbles and bursts, quite a little bit of frothy oil on the dish and quite a little in the pit," Al recalled. "So when the boys came out with my little bit of breakfast, why, we looked at it and sent Peck for . . . Captain Lucas."[39]

Lucas hurried from his house, demanding to know what they had found. Al told him it was oil.

"How much of a well do you think she will make?" Lucas asked him.

The only wells Al had ever seen were those in Corsicana, where a big producer flowed ten barrels a day. Based on that experience, he guessed as grandly as he could. "I think she'll make 50 barrels a day, Captain," he said firmly. In the wake of the coming discovery, that amount would be so small as to be of no account at all.

Lucas watched the slush pit for awhile, then suggested they put up another joint of pipe to determine the extent of the oil sand. It proved to be thirty-five feet in depth, lying at around 870 feet.[40]

They couldn't decide how to bring the well in. They had drilled right through the oil sand, and at the time, measures such as "cementing" a string of pipe with heavy mud or cement to harden and seal it, or using a perforated pipe, or "strainer," to strain out the soft sand, were unknown.[41]

They tried extracting the oil with perforated four-inch pipe, but the sand was too soft and fine. It kept fouling the pipe, perhaps as deep as two hundred feet inside. They even attempted using an ordinary bed sheet, then a fine metal mesh to strain out the oil, but nothing worked. The sand came right through. Lucas instructed them to hang four-inch pipe in the hole with one joint of six-inch on the bottom, reaching just to the top of the sand. Then he went back to town and wired John Galey to come immediately. It took Galey three days to reach Beaumont. In the meantime, the crew rigged the bailer and sandline, ready to bail the well the minute he arrived.[42]

They spent a week trying to bring the well in. The first time Galey directed them to run the bailer, they made a small flow of oil, reaching almost to the swivel boards, or "double boards" (the platform around twenty feet above the derrick floor). But there was quite a bit of sand in the bailer. When they went in again, the pressure had heaved the soft sand up into the hole. "The cussed thing stopped 300 feet from the bottom," as Al put it. They washed out the well and tried to bail it a second, then a third time, but with the same result. The well had sanded up again.[43]

This time, the hill nearly defeated them. Galey called an on-site conference with Lucas and the exhausted Al, and they stood in the December wind next to the derrick, weighing their options. Galey told them that he was considering abandoning that site and moving to another on the other side of the hill when Caroline Lucas, who had come out to the location, intervened.

"Mr. Galey," she said, "the contract calls for drilling this well to 1,200 feet. I'm not satisfied with this test. I feel that every effort should be made to carry this well down to [that depth]. We need to know what there is down that far."

There followed "some conversation" between her, Galey, Lucas, and Al. Al didn't report exactly what was said, but the result was that Caroline Lucas carried the day. They decided to keep drilling—to the full twelve hundred feet. As Curt said later, "She was a fine lady with a lot of determination."[44]

It was a telling incident. In that realm of high capability and forceful personalities, assignment of credit for a particular achievement often depended on viewpoint, but everyone seemed to have a deep respect for Caroline Lucas, apparently a peacemaker and a steadying influence in all situations.[45]

After Carrie Lucas had persuaded the men to keep drilling, they faced the

Carrie Lucas and Al Hamill, who always spoke of each other with great respect. *Courtesy Houston Metropolitan Research Center, Houston Public Library, Houston, Texas.*

problem of removing the drill pipe, which was carrying a six-inch joint at the bottom of the string with four-inch pipe just above it. Pulling it was going to be tantamount to threading a rope through the eye of a sewing needle.

Galey turned to Al. "Do you think you can pull that string of pipe?" he asked.

"I don't know, Mr. Galey," Al said, thinking to himself that it was going to be impossible.

"Well," Galey said, "I'll tell you what you do. You try to pull that pipe. Can't do anything with it the way it is. And set the six-inch through that and go on down and see if there's anything below. If you can get that done," he went on, seeing that the boys were completely worn out, "well, shut down for Christmas."

They did it, but it wasn't easy. "Well, we had a pretty tough time pulling that pipe," Al later reported. "Old Providence was with us. It would never happen again, I think."[46]

The December 21, 1900, edition of the *Beaumont Journal* carried an article by Anthony Lucas. It spoke of his persistence, his hope of presenting the citizens of Beaumont with containers of oil as Christmas gifts, and his disappointment when the oil sand could not be developed.

Captain Anthony Lucas and Caroline "Carrie" Lucas. *Courtesy Tyrrell Historical Library, Beaumont, Texas.*

The Captain declared that rumors that he had made a major oil strike and was hiding it were untrue; according to him, the oil floating on the top of the slush pit probably fueled the talk. Although it might have appeared to a novice to be a sea of oil, Lucas was more disappointed than elated, because salt water had been found in the well, always a bad sign.

The newspaper went on to say: "But all is speculation mingled with a disappointment to Captain Lucas . . . too keen to be appreciated and too delicate to find expression in words."[47]

On Christmas Eve, 1900, the Hamills safely landed their six-inch pipe at 880 feet on the hard formation below the oil sand. That day they set the pipe with no trouble and were able to shut down in time for Al and Curt Hamill to catch the train for Corsicana on Christmas Eve. They spent Christmas at home with their families—they had earned their holiday.[48]

When they returned to Beaumont on New Year's Day, Curt brought with him his wife and four children. They found a cottage between Sour Spring Mound and the "Pee Gee" railroad track.[49] Eva Hamill, with only a young African American man to help her, took care of the drilling crew; the men ate and slept at their house, and Al ferried Curt and Peck back and forth in his buckboard while they kept the well going.

They were drilling mainly through hard formations, making fairly good headway, when they hit another pocket of gas. With a great roar, it blew all the

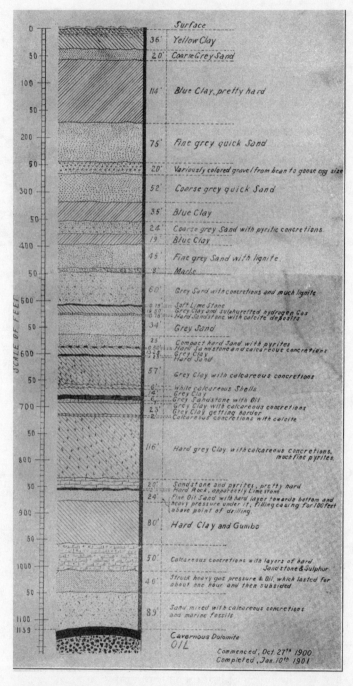

Well log, constructed and published by Captain Lucas after the fact. *Courtesy Tyrrell Historical Library, Beaumont, Texas.*

water and mud out of the hole. Luckily, it lasted only about ten minutes, doing minimal damage to the rig, but it furnished quite a welcome for Jim Hamill, who had come in from Corsicana that day for a visit. He had driven to the well site in a buggy, pulled by a pair of ponies. At the noise, the ponies jerked loose from the fence where they had been tied and ran all the way back to Beaumont.[50]

At around 960 feet, the crew hit a substance they had never encountered before. When it came to the surface, the yellow stuff floated on top of the water. The men gathered some of it and saved it in five or six fruit cans. When Lucas examined it, he pronounced it "floating sand." Later, they discovered that the substance was sulphur. It amused Curt to think that Lucas had originally come to Beaumont to look for sulphur, but he didn't recognize it when he found it.[51]

In the days after January 1, the crew made a total of 140 feet of hole, drilling through assorted layers of limestone, calcite, dolomite, and sulphur. They finally hit an especially hard rock.[52]

The hill had saved a last obstacle for them. At a little over a thousand feet, they ran into trouble. They drilled into the rock a short way, perhaps three or four feet, then the bit stuck in what seemed to be a crevice. If they turned it one way, it went down five or six inches; if they gave it a quarter turn the other way, it began to back up. When they drilled, the pipe hung up and jerked the rotary chain to pieces. With the pipe jammed in the rock formation, they kept grinding away without making much headway. They fought it for two or three days, then decided their bits were dull, "just nubbins, you might say," as Al put it. He wired Jim in Corsicana for a new fishtail bit.[53]

In the early morning of Friday, January 10, 1901, in the raw, stiff wind and clearing sky of a fresh Texas norther, Al hooked up the company buckboard and drove it into Beaumont to pick up the bit. Lucas was not at the well that day; he was in town, where he had set up an office of sorts at Louis Mayer's store, buying up more leases, as Guffey and Galey had directed.[54]

Coming into town on Park Street, Al encountered Pattillo Higgins, who was headed north into Hardin County to close a land deal. The men exchanged casual greetings, then went their respective ways. Al met the train, went to the freight depot to retrieve the new bit, and drove it back out to the well, arriving about mid-morning. He, his brother Curt, and Peck Byrd attached the bit to the drill stem and began running the string of pipe back into the hole. The weather was cold, and they wanted to push past this latest obstacle as soon as possible.[55]

Fifteen-year-old Earl Chaney, the son of the Reverend John Chaney, woke up that morning to the biting cold and realized that, with the new norther blowing in, the temperature was too low to do any plowing. Instead, he saddled his pony and loped it the mile and a half due west from his father's farm to Sour Spring Mound to watch the drillers at work.

The prairie was empty, even of livestock, except for the skeletal outline of the derrick on the crest of the hill, silhouetted against the winter sky. Young Earl reined in his horse near the derrick and propped one leg across the saddle horn to watch.[56]

He saw the three men, Al, Curt, and Peck Byrd, dressed for warmth and braced against the north wind. He watched as they changed bits, then begin lowering pipe into the hole. Al and Peck were working on the derrick floor and Al was running the draw works, as he usually did when they were coming out of or going back into the hole. Curt was on the swivel boards, putting on the elevators to lower the pipe.[57]

They ran around thirty-five joints of pipe back into the well, reaching seven hundred feet. Then a strange thing happened. The whole rig shuddered, and the machinery began to rattle violently. The drilling mud began boiling up through the rotary mechanism. The flow increased until it was flooding over the derrick floor in reddish brown rivulets that soon became rivers. From his ringside seat on his pony, Earl heard a gurgling noise, a "hissing, spewing sound."

A low rumble came from deep in the earth, and the gurgle became a roar. The mud blossomed into a fountain, then began to blow skyward until it spewed up through the top of the derrick. Intermixed with the mud, rocks began to shoot hundreds of feet into the air to rain down on the derrick and the surrounding countryside.

The first blast of mud and water blinded Curt, up on the swivel boards. He dived toward the ladder. By the time the second blast came, he had reached it, but his feet either slipped off the rungs or were knocked off by the force of the blast, he didn't know which. Later, he wouldn't remember how he reached the derrick floor. Apparently his descent was efficient in the extreme; Earl watched as he "came down off that rig so fast you couldn't figure it was a man."[58]

Al and Peck, who had dived under a nearby barbed wire fence, yelled to Curt to get into the clear. But he could see that the clutch in the draw works was still in gear. The machinery was still running, and the traveling block was cannoning toward the top of the derrick. If it went all the way up, it would crash into the crown block and tear the derrick down. Then gas began to spew out of the hole "to beat the cars," as Al would say later. The stench of the sulphur gas saturated the air; if the north wind had not been so strong, it might have overcome them.[59]

Somehow, in the rain of mud, water, and rocks, Curt made his way across the derrick floor and kicked the clutch out. He couldn't see, but the other two kept yelling to him. The roar of the well was so deafening that he could hardly hear them. Guided by their voices, he made his way toward them and off the derrick floor.[60]

By this time, the drill stem was moving up out of the hole, higher and faster by the millisecond. As the crew watched, stunned, several tons of drill pipe rocketed through the top of the derrick several hundred feet into the air, blasting away the traveling block, the elevators, and the crown block. As the joints of pipe reached the apex of their ascent, they twisted backward to the ground or broke off in sections as they fell heavily to the prairie beneath.[61]

With his shirttail, Curt wiped the muck out of his eyes. He must either have detected oil in the fallout or sensed what was to come, because he suddenly remembered the boiler—and the fire. The smokestack had been knocked from the boiler by the falling crown block, but the fire was still burning. He called for help, and the three men managed to put out the fire by dipping water out of the boiler pit and throwing it into the firebox. Then they turned and ran for their lives. By a miracle, no one was hit by either the rocks or the falling pipe.

As they stared in shock from a safe distance, the geyser gradually began to die away. The sudden silence assaulted their ears. Then, as Al put it, "We three boys . . . sneaked back down to the well and surveyed the situation . . ."[62]

Their operation was a shambles. Mud stood six inches deep on the derrick floor, and broken machinery and pipe lay in ruins all around the surrounding prairie. The drill stem, with the bit still attached, protruded from the ground where it had stuck into the earth. According to Al, all they could think about was that it was "Mr. Galey's drill pipe, but it was our responsibility." The pipe was now unsalvageable, and they didn't know how much of the hole was ruined. But they had to start somewhere. "I rather expect," the mild-mannered Al later admitted, "that I was pretty disgusted." He turned to grab a shovel.[63]

With an explosion like a cannon shot, a six-inch chunk of mud blew out of the drill hole. A little flow of "blue gas" followed, then all settled into quiet again. Al edged over to the hole and peered down it. He heard something

Heretofore unpublished shot of Lucas Gusher taken by Beaumont photographer A. L. Clark. Pictured are Charles and Will Roberts of Galveston, the grandfather and uncle of Patricia Giddings, who donated the picture to the Spindletop/Gladys City Boomtown Museum in Beaumont. *Courtesy Spindletop/Gladys City Boomtown Museum, Beaumont, Texas.*

"kinda bubbling just a little bit." He stared, transfixed, at "frothy oil" down inside the hole, rising and sinking back with the ebb and flow of the gas pressure. He said later that *the oil looked as if it were breathing.*[64]

That oil kept coming up, higher and higher, until it flowed over the rotary table—higher still, until, with a tremendous roar, it shot through the top of the derrick in a solid six-inch stream of greenish black crude oil. Al fled as it crested in a towering plume over 150 feet high, more than twice the height of the derrick, then feathered out to float southward in the stiff north wind. The hill had finally yielded its treasure, hoarded for so many eons. The giant slept no more. In Curt's words, "it come in a pure-D oil well."[65]

In all the excitement, the men hadn't even noticed Earl Chaney. When Curt had slid down from the derrick, he had landed quite near the youngster, but hadn't even acknowledged his presence. As Earl said later, "he was too busy getting out of the way of that oil."[66]

Young Earl watched the well blowing wild for about a half hour, then roused himself and ran his pony home. His mother, father, and seven siblings, who had heard the noise and had seen the black plume of oil, were standing electrified in their front yard, watching and listening. The Reverend John Chaney immediately mounted his horse and hurried over to the well to see if he could assist. He would later help to guard it and recruit mule teams to build levees for confining the oil.[67]

After the Hamills had pulled themselves together (in Al's words, "I imagine we were rather excited . . ."), they sent Peck Byrd on the run to fetch Anthony Lucas.[68]

"He's in town," Caroline Lucas told the breathless Peck, "but I'll try to get him."

Mrs. Lucas finally located her husband by telephone at Louis Mayer's Drygoods Store.[69] As Al told it,

> [Lucas] jumped in his old buckboard with his old horse and beat it to Spindletop . . . he came over the hill there where we could see him, the horse in a dead run . . . When he got so close . . . there was a gate down there, I guess . . . the old horse stopped and Cap fell out and ran up—of course, he was very heavy, you see, and time he got up to me he was just about out of breath.
>
> And he says, 'Al—Al—what is it?'
>
> And . . . when I says, 'Why, it's oil, Captain,' well, he just grabbed me and says, 'Thank God, thank God.'[70]

Curt reported that, in the Captain's excitement, he hugged every man on the job.

> He practically squeezed me in two as he did Al and Peck Byrd. And
> he was very much elated . . . over what had happened, but didn't
> know what he was going to do with the wild well . . . [71]

Lucas did have the presence of mind to issue instructions to the crew to keep the crowds away from the well; the danger of fire was huge, and it had by that time occurred to every man there.

As soon as he collected himself, the Captain mounted his buckboard, headed his horse northward, and hurried back to town. Once more, he wired Guffey and Galey in Pittsburgh, this time with far different news. When the news reached him, John Galey got on the first train heading to Beaumont.[72]

Carrie Lucas could see the well from the front porch of their house, only a mile away and in plain view. "There my wife stood in the door watching the display," Lucas later wrote, "and it was a heap of satisfaction to see her there. She soon came hurrying over to the gusher, and the look of joy which illuminated her countenance was reward sufficient for all the worry and work I had gone through." The Lucases' son, twelve-year-old Tony, had stayed home from school that day. He later remembered that he rode his three-dollar horse to see the well. (As he later explained, for five dollars you could buy a horse that was broken. His was not.)[73]

"I don't remember just what I did [after the well came in] . . . ," Anthony Lucas said afterward. "The men say I burst into tears. I know that an hour later I was at home with my wife and boy in my arms, and we were all crying for sheer joy."[74]

Chapter Seven

SPINDLETOP

"Captain Lucas has struck oil. His well has exploded and blowed h—l out of things. It's spoutin' oil so fast it's runnin' in rivers all over the prairie."[1]

YEARS later, witnesses still vividly recalled their first sight of the great plume of oil. The spectacle—and the accompanying noise—spread the word as quickly as the telephone.

About two hundred feet from the well, six-year-old Dillard Singleton sat in a parked buggy, waiting for his father. They had come driving out the old Beaumont–Sabine Pass road to see what was happening on the hill. His father was walking toward the location when the well blew in. "It just like to scared me to death," Singleton recalled later. The frightened horse "raised up as far as them [*sic*] shafts would let him go . . ."[2]

Around three hundred yards from the well, half a dozen carpenters were building a new barn for Perry McFaddin. "They come off that building," Curt Hamill reported, "just like rats when that well blew in . . ." Others, though farther away, also saw the oil drifting like a banner above the flat, bald prairie. Local drover Plummer Barfield, a boy at the time, was duck hunting with friends in the riverside marshes. He heard the roar, saw the geyser and rode over to see the phenomenon for himself. Perry McFaddin, in the midst of putting in a rice irrigation canal a mile away, hurried over to see the "big show." African American employees on McFaddin's land thought that "IT (the end of the world) had happened," recalling that the windows rattled in the ranch house where they were staying.[3]

The well emitted a steady, mind-numbing roar that could be heard for miles. The noise terrified farm animals (as well as their owners) and frightened passengers on a Beaumont-to-Sabine train three miles away. The oil soaked every blade of marsh grass within miles and saturated the ground underneath. It ran down the hill in torrents, collecting in the hollows and flowing out onto the prairie at the bottom of the hill. It enraged local farmers, whose crops were instantly drenched with a thick, greasy coat of tar-like crude oil.[4]

Local resident W. B. Fehl, whose family lived on the south side of town not too far from the hill, recalled,

> When it happened, people just come runnin' out [to the well], just crazy, just went wild, y'know, on horseback, and buggies . . . we all run upstairs, where we could see it just goin' up in the air, just makin' an awful noise, just a-roarin'. . . .[5]

Within the hour, men, women, and children began to flock to the drill site in all kinds of conveyances—horseback, wagons, buggies, bicycles, on foot. The citizenry of Beaumont, after making a "tremendous rush for the livery stables," streamed out to the well.[6]

It wasn't long before the first of the thrill-seekers showed up. One of the first was a man who paid no attention to the crew's instructions to stay away. As Curt Hamill told it, the man crawled through the fence and started for the well. Curt caught up to him and walked along with him, begging him to keep back.

"I was born and raised right here," the man said stubbornly, "and I'm going to that oil well." By the time he got there, three or four more had crawled through the fence, heading to the well.[7]

When Anthony Lucas returned from wiring John Galey, there were more than fifty people crowded close around the well, and there was nothing the helpless crew could do. According to Curt, Lucas lost his temper, "blew up" and threatened to authorize his crew to use a shotgun if they had to. (When asked later if he believed Lucas to be an excitable man, Curt answered that the Captain wasn't excitable at all, but at that time, he was definitely excited. The Captain had ample reason; the threat of fire was already haunting him.)[8]

Lucas recruited guards from among the local citizenry and put them under the command of town leader Perry Wiess. Fifty men were appointed to patrol the hill during the day and forty at night in order to control the steadily increasing crowds. They were instructed to allow no one to venture close to the well except with proper orders, and above all to strike no match. Securing gang plows and forty four-horse teams from the McFaddin-Wiess-Kyle company, Lucas gave orders to build levees and to plow under the oil-soaked grass.[9]

Dillard Singleton (right), who saw the Lucas Gusher blow in, pictured in 1902 with his father, Newton Singleton, the first law officer in the town of Nederland. From *Nederland Centennial History. Courtesy Michael Cate.*

At some point, one of Perry McFaddin's workmen remarked, "Mister,
that's some gusher, ain't it?" The nickname stuck. From that moment on, the
well was known as the Lucas Gusher.[10]

The *Beaumont Journal* received its first report of the discovery from oil
man W. R. J. Stratford, who, with his brother, was prospecting for oil in the
area. Only a few hundred yards from the drill site, Stratford had heard the distinctive "singing sound" the well made just before it blew out. Not long after,
local farmer Charles Ingalls rode into town, oil-soaked and angry because the
rain of oil was ruining his farmland. He announced that the oil was spouting
"at least 100 feet above the top of the derrick."[11]

To confirm the story, the *Journal* telephoned local resident Butch Wyatt,
who lived near the well. Wyatt reported that he could see the "oil flowing high
into the air" and being "wafted over the prairies by the wind." Finally convinced, the *Journal* jubilantly predicted that "the Queen of the Neches [Beau-
mont] can therefore prepare for a development and consequent commercial
excitement such as has never before been experienced by a Texas city." The *Enterprise* announced that Lucas had struck "A Geyser of Oil," adding that "this
will no doubt equal any ever struck in the best fields in the United States."[12]

The news reached Tony Lucas's classroom and cleared it of students. (Tony himself had stayed home from school that day.) Many local citizens climbed to the top floor of the Jefferson County Courthouse, four miles away in Beaumont, for a panoramic view, among them young Charles Berly, who climbed all the way to the cupola to see the phenomenon. "The [well] was going wild," he remembered,

> . . . probably spouting 150 feet in the air. . . . Nobody realized the significance of it at the time. We didn't understand oil in those days as a fuel. Oil was axle grease and kerosene for lamps . . . not fuel. . . . In fact, people were pretty disturbed about all that mess that was all over the face of the earth out there. . . . They were worried about the fact that it was going to kill all the fish in the creeks and inter- fere with agriculture . . ."[13]

Beaumont photographer H. I. Ostebee, who billed himself as "the high-priced photographer," missed the shot of a lifetime because of jury duty. Under the caption "Enforced Suspension," he ran an ad in the *Beaumont Journal* January 8, 9, and 10, declaring that "As I have been impressed on the jury, my place of business is necessarily closed for the present week. Will re-open as soon as the powers that be liberate me." He was held captive too long. It was Port Arthur photographer Frank J. Trost who made the shot of the Lucas Gusher, with Anthony Lucas standing proudly beside it, that would shortly become world-famous.[14]

That night, Carrie Lucas insisted that the Captain track down young Al Hamill and bring him home for a little rest and some home-cooked food. Al was eating breakfast with the Lucases the next morning when the first of the oil men arrived at the Lucas home on their way to see the well: T. J. Wood from Corsicana; S. M. "Golden Rule" Jones, the mayor of Toledo, Ohio, and manufacturer of oil field equipment; and none other than J. S. "Buckskin Joe" Cullinan.[15]

At one point in the conversation, Cullinan asked Lucas the depth from which the oil was flowing. According to Al, Lucas thought a moment, then replied that he believed the depth of the well to be 1,160 feet. Al, knowing that they had used fifty-one joints of twenty-foot pipe in the hole, which would bring the total depth to 1,020 feet, wondered if the Captain was deliberately misleading Cullinan, but he said nothing. Lucas spoke sincerely, however, be- cause the first version of his well log, published later, reflected a total depth of 1,160 feet. (In a later version of the log, he revised the depth to 1,139 feet.)[16]

The shot of the Lucas Gusher that would become famous throughout the world, made by Port Arthur photographer Frank J. Trost the afternoon of January 10, 1901. Anthony Lucas can be seen standing proudly to the right, and Jim Hamill is thought to be second from the left. *Courtesy Texas Energy Museum, Beaumont, Texas.*

Boomtown crowds congregating at the Crosby House Hotel, on left, across from the Southern Pacific Railway station. *Courtesy Tyrrell Historical Library, Beaumont, Texas.*

Lucas made another error, too. He had originally reported to John Galey that he believed the well to be flowing thirty-five thousand barrels a day, but he had gauged wrong. As it happened, that amount was only about a third of the actual volume, which was later estimated to be anywhere from seventy thousand to one hundred thousand barrels a day.[17]

The day after the well came in, Lucas must have been gratified to receive a telegram from Calvin Payne, the Standard Oil expert who had advised the Captain to return to his profession of mining engineering and who had been one of the direct causes of his "selling his birthright for a mess of pottage" to Guffey and Galey. The telegram extended Payne's warmest congratulations to Lucas for his success and informed him that he was coming down to see the "new wonder."[18]

By the end of that next day, all the liquor in town had been sold out and the news of the discovery was all over Texas. "Big Strike In Oil," read the January 11 *Galveston Daily News*. Within days, the world knew. The front page of the *New York Times* announced a "Big Oil Strike in Texas," calling it "A World Beater." Londoners learned of the "Lucas Oil Geyser" from *Lloyd's Weekly Newspaper*. "The rush is so great that it is impossible for the crowds to obtain

accommodation in and around Beaumont. . . . The fever has affected all classes of the community, even the lawyers, with the result that the courts have had
to close their doors and suspend business." The *American Lumberman* of
Chicago asserted that "Beaumont is now well known in St. Petersburg, Berlin,
Paris, London, Melbourne, and every capital in the world, because of this
great burst of oil."[19]

Anthony Lucas was the hero of the hour. Beaumonters on their way to
the well stopped by his home to congratulate him. (A local Italian grocer who
had recently sold his land near the well for five hundred dollars, more than
double the amount he had paid for it, even brought Lucas two heads of cab-
bage in gratitude for making him "rich.") The press fought to be the first to
interview the man who had brought about such a phenomenon.

One reporter caught him at his home shortly after the well came in. "It
would be difficult to imagine a more thoroughly happy man," the anonymous
journalist enthused. "He picked the reporter up in his arms and fairly carried
him into his handsome residence. Here a bottle of rare old wine was opened
and the success of the faithful oil investigator was drunk." The writer further
described Lucas as a "well-informed and well-educated gentleman, and in his
library has a collection of minerals and curiosities which is both interesting
and valuable."[20]

Wrote another: "The sanest man in this town . . . is the man who, in face
of discouragements that would have broken the spirit of a weaker man,
brought in the first gusher . . ." Newspapers hounded Lucas for quotes, even
when they were less than memorable. "We've struck oil is about all I know to
tell you," he told one reporter the day after the discovery. "You can tell almost
as much about it as I can tell you." (It is possible that the Captain had run out
of adjectives, or was simply tired of talking to reporters.)[21]

Pattillo Higgins heard the news and saw the geyser of oil erupting against
the southern sky when he returned from Hardin County late in the day of the
discovery. Bypassing his home, he headed directly for the hill. Seeing the
thundering column of oil, he probably experienced the whole gamut of bit-
tersweet emotions. He stood vindicated tenfold; the well was flowing more
than even he could have foreseen. In the course of a few hours, he had metamorphosed from fanatic to prophet. The populace of Beaumont would now
look at him with new respect. Yet he had been denied the satisfaction of direct
participation in the venture he had dreamed of and worked for so long.[22]

He must have derived some gratification, at least, from encountering his
old geological nemesis, William Kennedy, on the streets of Beaumont soon

Trade at the Crosby House, the "center of the oil world," during the boom. *Courtesy Tyrrell Historical Library, Beaumont, Texas.*

after the Lucas well came in. "Now, there was a mortified man," Higgins remembered. "I can still hear him saying, 'Well, Mr. Higgins, I was a little wrong about the oil, wasn't I?'"A little wrong!' I exploded. 'Ye gods, man, you were just a few billion dollars wrong—that's all!'"[23]

With the word out, the citizens of Beaumont braced themselves for the first wave of strangers eager to view the phenomenon for themselves. Six trains made daily runs into Beaumont, but within twenty-four hours of the discovery, railroads were forced to organize special excursions. Even with the augmented schedules, the trains still could not keep up with the crowds. "The gusher has been a regular Klondyke for the livery stables and hotels," reported the *Beaumont Journal.* Thousands, including a sizable number of women, poured into town, where they willingly paid ten dollars for a hack to take them down the Beaumont–Gladys City road to the field. Once there, they tramped about in the oil and the mud and gazed, mesmerized, at the spouting well, which the *Beaumont Journal* described as " . . . too grand for intelligent description . . . it is the sight of a lifetime."[24]

Other visitors came with more serious intent—and wasted no time. In addition to oil men Wood, Jones, and Cullinan, who had already shown up at the Lucases' door the morning after the well had come in, the *Enterprise* of January 12 reported the morning trains "crowded with oil men from all parts of the country." They created "a general stir, hunting transportation to the well." Operators and promoters of every stamp came from oil fields in Corsicana, California, Pennsylvania, Ohio, and Indiana, and from the business centers of New York and Chicago.[25]

One early arrival was J. L. Caldwell of Huntington, West Virginia, a prosperous coal, railroad, and banking magnate, who heard the news from his son-in-law, Perry McFaddin. Leaving Huntington January 14 on the 3:30 A.M. train, he arrived in Beaumont January 16 and was soon writing enthusiastically, "Biggest oil well I ever saw . . . the oil I think is good."[26]

Caldwell immediately met with oil men in Beaumont, among them Guffey, Galey, and Lucas, as well as the "Standard men," Joseph S. Cullinan and Elgood Lufkin. A few weeks later Caldwell, McFaddin, Valentine Wiess, and others formed the McFaddin-Wiess Oil and Gas Company, which forthwith elected officers, leased twenty-four thousand acres of land from the McFaddin-Wiess-Kyle interests, and applied for a charter from the state.[27]

The oil men were soon followed by land agents, newspapermen, and all manner of profit-seekers, honest and dishonest, wealthy and desperate. "The town continues to fill up," reported the *Galveston Daily News*.

> The streets resemble a great holiday event. Business is seriously impeded by the excitement. Physicians are becoming real estate men. The lumber industry is forgotten in the wild rush for oil land. . . . Throngs of people frequent the streets until late at night and everything is oil.[28]

The Crosby House, Beaumont's best hotel, became

> the center of the oil world. . . . The lobby was a seething mass of excited prospectors and individuals who had come to see the greatest wonder of the twentieth century, while many rooms were occupied by parties who were critically scanning the map of Jefferson county . . . to see if the lands they had been offered were desirable locations."[29]

Beaumont's hotels and boarding houses, of all sizes and degrees of respectability, filled beyond capacity. Clerks rented out every room, then lined

"A. Broussard, Undertaker [and] Livery and Boarding Stable" in Beaumont, used as lodging for the human species during the oil boom. *Courtesy Tyrrell Historical Library, Beaumont, Texas.*

the halls with cots. Even the chairs in the lobbies were reserved, often for months in advance. Some strangers were fortunate, and prosperous, enough to find space in private homes.[30]

The majority of newcomers, lacking money or perhaps forethought, walked the streets, unless they found a spot in a barber chair, a hayloft, a saw-dust pile, a tent or shanty on a vacant lot, or on an open pool table. H. P. Nichols paid three dollars a night to sleep in the loft of Broussard's livery barn, the bed consisting of a little straw covered with a tarpaulin, where millionaires and working men alike tried to steal a few hours sleep. "I'm certain I never heard a more wonderful exhibition of snoring," Nichols commented later, "from *basso profundo* to coloratura soprano."[31]

Each afternoon, boomers filled outgoing trains, seeking accommodations in the nearby towns of Sabine and Port Arthur or farther off in Houston or Galveston. Others slept on the train, taking the late-afternoon run to Houston, then catching the Pullman that returned to Beaumont at six o'clock the next morning. Prosperous businessmen from the North and East chartered their own Pullman cars.[32]

Eating establishments suffered the same rush of business. Restaurants and cafes were, in the words of one newspaper, "cleaned out." At one point,

Oil lake at Spindletop, pooled from early gushers at the field before oil tanks were built. From William Battle Phillips, *Texas Petroleum* (Austin, 1901). *Courtesy Mary and John Gray Library, Lamar University, Beaumont, Texas.*

armed guards corralled lines waiting to enter restaurants. Not even Beaumont's twenty-five saloons, ample for a population of ten thousand, could handle the hordes that descended upon them, though they were overjoyed to try. All hospitality establishments could name their prices.[33]

In the meantime, the spouting well continued to saturate the landscape. Fog carried greasy mist and sulphur gas from the well into the south end of town, turning the white houses a "sullen hued yellow," discoloring the exteriors of the buildings in Beaumont, besmirching paintings on the walls of the residences, and tarnishing silver. "I painted their houses," Pattillo Higgins was heard to remark with pardonable pride, "every one of them." No self-respecting housewife dared hang out her laundry. The morning after the discovery, the *Enterprise* reported "oil all over the prairie around the well" and the surrounding atmosphere as being "impregnated with the smell of oil."[34]

The liquid collected in a natural low area at the eastern base of the salt dome and in great, ever-increasing lakes in the surrounding prairie. In an effort to save it and to protect his nearby grazing land, Perry McFaddin diverted men and mule teams from their canal work to scrape up dirt levees into a makeshift reservoir. The next day, they had to build a second one. John Galey, arriving in Beaumont on January 13, put out a call for all available men and scrapers, no matter what the cost. Dikes soon circled the well by a quarter mile.[35]

As the huge lake of oil grew, Galey, Lucas, and the Hamills worried constantly over the waste and especially the danger of fire. "There was no rest or

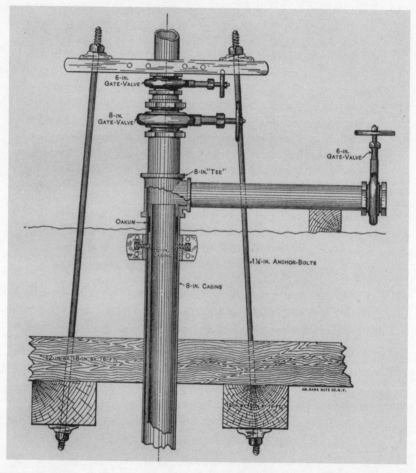

Drawing of gate valve assembly used to close the gusher. From Reid Sayers McBeth, *Pioneering the Gulf Coast: A Story of the Life and Accomplishments of Capt. Anthony F. Lucas. Courtesy Tyrrell Historical Library, Beaumont, Texas.*

sleep for me until the well was closed," Lucas later recalled. "If that fluid should take fire it would mean the utter demolishment of the entire town."[36]

On Sunday, January 13, the worst almost happened. The morning had dawned clear and cold, with a heavy frost. Curt and Peck Byrd, who stayed at the well from sunup to sundown every day, had put on slicker suits over their other clothes for warmth. During the morning, five or six hundred people had gathered behind the barbed wire fence on the adjoining Higgins land. Someone dropped a lighted match onto the oil-soaked grass near the well. The oil instantly burst into flames.

Lucas was dining at home with his family that day. Around noon, Carrie called his attention to dense black smoke billowing from the direction of the well. He looked out the window to see columns of flame shooting many feet in the air. For a moment, by his own admission, he stood stunned. He knew that, if the well was on fire, it lay beyond their capabilities to put it out. He said a hasty prayer, then bolted for his horse, which was standing saddled at the front door of the house. He rode like a madman to the well to find, to his immense relief, that it was only oil-saturated grass that was burning, not the well itself. But the danger wasn't over; the fire could still reach the well.[37]

Most of the spectators were running for their lives, but Curt and Peck Byrd had pulled off their slicker coats and were fighting the fire. Seeing them, many came back to help them fight it with coats, blankets they jerked from under their saddles, boards from McFaddin's barn, and anything else at hand. By the time they put out the fire, more than an acre had been burned. Although it never reached the well and no one was seriously injured, it underscored the urgent need to harness the gusher, which was presenting problems new in the annals of oil history. "Now that we've got her, boys, what are we going to do with her?" Lucas is supposed to have asked the crew in sheer bewilderment.[38]

After John Galey arrived in town and had duly pronounced himself elated over his new well, harnessing it became his first order of business. Lucas, Jim Hamill (who had come into Beaumont the day after the gusher blew in), Al, and Curt met with Galey in his room at the Crosby House. Lucas reviewed the propositions he had received to close off the well, some from as far away as San Francisco. All were expensive. A woman in Illinois had even offered to use her occult power "to discipline nature"—for ten thousand dollars.[39]

Galey listened awhile, then turned to Jim. "What do you think about shutting it in?" he asked.

"Mr. Galey," Jim said, "I think we can do it."

"All right, Jim," Galey said in his quiet way. "Go to it. You boys drilled the well; you should have the chance to do the rest."[40]

It was Jim Hamill who masterminded the project. Lucas approved their plan, and they moved the rotary equipment away, straightened the bent, twisted pipe as best they could, and wired quick orders for fittings. Al swiped two railroad irons (lengths of track) from the Southern Pacific, and the crew fastened them to the girths of the derrick.[41]

On January 14, a T-valve, consisting of a vertical pipe and a horizontal joint, arrived by train from St. Louis. The crew built a heavy carriage assem-

Anthony Lucas (left) and John Galey in front of the Lucas Gusher on January 18, 1901, the day before it was capped. From William Battle Phillips, *Texas Petroleum* (Austin, 1901). *Courtesy Mary and John Gray Library, Lamar University, Beaumont, Texas.*

bly to house it, then secured the entire device to the railroad irons, in position to be dragged over the well's spouting jet of oil. The gusher was still heaving occasional chunks of rock, and Galey cautioned them that, to avoid damaging the gate-valve mechanism, they had better wait until the flow was clear.

The morning of January 19, around 10:00 A.M., he came out to the well. "How's it been acting?" he asked. They told him the well hadn't thrown any rock that morning."Well, boys," the old wildcatter said, "let's shut her in."[42]

They devised a series of hand signals in order to communicate above the roar of the oil. All donned protective gear—slicker suits and hats, goggles sealed around the edges with adhesive tape, gauze over their noses, and plaster over their ears, because they would be working in a deluge of oil. Al Hamill, as the bachelor, volunteered to perform the most dangerous task— cutting and rethreading the protruding end of the existing wellcasing to receive the valve assembly. J. S. Cullinan, an interested observer, warned Jim Hamill that Al was in "great danger." "Jim, you watch that kid," Cullinan said. "If he hits a spark there, why . . . it would be impossible for him to get out."[43]

While the other men held their breath, Al took a hacksaw and cut the protector off the top of the eight-inch pipe, then "dressed . . . up" the threads, all in the rain of oil. The job took several slow, agonizing hours. Once he had readied the pipe, the crew rigged a windlass, block and tackle and hitched up a team of horses. At the signal, they drove the horses forward at rapid speed, and the animals began to drag the carriage assembly, containing the open gate valve, across the shooting stream of oil. As the apparatus cut into the stream, the force began to rock the derrick, and Lucas recalled picking up a fossil from the ground and throwing it at the horses to urge them to greater speed.[44]

Although the whole derrick shook under the tremendous pressure from the column of oil, it held together. The boys from Corsicana had built it well. They anchored the assembly in place, then gradually closed the vertical valve, diverting the oil flow into the horizontal pipe.

"Curt," Al said, "you turn the valve there, will you?"

Curt rushed in and closed the valve to the horizontal pipe, shutting off the flow completely.

"Just like that," Al said, "it was over." To wild cheers and thunderous applause from the onlookers, the exhausted, oil-soaked crew lined up and bowed to their audience, and Lucas is said to have pitched his hat into an oil pond in celebration.[45]

They constructed a heavy iron casing around the well and banked the wellhead assembly with sand to protect it from fire. On January 19, 1901, nine

Drawing of derrick and gate valve from Curt Hamill, *We Drilled Spindletop. Courtesy Tyrrell Historical Library, Beaumont, Texas.*

days after it blew in, the Lucas Gusher, that "mighty belching of nature," as one journalist had called it, was finally brought under control.[46]

Contemporary accounts of the amount of oil the well had produced varied wildly, but later estimates put it at one hundred thousand barrels a day—during those nine days, almost a million barrels had poured out onto the prairie, most of it either burned or absorbed into the earth.

At first, capping the gusher did not stop the flow of visitors. The next day, over five hundred sightseers from Galveston packed into a special thirteen-coach excursion train to Beaumont. On discovering the gusher had been shut down, they tore down the protective fence, swarmed up to the derrick, and would have opened the valve had it not been covered with sand. "Altogether, it was a most exciting day," reported the *Galveston Daily News* with satisfaction. "The weather was fine, and the Beaumont people were on the streets in thousands. All manner of carriages, buggies, and fashionable traps and auto-

The capped Lucas Gusher, in foreground, its derrick already removed. Later, when the well was reopened, it never paid for itself. *Courtesy Texas Energy Museum, Beaumont, Texas.*

mobiles were whizzing through the throngs. . . ." The reporter explained that Galveston had "oil fever," and that Galveston bartenders had gone so far as to name their drinks "gusher punch," "oilerette," "geyser julip," and "spouting fluid."[47]

For weeks, the crowds pouring into Beaumont ebbed and flowed, governed only by excursion-train schedules and every scrap of news or rumor that issued from the oil field. Inevitably, however, the excitement began to die down. Two months after the discovery, the *Kansas City Star* correspondent reported with some relief that

> [t]he windjamming land traders who [mounted] boxes or railings at
> every opportunity to call their lists, are gone; their megaphone
> voices are stilled and the people who fill the sidewalks are dealing
> like sane beings. The map and button fiends, lusty loungers, every
> one of them, are quiet and the photograph and souvenir vendors
> have ceased to howl. The spectacular side of the boom is disappear-
> ing fast. But if—so much hinges on 'if' in Beaumont . . . these out-

side wells come in[,] the boom may rise again on the spectacular and speculative side.[48]

In fact, everything hinged on the "if." The day of the discovery, the *Beaumont Enterprise* had briefly interrupted its own exuberant narrative to issue a single, small warning: "Of course it is too early to predict the value of the discovery."[49] The worth of the field depended entirely on the quality, as well as the quantity, of the oil. If it proved to be a light grade, suited for illuminating or lubricating purposes, a small field would be profitable; a large one could actually ruin the existing market. If the grade was a heavy one, usable only for fuel, the field would have to be a large one to be able to supply the industrial market.

Early evaluations of the oil varied widely. Driller W. R. J. Stratford, in his capacity as a "well-known chemist," pronounced the oil to be "very superior [containing] lubricating oil and also illuminating qualities." J. S. Cullinan first judged the "grade heavy and the quality indifferent," while another Corsicana oil man pronounced the grade to be superior to that field's oil. In a possible sour-grapes evaluation, a reporter from a Pennsylvania newspaper called the gusher "overrated," declaring crankily that by its dark green color and strong odor the oil "would make a good disinfectant for some of the garbage wagons in Bradford."[50]

Before long, however, it was determined that Beaumont oil was of a heavy grade, therefore not of much use in the manufacture of kerosene. Initial disappointment was mitigated somewhat, however, by the fact that it was indisputably suited for fuel, a finding applauded by those connected with the Lucas well. Anthony Lucas observed that "[t]he heavy oil is much more valuable to the producer and the country than would be the illuminating oil."[51] John Galey maintained that

> if it had been a light oil, the oil markets would have been demoralized and the oil could not have been sold at the cost of production. As it is, there will be a good market for fuel oil when the country has had time to adjust itself to using liquid fuel.[52]

Others shared Galey's belief in a future market. The *Houston Post* asserted that "[f]or fuel oil a great demand can be developed." The *Galveston Daily News* predicted a "revolution . . . for the people of the west who use fuel." One Philadelphia oil man called the oil discovery "providential," because "a fuel crisis is gradually approaching the industrial world." In February of

1901, Lucas himself made the first sale of oil for Guffey to a mining company in Louisiana.[53]

The catch was, of course, that the field had to be a big one to justify a fuel changeover from coal to oil—and only more gushers would determine that. While some oil men held back for the verdict, others, trusting to faith or gambler's instinct, moved full speed ahead, even before the Lucas well was capped.

Those with land already under lease had a head start. Lucas, Guffey, Galey, and the Hamills prepared to drill a second well some six hundred feet east of the Lucas Gusher. W. R. J. Stratford and fellow oil prospector J. A. Paulhamus, with Jefferson County wells already in progress, continued drilling with renewed enthusiasm, though both were drilling off the hill.[54]

As it happened, Pattillo Higgins was the first to drill on the hill after the Lucas well came in. He had wasted no time in organizing the Higgins Oil and Fuel Company, which included prominent Beaumonters John N. Gilbert, W. S. Davidson, and L. B. Pipkin. He sold his thirty-three-acre pasture, which was located in Spindle Top Heights, the subdivision on the northeast flank of Sour Spring Mound, to his own company and announced that he would drill two wells in Block 29, the boundary line of which lay only one hundred feet north of the Lucas well.[55]

For those just getting started, finding land to lease or buy was the first priority—and a challenge of no little magnitude. Lucas, Guffey, and Galey had leased the lion's share of the acreage on and around the hill; enough remained, however, to cause a scramble. Lucas was learning a number of hard lessons; in his excitement, he had failed to follow Galey's previous orders to secure leases on the rest of the hill, assuming that the given word of the landowners would be sufficient. After the gusher came in, the only additional lease he had been able to obtain outside the original Gladys City and Mc-Faddin-Wiess-Kyle leases was the fifteen-acre Page tract. The other leases had gone in record time, to the highest bidders. Al Hamill said later,

> Lucas had it all promised to him, all those tracts . . . and all he
> thought he'd have to do when he wanted it was go down here and
> say, 'Here, Charlie Ingalls, I want you to sign this lease. Here,
> Adams, I want you to sign this." Well, this boom came on, and
> heck! There was [*sic*] thousands of dollars offered to them the next
> day or maybe that afternoon.

Al further speculated that "if Mr. Galey had . . . known the condition those leases were in, he would never've let us start up when he did at Christmas."[56]

On the very afternoon the discovery well came in, four Beaumont businessmen—O. B. Greeves, C. A. Hageman, and brothers Marion K. and Emmett A. Fletcher—kicked in a thousand dollars each to buy Charles Ingalls's oil-saturated seven acres near the gusher. (Ingalls would have sold for two thousand dollars, but his wife wanted an equal amount.) The four, none with prior experience in oil, formed the Lone Star and Crescent Oil Company.[57]

J. A. Paulhamus warned Beaumonters not to "get excited and sell too quickly to curbstone brokers." Some, however, chose not to wait. Land prices skyrocketed, not only on the hill but all around Beaumont and Jefferson County. The *New York Times* reported "fabulous offers" for land, as high as fifty thousand dollars for ten acres, and other high prices paid by "wealthy oil syndicates." One reporter, citing the ridiculously inflated land prices, pronounced the oil men to be "disgusted" with local landowners.[58]

If so, they hid their feelings well. Early arrivals among the oil men made their leases or purchases as near the gusher as possible and got rigs up and running. David R. Beatty, late of Galveston, where he had played a major role in recovery efforts from the Great Storm, arrived in Beaumont January 11 with only twenty dollars cash. He quickly leased ten acres about one-half mile north of the well from an unemployed lumber millwright named Lige Adams, who in turn promptly landed a job cooking for the drilling crew. Beatty hired two experienced drillers from Corsicana already drilling for Paulhamus, brothers Jim and Bill Sturm, and commenced drilling February 10.

Hard on Beatty's heels came the Heywood brothers, well known in the vaudeville and music world, to trade one show for another. Scott Heywood, who had dabbled in Alaskan gold and California oil, arrived in Beaumont as the Lucas well was being capped. He contacted his brothers—Dewey, Alba, and O. W.—and the four joined forces with Iowa entrepreneur Captain W. C. Tyrrell, who had landholdings in Port Arthur, to form the Heywood Brothers Oil Company.[59]

Conspicuously absent from the early rush to find oil was Standard Oil Company, John D. Rockefeller's feared and hated industry monopoly. Standard had been officially unwelcome in Texas since 1900, when its subsidiary, Waters-Pierce Oil Company, had been convicted of unfair marketing practices under state antitrust laws and ousted from the state, but legal action did not stop Texans from seeing a Standard man behind every bush. (In fact, after Lucas's first visit to Beaumont in 1899, the *Beaumont Enterprise* had

The Beatty, Heywood, and Lone Star and Crescent gushers, in a possibly enhanced shot. It is extremely unlikely that the three gushers ever actually spouted at the same time. *Courtesy Tyrrell Historical Library, Beaumont, Texas.*

warned of a possible Standard agent trying to lease land, not for drilling rights but to keep out other oil companies. The reporter warned land owners against making "indefinite leases.")[60]

By turning down both Higgins and Lucas, Standard had missed its chance to get in on the ground floor of the action, but it was common knowledge that the company had the power to jump in at any time. The *New York Times* reported that individual drillers and small companies planned to form a combine "with a view of shutting the Standard Oil Company out of Texas entirely." The early and continued presence of Standard men in Beaumont constantly fed rumors, one of which asserted that John D. Rockefeller himself was on his way to see the well. It never happened.[61]

When the Lucas Gusher had come in, Standard's only immediate response had been to cut the price it was paying for Pennsylvania crude from $1.25 to $1.20 per barrel, forcing oil producers to sell before the price dropped even lower. In the meantime, the company kept close tabs on the developing industry, but chose to bide its time.[62]

By February 20, 1901, thirteen rigs were up at the oil field, drilling their way into the hill. Besides the Lucas Gusher and Guffey and Galey's two additional rigs, these included derricks belonging to the Higgins Oil Company, the Heywood brothers, Wynn and Broughten, Sabine Oil and Gas, and D. R. Beatty.[63]

In the early morning of March 26, just under eleven weeks after the Lucas discovery, the Beatty well blew in as the second gusher of the field, estimated to be capable of producing seventy thousand barrels per day. The location, a full twenty-five hundred feet north of the Lucas well, was a good sign that the oil field was not a "freak" located in a "mere pocket," but large enough to provide "an almost unlimited supply of oil."[64]

Shortly afterward, the Heywood brothers brought in their first. Then Guffey and Galey, in partnership with Lucas, brought in two more, and on April 18, the Higgins Oil Company's first well made the sixth gusher on the hill. The Lone Star and Crescent Oil Company brought in its first well on May 3, and the Hogg-Swayne Syndicate its first in June. By late June, the *Beaumont Journal* reported a total of thirteen gushers. Beyond any doubt now, Lucas's well was not a fluke. The field was real.[65]

In a final irony for Pattillo Higgins, it is probable that, when he decided to drill in Spindle Top Heights, he inadvertently gave the field its name. His dream had been of Gladys City, but the oil field he had envisioned would not carry the name he gave it. The sobriquet of Spindle Top was already associated with the area; the old landmark on the river had lent its name to the subdivision on the hill and to Spindle Top Avenue, the road running northeast and southwest that bisected it. Doubtless the name also appealed to journalistic imagination; the *Beaumont Enterprise* theorized that the transfer must have come about "through . . . the fertile brain of a newspaper correspondent or reporter."[66]

Once the press laid hold of it, the field irrevocably became known by its new name: Spindletop.

Chapter Eight

BOOMTOWN

"Beaumont is today the center of the universe and is being mentioned more frequently through the papers than New York, Chicago, or any of the other great cities."

—Houston Post, *April 21, 1901*

"Beaumont was a mighty tough place for a good while . . ."

—Al Hamill[1]

THAT spring, as the new Spindletop gushers blew in one after the other and the field emerged as a reality, madness reigned. As the newspapers had predicted, the boom began all over again.

West Virginia businessman J. L. Caldwell spoke for the town—and for history—when he noted in his journal: "Big excitement—went to see the Big Gushers. . . . Sayed [sic] by old men never equaled by the wild excitements of 1849 or the wild days of Oil City Pa . . . great crowdes" [sic].[2]

What effect does a phenomenon of such worldwide import have on the place where it occurs? What happens to a small riverside lumber town, set on its predestined course, when faced with an event of such magnitude? Suddenly Beaumont, with a population of a little less than ten thousand, became the center of worldwide attention, hosting thousands of strangers. The *Houston Daily Post* reported at one point that "The depot and galleries of the Crosby Hotel were all black and moving like an ant hill."[3]

One correspondent described the atmosphere:

Excitement was slow to commence, but, like heavy machinery, more terrible and uncontrollable when under way. Strange faces began to be seen in the streets, the postoffice and telegraph employes [sic] were put on their mettle, shipments of cots went round

"Lodging 50¢," photograph from *Harper's Weekly*, circa 1901. The tenants of these tents probably felt royally accommodated. *Courtesy Tyrrell Historical Library, Beaumont, Texas.*

to the hotels, and then day by day the fever grew till the city roared like a hive and trains came in crowded with impatient men who leaped off before the station was reached. And behold, Boom and Frenzy ruled the day![4]

According to Perry McFaddin,

Everybody was selling and buying land. A man couldn't lie fast enough to keep ahead of what actually happened. Tents and shanties were put up as fast as men could do it; the trains were dumping from 300 to 400 new people every day, and you never saw so much excitement in all your life. Everybody was getting rich . . . Every hotel and rooming house in the city was overcrowded and people slept every which way. It was a second Klondike rush. . . .[5]

The boom mushroomed, then spun out of control. At its height, the population of Beaumont soared to an estimated fifty thousand, although the number changed hour by hour. Excursion trains brought in thousands of people daily, disgorging fifteen thousand one memorable Sunday. Night brought only a slight reduction in the crowds; while many of the strangers were sightseers, many more came determined to stay until they got rich.[6]

The amazed and bemused little town found itself entertaining types as

Train disgorging crowds in boomtown Beaumont. Note hacks lined up to ferry passengers to Spindletop Hill. *Courtesy Tyrrell Historical Library, Beaumont, Texas.*

foreign to its streets as Buffalo Bill Cody's Russian Cossacks. In the overnight avalanche of humanity, the greedy, the criminal, and the bizarre jostled elbows with big oil men and hometown boys. A reporter likened the scene in Beaumont to a "street fair." "A new class of people walk the streets," one newspaper noted. "New enterprises are on every hand, street fakirs, museum attractions, and all sorts of little money-making schemes abound in almost endless variety." Everywhere there was the "aggressive hustling of the male bipeds who have everything on earth to sell from a peanut to that earth itself . . . "[7]

Some of the most successful of these hucksters were those who claimed to be able to find oil, and they were not all males. From her room in the Cordova Hotel, one Madame LaMonte, of unknown origins, charged ten dollars for her advice on land and stock transactions. She made enough to consider purchasing the entire hotel block, but unexpectedly left town with her earnings, probably to avoid retribution.[8]

A thirteen-year-old from Uvalde, Guy Finley, billed as "the boy with the X-ray eyes," claimed to "see" oil in the ground. He located at least one

Boom crowds at the Crosby House, where maps of oil fields covered the walls and the lobby resembled a miniature stock exchange. *Courtesy Tyrrell Historical Library, Beaumont, Texas.*

successful well. He and his father were in the process of negotiating a contract with a prominent Beaumonter when he quit, believing that he was not meant to capitalize on a natural gift.[9]

One newcomer who sought his fortune at Spindletop was George Parker Stoker, a young physician who left a successful practice in the eastern United States to come to Beaumont at the height of the boom, lured by "thrilling tales of the Croesus-like fortunes" to be made. Stoker later wrote a vivid account of his days in the boomtowns entitled *Oil Field Medico*, published under the pseudonym of George Parker.[10]

Stepping from the train on a drizzly spring day, Stoker watched mule teams pulling heavy oil field equipment through belly-deep mire, "plunging, falling into the mud, getting up to lunge again, as the singing whips tore at their backs, and the raw curses of the mule-skinners filled the air."[11]

Stoker headed toward the Crosby House, which to him looked like "an old scow pushed up against the banks of a river." The hotel gallery and surrounding flower bed had been divided into numerous temporary stalls by planks nailed between the front wall and the gallery bannister. Maps of oil fields or likely locations covered the makeshift walls and the tops of tables and desks.

A "sidesaddle" gusher, or capped well whose flow was reopened on command for the benefit of investors and sightseers. *Courtesy Texas Energy Museum, Beaumont, Texas.*

Stoker, fascinated, watched the proceedings:

> An intense air of excitement pervaded the place. Men and women,
> gesticulating wildly, ran from one stall to another. Stacks of green-
> backs stood out in vivid contrast against the blue of the maps. I
> had never seen so much money.[12]

More chaos confronted him inside the Crosby. The lobby resembled a
miniature stock exchange run amok. Brokers and traders stood on tables and
chairs, shouting out what they wanted to buy or were offering for sale in the
way of stock, leases, or land. "Well-dressed, prosperous businessmen stood
talking to the rough-neck in high boot and slicker suit. Disheveled, hard-
faced women screamed at each other above the din." Those unable to find a
spot at the Crosby rented space in saloons or made do with makeshift furniture in barns, abandoned buildings or even along the sidewalk.[13]

Becoming an oil-boom broker required only energy, panache, and a limited amount of business sense. Land and leases were sold and resold, usually

Investors in the Big Four Oil Company, dressed in Sunday best, unusual for most oil field photographs. *Courtesy Gary Volbirding.*

for cash, with values increasing exponentially. A small tract of land that once would not have brought $150 was sold for twenty thousand dollars in the wake of the Lucas Gusher, then resold instantly for fifty thousand. After the Beatty well came in, the land went for one hundred thousand dollars. J. L. Caldwell sold twenty-four and a quarter acres of McFaddin-Wiess Oil and Gas Company land, property the company had originally purchased for slightly over two dollars an acre, for twenty-five thousand dollars. Land on Spindletop Hill remained the most coveted, especially when, to tantalize visitors, owners of capped gushers obligingly opened the valves to bring them roaring into life.[14]

Countless sales were made without benefit of abstracts or titles, only a small-scale map and the seller's assurance that the transaction was legitimate. "There is going to be a great deal of litigation grow out of this oil business,"

The Beaumont Oil Exchange and Board of Trade. *Courtesy Texas Energy Museum, Beaumont, Texas.*

prophesied the *Galveston Daily News.* "Some leases have been noted in which there is no royalty consideration specified. . . . Other leases do not definitely specify the land."[15]

The discovery triggered a frenzy of charter applications for stock companies. By the end of 1901, over five hundred land and oil corporations chartered by the state of Texas and hundreds more chartered in other states were operating in Beaumont. Corporations were chartered under an endless variety of names, some predictable, some whimsical—the Commercial Oil Company, the Sour Lake Franco-American Oil Company, the Bay Shore Oil Company, Old Glory Oil Company, Grace Oil Company, Federal Crude Oil Company. The Lucky Dime Oil Company and One-Penny Oil Company were named for the price of their stocks.[16]

Although many stock companies were legitimate, more were fraudulent. Anyone could, and many did, organize a corporation, capitalize it, and sell certificates without knowledge or even intention of actually drilling wells, then take the money and run. Some promoters organized multiple companies at the same time. Magazines gave out oil stock with subscriptions. So many people lost money on bogus stocks and other crooked schemes that the oil field finally earned the nickname of "Swindletop."[17]

Anthony Lucas himself fell victim to some of these shady operations, not as investor but as unwitting endorser. Promoters knew that his name on anything would guarantee sales, hence the Lucas Oil Company was chartered without Lucas being listed as a director. Perhaps this was the same company that reportedly sent a representative to Lucas's office to gain permission to use his name. When Lucas protested that the land had not been proved, the caller declared that it didn't matter—Lucas's name alone would ensure stock sales. The Captain was a big, well-muscled man, in excellent physical shape. The promoter made it to the door in record time, and not under his own power.[18]

In a desperate effort to provide investors with some protection, a group of Beaumont businessmen, led by "Colonel" Sam Park, founded the Beaumont Oil Exchange and Board of Trade on May 15, 1901, selling one hundred seats at three dollars each and admitting only those companies regarded as legitimate. By 1902 the Beaumont Oil Exchange had been joined by others in Galveston and Houston.[19]

Even before the initial shock of the phenomenon wore off, the Beaumont populace began preparing for the many benefits that oil would bring to the town—shipping, railroads, ironworks, foundries, retail businesses, and more. A cheap and plentiful fuel could power local industry, process resources, and assure the town's future as a manufacturing center. After passing an ordinance prohibiting oil drilling within the city limits, the City Council instantly granted a franchise to a group of Beaumont investors (three of whom were Lucas Gusher landowners) to pipe natural gas and oil directly from the field into Beaumont.[20]

Town leaders determined to create a climate attractive to potential investors. When hotels overflowed, the *Journal* suggested that the city auditorium, then used as a shelter for the homeless, be converted into a "lodging house" for several hundred. Real estate agent C. L. Nash encouraged the Chamber of Commerce to form a "public comfort committee" to connect boomers with citizens willing to rent space in their homes, urging that rates be set at a "reasonable" price. Nash also reminded locals to sell property, whether in the city or near the well, at prices that would attract investment.[21]

Local businesses wasted no time in exploiting the new market. Just days after the gusher had come in, fabricators of cisterns, both wood and metal, added oil tanks to their advertised inventories. C. W. George Manufacturing Company actually constructed the first tanks in the oil field; they were made of cypress wood and located near the Lucas well. Beaumont's three brickyards, anticipating a building boom, planned expansions; in an uncanny echo of Higgins's earlier idea, at least one announced plans to use oil for fuel.[22]

To broadcast the town's good news to the world, the *Journal* proudly published a special "Twentieth Century Oil Edition" for distribution at the Pan American Exposition in Buffalo, New York. Newspapers in other cities praised the town's quick efforts to capitalize on its new industry. "The Beaumont People," proclaimed the *New Orleans Times-Democrat*, "have gone to work energetically to develop this business—to bring their oil into general use as a substitute for coal."[23]

Indeed, Beaumonters intended to do just that, predicting that oil would fuel the transportation and industry of the world and that railroads and steamships, as well as manufacturing, could save money by switching from coal to oil. Every day brought new prospects for future industries that would use Beaumont oil, including a center for smelting ore from an "iron mountain" located in nearby Jasper County and a rice mill and adjacent brewery in Beaumont. By the end of the year, locomotives from several railroad companies, including the Southern Pacific Railroad, were being converted into oil burners, and fuel oil was being used to fire boilers in sugarcane refineries in Louisiana. [24]

Faced with the whirlwind chaos of the boom, most Beaumont folk reacted philosophically—and pragmatically. Perry McFaddin would not allow his wife, Ida, or their young daughter, Mamie, to go to town alone. Some rented their spare bedrooms; the mother of Mayor D. P. Wheat occupied the entire second floor of her son's house and let all but one of the rooms on that floor to boomers. "She was just goin' to town at a dollar a night," her grandson recalled. Others opened full-blown boarding houses. Enterprising individuals set up tables in empty lots or hawked sandwiches or pie on the streets to feed the hungry hordes.[25]

With all hacks taken, family carriages or buckboards—anything that would make it to the oil field—were pressed into service, charging as much as the market would bear. Boys sold small bottles of oil from, and photographs of, the Lucas Gusher. They charged fifty cents for copies of Pattillo Higgins's map of Jefferson County, the same that he had once handed out for free.[26]

The same boys profited from the town's woefully inadequate sanitary facilities. In a vain effort to accommodate the huge crowds, civic officials installed outhouses downtown. The boys waited in the endless outhouse lines and, as their turn came near, sold their spots to desperate boomers. Lines became even longer as a gastrointestinal condition known as the "Beaumonts"

Open-air cafe in boomtown Beaumont. Beaumonters capitalized on the boom in any way they could. From *Harper's Weekly*, circa May 1901. *Courtesy Tyrrell Historical Library, Beaumont, Texas.*

affected boomers who drank from Beaumont's public water supply, which came unprocessed from the river and was described as "soupy" and smelling like "alligators, bullfrogs, and fish."[27]

Health facilities were hopelessly overloaded. Since the 1898 opening of Beaumont's Hotel Dieu Hospital, its administrative order, the Sisters of Charity of the Incarnate Word, had already dealt with a smallpox epidemic, but that hardly prepared them for the oil boom. The forty-bed facility's staff of seven nuns, eight graduate nurses, and six trainees worked nonstop, treating everything from oil field injuries to gunshot wounds to typhoid fever to widespread venereal disease. Overworked or underqualified oil field doctors often sent their patients to the hospital to die. In March of 1901, the Sisters held a benefit concert to pay for the addition of private rooms and a badly needed charity ward. Before long, the hospital contained eighty beds, desperately needed and constantly occupied.[28]

Local forces of morality and religion had long faced more than they could say grace over in the rough little lumber town, but the population explosion that came with the oil boom brought newer and bigger problems. Customers stood in front of bars six to eight deep. Beaumont's "Sunday Laws" were generally ignored, since a given day's profits amounted to far more than any fines that might be levied. Temperance enjoyed some support, but during this period only a small minority actually favored prohibition.[29]

Long before Spindletop, the Woman's Christian Temperance Union had offered free ice water on downtown streets as an alternative to alcohol for lumber and river workers. After the gushers blew in, the organization became even busier, competing not only with the burgeoning numbers of saloons but also the increasing scarcity of safe drinking water. To bolster support for its cause, the W.C.T.U. held a temperance lecture in the city auditorium. Because the building had until recently served as a shelter for boomers, it had to be fumigated first, to banish any unsavory reminders of its former occupants.[30]

A few weeks after the boom began, the Salvation Army arrived in town to set up permanent headquarters. Local commander Ensign Walter Yager rented the Millard Hall on Pearl Street for services each evening because the city auditorium was inconvenient, "uncomfortable, and unclean." The Salvation Army also planned a series of street services and benefits, including a "graphophone entertainment" that cost adults twenty-five cents and children a dime to attend.[31]

Vice during the oil boom provided Beaumont's ministers with endless fodder for sermons. Saloons and bordellos became prime targets. The Reverend C. M. Davenport of the First Methodist Church exhorted parents to be aware of the "evil dens" that tempted their sons and to realize that "none were free from danger," naming the "gambling dens and the saloons with all their glitter and glare and every inducement to entice the boys and young men and the different so-called amusements to hold them when once inside."[32]

The newspapers also garnered new material for metaphors; in reviewing Davenport's sermon, the *Beaumont Journal* reporter remarked that "oil spouts, and big oil fires" were nothing in comparison to the minister's inspired prose. Shortly thereafter, possibly out of gratitude, the good Reverend asked God's blessings on editors and reporters of Beaumont newspapers.[33]

Davenport's successor, the aptly-named Reverend V. A. Godbey, thundered, "When we talk of immoral occupations in our city, will it bring to your mind that you rent property for immoral purposes? Are we *particeps criminis* in the wickedness of this city?"[34]

Saloons and bordellos, with their accompanying activities, had long been an accepted, if not always welcome, fact of life during the town's lumber days. During the oil boom, the number of saloons burgeoned from twenty-five in 1900 to eighty-one by 1903. They were also, in the words of Beaumont physician D. W. Davis, "scattered all over town"—throughout the central business district, near the railroad depot, and in residential areas.[35]

The unsavory and often illegal nature of saloon activities did not prevent socially prominent Beaumonters from enjoying the pleasures to be found there, or occasionally cashing in on profits. The *Journal* editor wrote,

> Distinguished Beaumonters who are deriving revenue from gam-
> bling houses by permitting their buildings to be used for such pur-
> poses need not ask mercy in the event of indictment or prosecution.
> They are not violating the law ignorantly. A greed for gold has
> deadened their conscience and they will have no just cause to com-
> plain of punishment both by the courts and by publicity.[36]

Policeman Will Armstrong, following mayoral orders, attempted to shut down a saloon that, one Saturday night, was operating past midnight. The woman running the establishment refused. "You better wait and find out who's in here," she threatened. She proceeded to call the chief of police, then the mayor pro tem, from the back room. They declined to support her, how-ever, and since they themselves were not violating the law, Armstrong took only the woman to jail. The next morning she was assessed a two-hundred-dollar fine and released.[37]

In spite of the additional wealth the boom had brought him, the consci-entious George W. Carroll deplored the vice it had generated. Known for his stance against saloons, in 1903 he decided to challenge the widespread gam-bling in Beaumont, to which he felt local law was turning a blind eye. He chose as his target one of the town's most thriving saloons, the Ogden. To gain admittance, he disguised himself by shaving off his beard of many years and donning old clothes. Once inside, he quietly observed the blatant gam-bling for a short time, then climbed onto a nearby table and announced a raid. Once the crowd recognized him, the room cleared instantly. Though he ef-fected little long-term reform, for the next few weeks there was a marked de-crease in the gambling in town. At least one local citizen opposed Carroll's reform movement; Pennsylvanian Jack Ennis, who had come to Beaumont as field manager for Guffey and Galey and later managed both the Parkersburg Tank Company and the new Enloe Hotel, pronounced himself afraid the town would be "run by preachers and prohibitionists," then packed up and left.[38]

Undeterred, Carroll intensified his reform efforts, ultimately becoming the vice-presidential candidate on the Prohibition ticket in the 1904 presi-dential election.[39]

Saloons were not the only local dens of iniquity. The red light district also

covered "quite a territory" in town. Even back in 1898, townsmen, condemn-
ing the houses of ill repute along Forsythe Street as "nuisances to women and
children," had petitioned the City Council, not for eradication, but removal
to "some retired corner." With the influx of new people—and new customers—during the boom, they became even more of a "nuisance."[40]

The law eventually managed to confine most of the bordellos to a smaller district along Crockett Street, which came to be known as Deep Crockett,
or the Reservation. Some Deep Crockett prostitutes still slipped out and went
by hack or horseback to the oil field to do business or to make appointments
with workers for their next trip into town.[41]

Like those of morality and religion, supporters of law and order faced
new challenges. People crowded into town to make money. Some were on the
up-and-up; others operated, if not on the wrong side of the law, at least on the
edge of it. The sheer increase in population was bound to cause greater social
disorder. However, contemporary reports varied on the severity, and Beaumont may not have earned quite the wild reputation it received over the years.
During the boom the *Beaumont Enterprise* claimed to have found a "total absence of drunkenness on the streets with a possible few exceptions." *Harper's
Weekly*, while calling it the "dirtiest, noisiest, busiest, and most interesting
town on the continent today," nevertheless maintained that, given the large
"wads" of money the boomers carried with them, "it is remarkable that there
have been so few thefts and so little crime of any sort."[42]

Whatever the realities, the time of the boom stood out as being rough
and disorderly in the memories of some. One Beaumonter's memory of law
and order was its total absence: "why, during those days, they didn't have it.
Everybody was his own boss . . . and humanity was plumb tore up at that
time." Killings were "quite common, quite frequent those days," remembered
Dr. D. W. Davis, a Beaumont physician. Another resident recalled that, for
nine consecutive mornings, a dead man was found in the "muddy waters of the
Neches River," and that the murderers turned out to be a bartender and his
accomplice.[43]

The gushers kept blowing in and the oil field continued to grow, but during the late spring and summer the frenzy began to ebb. The *Journal* for May
7 remarked with relief that "Sunday was more generally observed in Beaumont yesterday according to the Biblical proscription, than it has [been] in
several weeks." The crowds in town and out at the oil field had thinned; brokers sat in their "offices" on the street and read their newspapers. The worst
of the boom was winding down.[44]

Men at the Crosby House finding a moment of leisure, however brief, to catch up on the news. *Courtesy Tyrrell Historical Library, Beaumont, Texas.*

By August the *New York Journal* could describe Beaumont as a town approaching a normal state.

> Aside from the lack of conveniences consequent upon its rapid growth and feverish condition, Beaumont is a pleasant city to live in. The people are hospitable . . . the temperature never rises above 100 degrees and the nights are cool . . . plans are already proposed for making Beaumont a seaport by the cutting of a deep-water channel . . . the railroad facilities could hardly be better . . . there are large lumber mills in the city. . . . As a rice center Beaumont is also famous.

The reporter predicted that "Beaumont will in a short time be one of the greatest cities of the great Southwest." By the end of the year the town's population had stabilized at around twenty thousand.[45]

The boom that had so benefited the town—and the rest of the world—had taken its toll on the man responsible for it. The ballyhoo, the chaos, and the fraud not only ran counter to Anthony Lucas's purpose, but to his very nature. As an engineer and a scientist, he was concerned with finding oil, not endorsing stock companies. Yet, ironically, he was a magnet for publicity. His knowledge, his integrity, his imposing physical appearance, his dynamic personality—all made him an irresistible subject for the ravenous press, who proceeded to romanticize him as if he had been a latter-day movie star. Wrote one reporter:

> Captain Lucas is . . . over six feet, straight as a gun barrel, power-fully built and has a pair of eagle eyes set in a head full of A-1 brains. . . . strong chin and firm mouth. . . . forgetting that he had made himself rich; thinking only of the riches he had added to the world."[46]

Another reporter rhapsodized about his "massive, protruding chest" and his shoulders, which were "square as any that ever adorned a prizefighter." Yet another stated reverently at the end of an interview with Lucas: "He was splendid." According to still another source, Lucas had a "hearty, cordial man-ner about him . . . [he] has a handsome, open face, a keen, bright eye, and when he becomes earnest in his conversation, looks you square in the eye."[47]

Lucas hated the loss of his privacy. A few months after the gusher came in, an article in the *Atlanta Constitution* reported that he was the "wandering" husband of a Mrs. Anna Lucas and the father of her two sons. Although the story was discredited even before it was printed, it was widely repeated in other national publications. Lucas, declaring that it would have been "rather funny if it had not been somewhat annoying," was still greatly concerned for his wife's sake. In fact, the enormous commotion began to tell on even the in-domitable Caroline Lucas. In the late spring of 1901, she went to visit rela-tives in Dahlonega, Georgia, "where she [withdrew] for a temporary respite from the Beaumont excitement."[48]

Just before the boom began to wane, an Englishman whose name has been lost to posterity presented Lucas with an expensive diamond scarf pin. He told the astounded Lucas that he had been in Bombay, India, when the news of the gusher flashed over the world—and because of the International Date Line, the date in Bombay had been *January 9*. In a scenario worthy of Phileas Fogg, the man had rushed by steamer to Liverpool and then New York in time to capitalize handsomely on the discovery. The scarf pin was his expression of gratitude to Lucas for bringing it about.[49]

As 1901 wore on, Anthony Lucas appeared less and less on the streets of Beaumont. In May of that year, he sold his stock in Guffey Petroleum for four hundred thousand dollars plus one thousand shares of Guffey stock when the Mellon family agreed to finance the formation of the new J. M. Guffey Pe-troleum Company. Always seeking to bring a rational, scientific approach to the mystery of oil prospecting, Lucas continued his search for oil fields in

Medal presented to Anthony Lucas by a hundred of Beaumont's most prominent citizens. *Courtesy Tyrrell Historical Library, Beaumont, Texas.*

Southeast Texas, Louisiana, Alabama, the Carolinas, Georgia, and Kentucky, then eventually into Mexico.[50]

Months after the wild days of the boom had calmed, a hundred of the town's most prominent citizens presented Lucas with a gold medal containing a "first water diamond," crafted by Tiffany of New York. It was inscribed, "Beaumont: To Lucas from 100 Friends."[51]

Pattillo Higgins never received the widespread recognition accorded to Lucas, recognition that he felt he deserved. Some of his vindication came, according to his biographer, at his own instigation; he persuaded thirty-two community leaders to sign a document, dated December 3, 1901, giving him complete credit for the discovery at Spindletop. "Mr. Higgins," it read, "deserves the whole honor of discovering and developing the Beaumont oil field." Higgins then had the document printed and distributed.[52]

By then, he was already off on his next adventure. Angered when his partners in the Higgins Oil and Fuel Company sold a large number of shares to the Houston Oil Company (whose major stockholder was lumber baron John Henry Kirby) for three million dollars in a corporate takeover, he sold his own stock back to the company. In November of 1901, he chartered the Higgins

A sightseeing excursion to Spindletop oil field. *Courtesy Texas Energy Museum, Beaumont, Texas.*

Standard Oil Company, Ltd., to enter into all phases of the oil business from top to bottom—production, transportation, refining, and marketing. Ever the salesman, he put out an expensive seventy-two-page promotional booklet, loaded with propaganda on fields he intended to bring in and pipelines and re-fineries he intended to build. He also took the opportunity to blast the Beau-monters who had failed to support him and the geologists who had told him he was wrong.[53]

Higgins took legal vengeance as well. In May and June he filed three suits, one each against Lucas, Guffey, and Galey for four million dollars, representing the one-tenth interest in the Lucas Gusher he felt he should have received. He also sued Lucas personally for ten thousand dollars in damages in unpaid rents and revenues on the land. Shortly afterward, he sued George W. Carroll for two million dollars, alleging that Carroll and Lucas had based their contract on his, Higgins's, predictions of oil at Spindletop. In return, Carroll sued Higgins in an effort to clarify owner-ship of the mineral rights on the Caswell portion of the Gladys City Com-pany, when Higgins would not respond to unofficial overtures. The suits were later settled out of court for an undisclosed amount, but the personal friendships came to an end as well.[54]

Stock fraud still ran rampant. The Beaumont Oil Exchange and Board of Trade could contain it to some extent, but it could exercise no power over fluctuations in price and market. Nor could it control the capriciousness of the field—variations in gas pressure, for instance, or dry holes next to gushers. Well pressures waxed and waned crazily; every drop in pressure, and every dry hole, triggered fears that the field was playing out. Still, by October of 1901, the Spindletop oil field boasted 440 wells, sixty-seven of them gushers. November and December saw the most spouters yet for a single month, with twenty and twenty-two respectively. At the end of the year, the field boasted 138 gushers and forty-six rigs in the process of drilling, with the search as intense as ever. In January of 1902, driller Walter Sharp brought in the New Year by completing a well in twelve days—a record. The Spindletop oil field was very much alive.[55]

With relative calm restored, Beaumont found itself in possession of a brand new future. Because of Spindletop, possibilities now existed for electric streetcars, paving, water mains, purified drinking water, and other benefits that had only been dreamed of before. And a deepwater channel would make the town accessible to the waiting world market.[56]

Spindletop had already brought a building boom. Names from the Spindletop oil field appeared throughout the list: Valentine Wiess's $150,000 office building, W. W. Kyle's $100,000 opera house, a $50,000 Southern Pacific depot built by Perry McFaddin, and $40,000 buildings for John N. Gilbert and C. T. Heisig. The boom created a temporary shortage of architects. "Building has been considerably hampered in Beaumont for several weeks past on account of the lack of architectural help," reported the *Beaumont Journal* in May 1901. To help him take care of business, architect U. O. Long hired five "expert" draftsmen, some of whom went on to design some of Beaumont's finest homes.[57]

In November of 1901 a *Saturday Evening Post* reporter came to Beaumont, looking for "true" stories of the town's "great oil excitement," especially rags-to-riches tales. "Unfortunately," the *Journal* commented, "there are not many of these since the outside territory was found to be without oil and the land on Spindle Top [*sic*] was all owned by men of more or less wealth." To a large extent, oil wealth followed existing land and timber interests.[58]

The get-rich-quick tales existed, but they were rare. The first frenzied days of the boom, when everyone aspired to become a millionaire, had quickly

Cover of a 1907 pulp novel, as Beaumont, Spindletop, and Texas became a part of the American myth. *Courtesy Tyrrell Historical Library, Beaumont, Texas.*

given way to reality. A relatively small number of survivors would continue in the oil business. Many more—sadder, poorer, but presumably wiser—gave up the cause. "A half or whole interest in a drilling outfit," read one telling ad in the *Enterprise*, "complete with boiler, pumps, rotary table, engines, tools, ropes, blocks, pipe and pipe connections to operate same, and a drilling camp kitchen outfit. Everything in good order and entire."[59]

By the end of 1901, Beaumont's boomtown ordeal was essentially over. But the ripple effect of Spindletop was already spreading from the epicenter at Beaumont to move outward in all directions. Inevitably, attention turned to other upper Gulf Coast salt domes, with their accompanying mineral springs and oil seeps. There was more oil to be found, and in greater quantity than anyone would have dreamed a short year ago.

The partnership of Lucas, Guffey, and Galey began explorations at High Island, a promising salt dome located on Bolivar Peninsula near Galveston Island. The Big Thicket, lying just to the north of Beaumont, would spring its own surprises in Sour Lake, Saratoga, and Batson. In mid-June of 1901, James Guffey brought in a moderate-sized gusher at Sour Lake, renewing interest in the old Big Thicket spa town. After a small strike in November of 1901, the Hooks brothers brought in a gusher at Saratoga, about ten miles northwest of Sour Lake, on March 13, 1902. At five hundred barrels a day, the well was small compared to the Lucas well, but it sufficed to establish the oil field there. In the fall of 1903, the Batson field came in a few miles from Saratoga.[60]

In October 1901, developments also moved eastward. The Heywood Brothers Oil Company brought in a gusher at Jennings, Louisiana, that "spouted to the top of the derrick for seven hours." More discoveries would soon be made on other parts of the Gulf Coast, then the rest of the country, then the world.[61]

Chapter Nine

THE OIL FIELD

"There's something peculiar about a boomer. He will be working . . . on a good job and getting good wages . . . but if a boom starts someplace else, I have known them to quit good jobs, good positions, good living conditions, their families, and go to the boom."

—Oil field worker James Donahoe[1]

THE calm that eventually prevailed in the town of Beaumont in no way extended to the oil field itself. There the boom began to assume a life and an identity of its own.

Long before the second gusher came in, a settlement called Spindletop began to form on the hill. As early as February of 1901 the *Galveston Daily News* reported that "stores are springing up [near the Lucas well] and soon it may be expected that it will become an active and characteristic mining village." Whatever the *News* might have defined as "characteristic," Spindletop would soon earn a reputation for being as rough as any mining town California or Alaska ever saw.[2]

As the gushers blew in and drilling activity became more frenzied, job hunters poured into the field. Word got around that the pay, even for beginners, was well above the going rate of other places. Even inexperienced workers made two or three dollars a day, twice what they could get in any other industry. Experienced drillers might make up to fifteen dollars a day. Given those incentives, men swarmed in from Texas and Louisiana and even farther away, including the West Virginia and Pennsylvania oil fields.[3]

At first there were no real living quarters on the hill, only derricks and crude drillers' shacks. Early drilling crews slept on cots in open, screenless tents or in long wooden structures called bull pens. Sam Webb, who riveted

"Tent Town," workers Walter Leonard Gober and William Louis Gober in the oil fields of southeast Texas. *Courtesy Spindletop/Gladys City Boomtown Museum and Tyrrell Historical Library, Beaumont, Texas.*

tanks for the firm of Harris Brothers, recalled that the oilfield "camp" where he lived consisted of a group of wooden shacks and a cooking area. Alice Slausen, who as a child moved with her family from Houston to Spindletop soon after the Lucas Gusher came in, recalled that "it was so crowded you couldn't get around . . . people milling around and sleeping on the ground and anywhere they could." Most returned to Beaumont each night until sufficient tents and shanties could be thrown together, anywhere and everywhere in the field.[4]

Boarding houses provided some workers with a slightly more homelike atmosphere. Alice Slausen's mother, Polly Ann Shockley, at first ran only a restaurant in her home, where men ate on benches at makeshift tables made of boards laid across nail kegs. But Shockley quickly realized she could turn a profit from the single large room that took up the second story. "Mama put cots up there," Slausen remembered. "She just filled that place as tight up as she could—with just army cots. . . . They was glad to get it."[5]

With the workers came a hoard of support businesses hoping to share in the wealth. Slausen's father, livery stable and saloon operator John Thomas Shockley, told his family, "we may not get rich off of any of this oil, but we're going to get money spent by rich people." Like the houses, most retail busi-

Spindletop boarding house owned by Charlotte Kramer Inkster Sanborn, standing. The child is her daughter, Elizabeth Inkster Sanborn. *Courtesy Charlotte Yust.*

nesses were first located in rough, slapped-together quarters in the midst of the oil derricks. The *Galveston Daily News* described one of the first restaurants: "The ever present restaurant was already on the ground, though there was every evidence that it had only been built a day or so. For it was only a hastily-constructed box house, that is, a house of upright planks, while its new iron roofing had every evidence of having just come from the store." Curt Hamill recalled that among the first merchants to set up shop in the oil field were two Jewish men who sold notions and work clothes from "a very small shack."[6]

While adult males still predominated in the boomtowns, a substantial number of the oil field boomers brought their families with them "to live their days and nights in the mud and sweat and sound of the oil fields." Often they lived literally right next to the derricks, because there was nowhere else for them to go. They set up housekeeping in tents or built tiny box-like shacks out of one-by-twelve boards, batting up the cracks with one-by-fours because they couldn't afford anything else. One man recalled his childhood home at Spindletop as "three rooms, two in the main part and a lean-to in the back," located only about a hundred feet from the nearest well.[7]

The real Gladys City, the tamest part of Spindletop Hill but a far cry from Pattillo Higgins's dream. *Courtesy Texas Energy Museum, Beaumont, Texas.*

Within weeks of the Lucas discovery, a strange, ragtag town began to take shape amidst the derricks, stacks of pipe, and boilers at Spindletop—not a single settlement but three tiny separate ones. Originally Pattillo Higgins, in keeping with his and George Carroll's Baptist beliefs, had designed his dream town so that the property of any landowner who sold alcoholic beverages would automatically revert to the Gladys City Company. The Gladys City that actually sprang up on the old town site, although far short of Higgins's dream, became the tamest part of the hill, at least, and the area where many men located their families. The post office and depot were also built in the vicinity of Gladys City, though the post office carried the name of Guffey, Texas.[8]

A second, larger town, usually called Spindletop, grew up on McFaddin land a few hundred feet east of the Lucas Gusher. There, because of the lack of restrictions, saloons alternated space with boarding houses, restaurants, retail establishments, and offices. This became the roughest part of the hill.[9]

The third settlement, known as South Africa, or Little Africa, was the home of the African American and Mexican laborers. It lay across the tracks of the Kansas City, Pittsburgh, and Gulf, or "Pee Gee," Railroad, near the Neches River.[10]

R. C. Grinnell's Log Cabin Saloon in the settlement of Spindletop, known as the roughest area of Spindletop Hill. *Courtesy Texas Energy Museum, Beaumont, Texas.*

Newcomers looking for hotel rooms got a rude awakening. Physician George Parker Stoker discovered in short order the paucity—and the poor quality—of accommodations; on his arrival in Beaumont during the height of the boom, Stoker, unable to rent a hotel room, a cot in the hall, or even a lobby chair for the foreseeable future, decided to try his luck on Spindletop Hill. He finally secured a hack and driver, who claimed to be able to make the trip "in nothing flat, or better," and assured Stoker that they "would neither flounder nor sink."[11]

They struck out for the oil field at a gallop, the muddy streets of Beaumont soon giving way to a shell road pocked with huge holes. Lurching wildly, the hack flung Stoker from side to side in his seat, while the driver with unerring aim arched long streams of tobacco juice at objects along the road, regaling Stoker with oil field stories. Having asked to be taken to Spindletop's "best" hotel, the young doctor found himself at what was little more than a shack of unpainted planks, with a carpet of mud in the lobby. The furnishings in his tiny room comprised a half-size, sagging bed, unwashed sheets, and one broken chair.[12]

Stoker "inherited" a practice from a middle-aged physician who seized

The shell road to Spindletop Hill, with the oil field in the background. *Courtesy Tyrrell Historical Library, Beaumont, Texas.*

the opportunity presented by the younger doctor's arrival to go on an extended drunk. At first Stoker fought his own disgust at not only the filthy, inadequate office and equipment, but also the "brutality, the gross and flagrant bestiality, the crass ignorance of the people, the loss of life through lack of sanitation, indifference, and violence." But soon after he stitched up his first patient (a worker with a badly cut leg), receiving an unheard-of twenty dollars for his services, he was getting more business than he could handle. Working day and night, he made a great deal of money and soon found himself rushing through the days like all the other boomers.[13]

For the rest of 1901, the settlement at Spindletop continued to grow, commensurate with the constantly increasing number of gushers on the hill. By August of that year, one estimate put the head count of Spindletop at between four hundred and five hundred people. *C. B. Hice's Spindle Top Guide and Directory*, undated but probably published about 1903, lists a population of over fourteen hundred. Like those of any boom, however, the Spindletop boom's days were numbered. When the field was "drilled out," it inevitably died, and the mass of the population moved on, leaving a skeleton crew of pumpers and gaugers, with a few support businesses. By the time Spindletop

"Boiler Avenue," Spindletop Hill. *Courtesy Texas Energy Museum, Beaumont, Texas.*

ceased to produce gushers and became a pumper field, the settlement there had become relatively quiet, although its rough reputation endured for years.[14]

When they left Beaumont, boomers did not have far to travel to find greener pastures in the new fields in the Big Thicket area of Hardin County—Sour Lake, Saratoga, and Batson. They were followed by legitimate retail merchants, as well as the more unsavory element of "gamblers, con men, street walkers, bartenders, madams, robbers and thugs." "After the boom ended in Beaumont," recalled V. B. Daniels, a Sour Lake oil field worker, "all of the riff-raff that was left over there came over here [to Sour Lake]. And from here they went to Batson, and Saratoga and on, further on."[15]

Sometimes the increased influx of "riff-raff" in one town was directly related to cleanup efforts in another. "After we [in Sour Lake] all decided to straighten up things," Daniels commented, "that other class could not live if they didn't get something off of somebody that was earning something." So they migrated to the next booms: Saratoga, then Batson.[16]

Others joined the exodus from Spindletop simply to satisfy their need for excitement. So completely was George Parker Stoker pulled into the oil field's "intangible, sinister, and hypnotic wildness" that after a major fire brought on a lull in drilling activity, he left. "Life had become so exciting for me, both as to experience and earning money," he confessed, with the mind-set peculiar to the boomer, "that the increasing quiet of the place made me nervous." Leaving his practice with one of the local druggists, he headed to the Big Thicket.[17]

Sour Lake was the largest of the three Thicket boomtowns, both before and after oil was discovered. At the peak of the boom, the population jumped to a number estimated at anywhere between three thousand and ten thousand, the majority of them men. Stoker bypassed Sour Lake, opting instead to try his luck in Saratoga. He described that other old spa town, where in November of 1901 the first well came in, as consisting of a two-story frame building, a log house, and a general store, where he set up his office. A few days after he arrived, the onslaught of humanity began. "As quickly as men could hammer the planks in place," he recalled, "saloons, stores, residences, gambling-houses, and red light shacks sprang up."[18]

In the fall of 1903, while Stoker was living in Saratoga, the first gusher came in on Batson Prairie. The actual town of Batson, unlike the other two Thicket towns, came into being only after oil was struck, but within days of the strike, humankind came flocking in from Saratoga, Sour Lake, Beaumont, Houston, and the world. A "business district," consisting of gambling houses, saloons, bawdy houses, and grocery stores, occupied a three-quarter-mile stretch on the main street. "The doors was [*sic*] never hung on the hinges," Batson oil field worker James Donahoe remembered of one establishment. "It was a 24-hour operation." Another boomtown was born.[19]

Donahoe shared the view of many that Batson was the roughest of the Southeast Texas boomtowns. He recalled a gambler's words as he was leaving: "I do not say that everybody here in Batson is a son-of-a-bitch, but I do say that every son-of-a-bitch is here that could get here." In Donahoe's memory,

> . . . the people in Batson at that time apparently came from all over the United States and they was gamblers, whores, and the very lowest class of people that you could think of. And so many went under an assumed name . . . they was all under a cloud.[20]

Indeed, assumed names and colorful nicknames seemed more common than given ones in the oil field. A woman called "Mooch," described as a good fighter and a hard drinker, worked at a Sour Lake saloon, and if any roughneck got down on his luck, "she'd go out and mooch all the oilmen in the country" for his bail money. In Saratoga, bartender Pinky Pete conducted a

RUCKER'S
BOARDING HOUSE.-BATSON
THANKSGIVING-1904

Rucker's Boarding House in Batson, Thanksgiving 1904. *Courtesy Tyrrell Historical Library, Beaumont, Texas.*

running feud with Pug Mulligan, one of his customers. At Batson, everyone knew gamblers One Quarter Lawson and Monk Fife, as well as Six-Shooter Kate, a prostitute and "quite a fighter." Two Gun Bill and Long Jim were saloon men, and Big Thicket Kid and Mexican Joe killed each other in a fight.[21]

One man who came to Batson "under a cloud" was a man known as "Doc" Harris. Harris actually held a medical certificate of some sort, but made his living by keeping a saloon. A neat, flashy dresser who carried both a double watch chain and a gun, he had operated a saloon at Beaumont but moved to Batson after he had "some trouble." (This was probably the same Doc Harris, co-owner of the Metropolitan Saloon in Beaumont, who shot a constable in Beaumont in May 1903 while the lawman was attempting to enforce a Sunday law. In Batson, however, he was remembered as "a tender-hearted man.")[22]

Like mining towns, oil-boom towns were rough, uncomfortable, unhealthy, and dangerous. Southeast Texas oil towns added their own distinctive ingredients to the mix—mud, mosquitoes, and snakes. Moreover, Big Thicket boomtowns could be especially difficult to operate in, because not all of the older residents welcomed the coming of oil. To them, the wealth from the black gold unearthed in their isolated corner of the world did not sufficiently compensate for the chaos, pollution, noise, and general intrusion from the outside.

> Salt water and thick black scum crept over the pastures and contaminated the bayous. Escaping gas was insidious [by nature] and was flared for safety's sake, lighting the woods and driving off game. . . . One astonished [drilling] crew found their horses daubed with assorted colors of barn paint by indignant natives who hated oil in any form. Night watchmen were posted on rigs because the natives took a very dim view of this so-called "progress."[23]

Mud presented the biggest problem in the fields, hindering or actually halting drilling operations. Compounding the problem were heavy rains, beginning shortly after the Lucas Gusher had come in and continuing off and on for months. At one point the *Beaumont Age* reported that the land all around the Spindletop field was

> almost impassable. . . . Teams are dragging wagons loaded with pipe and lumber across the prairie with the wheels buried to the hubs in the mud, while the men are wading about in the marshy ground knee deep in water and slush.[24]

The mud in a slush pit at the Hogg-Swayne tract nearly inundated one Dr. Griffith, described as an "oil operator" at Beaumont, Sour Lake, and other fields. Former gauger W. M. Hudson described him as always dressed in a "hard derby and a long, Prince Albert black coat, and a large, long black beard." During drilling, sand had been blown on top of a thick layer of mud in the slush pit. The wind then spread the sand into a smooth surface that appeared hard and dry. The immaculately dressed Griffith, thinking the pit was solid ground, stepped off "almost to his neck in mud." He was subsequently rescued, his person intact but his image as an immaculate dresser much besmirched.[25]

One inventive saloon keeper at Batson, instead of fighting the mud, turned it into a business asset:

> . . . there was a low flat between the town proper and the field and one man built a walk across that so that they could walk without going through this flat and going through all that mud. And right out in the middle of the walk, he built a saloon, and anybody that went from the field into town had to go through his saloon.[26]

Boomtown residents were forced to share space with vermin and other creatures of the wild. Mosquitoes, the scourge of Southeast Texas, were, in the single word of one Batson woman, "terrible."

> We had to have a mosquito bar over our bed . . . and then at night
> before we would go to bed, we would put a smoke under the bed
> and let it smoke good and shake the mosquito bar good before we
> pulled it around the bed and then usually we would use just a little
> kerosene and rub it all over our bodies and then about midnight,
> we'd get up and smoke again and get all the mosquitoes out from
> the bar.

In addition to mosquitoes, Big Thicket residents coped with alligators, water moccasins "eight and ten feet long," and even sand fleas. "[In Batson] the sanitary conditions was terrible," James Donahoe lamented. "No sewers, nothing . . . I have often wondered why we all didn't die of the cholera. And no screens, and flies by the billions."[27]

Danger in worse forms—fires, blowouts, explosions, poison gas—was never far away. George W. Carroll won a lawsuit forcing safety measures at Spindletop, attempting to persuade everyone to use fire extinguishers (probably nothing more than buckets of sand). His efforts to make it less perilous resulted in part in the formation of a safety committee for the field that established practices, monitored activity and issued rulings. But the fact remained that the oil field workplace was a rough arena indeed, and exacerbating the danger was the constant pressure to produce quickly.[28]

> To get the oil out of the earth and get it converted into money was
> the sole thought of the acreage owners. . . . Employers paid good
> wages for what they had done and slam, bang, clang! They had to
> have immediate results . . . well crews had to work with "rattletrap"
> outfits . . . men worked in the tops of the derricks, hanging on with
> one hand . . .[29]

Every night workers fell into bed exhausted, only to be jarred awake by an emergency call to fight a fire, or a well threatening to blow out. "If you didn't get to bed in 36 to 48 hours," Donahoe remembered, "it wasn't unusual. . . ." Sam Webb's crew usually slept in their clothes. "Stay up all night and go to work the next morning," Webb recalled. "Night in and night out." As to catching up on his sleep, "Didn't catch up," he declared. "Got used to it."[30]

Fire was such a constant threat as to be a virtual certainty, started either

A blaze in October 1902 ignited when oil from a collapsed wooden tank spilled onto a boiler. This view shows the north end of the densely populated Hogg-Swayne tract after the fire. *Courtesy Texas Energy Museum, Beaumont, Texas.*

from human error or acts of God (lightning being a frequent culprit). During its first year of existence the Spindletop oil field suffered several fires, the first occurring the Sunday after the Lucas Gusher came in, when the quick action of the Hamill brothers and assorted spectators extinguished it before it could ignite the still-spouting well.

By the time the danger of fire reared its head again, the gusher had been capped and banked with its protective covering of sand, but an estimated three hundred thousand barrels of oil, part of the overflow from the nine days the well had flowed uncontrolled, lay in an oily lake surrounding the well site. On March 3, 1901, stray sparks from a switch-engine smokestack, driven by a steady west wind, fell into the oil-soaked grass on the west side of the hill, igniting a fire.[31]

Like chain lightning, the fire snaked up a small rivulet to the inland lake of oil. Within seconds, the lake exploded into an inferno, shooting fingers of flame high into the air and belching mushroom clouds of black smoke that

Burning oil tank, possibly ignited by lightning. *Courtesy Texas Energy Museum, Beaumont, Texas.*

darkened the sky for miles around. Men shouted, horses screamed, and confusion and fear reigned as the flames licked eastward across the lake with terrifying speed. At Anthony Lucas's hasty order, Cap Forney, the Guffey and Galey field superintendent, jumped into his buckboard and ran his horse around to the east side of the lake to set a counter-fire. The east side blossomed into flame and began to race west. Al Hamill remarked later that the two fires looked like large buildings, and the space between them like Wall Street. As the two cliffs of flame roared toward each other, the resulting vacuum periodically sucked oil into the air in huge sheets from the surface of the oil lake, where it ignited in giant fireballs that exploded high above the ground, sending flashes like lightning clear across the sky.[32]

When the two conflagrations met in the middle of the lake, skyrockets of flame shot into the clouds to arc flickering to earth like spent Roman candles, and the explosion "shook the countryside," in Lucas's words, "affording a spectacle of unparalleled grandeur." Several local churches, believing that Armageddon had arrived, convened to urge the discontinuation of oil explo-

Multiple fires on Spindletop Hill. *Courtesy Texas Energy Musuem, Beaumont, Texas.*

ration on the hill, predicting that if other wells were brought in, the entire coast of Texas would be submerged in a sea of oil, which would "ignite and destroy all living beings."[33]

As it happened, the final pyrotechnics extinguished most of the fire. No lives were recorded as lost, but damage to surface equipment was extensive—crew housing, rail cars, lumber, pipe, and several rigs were destroyed, as well as numerous livestock. But with the oil lake gone, the safety level of the field actually improved. A new policy was adopted: waste oil, rather than being allowed to accumulate, was thereafter burned weekly.[34]

Inevitably, fire continued to break out regularly on the hill. The field's worst fire, occurring in October of 1902, actually consisted of several fires. A section of the impossibly overcrowded Hogg-Swayne tract, with its dense thicket of derricks, caught first, when oil from a collapsed wooden tank spilled onto a boiler. Before that fire was brought under control, a lantern ignited gas fumes from a well in another section of the Hogg-Swayne. This time, tragedy struck; a roughneck died, caught between the walls of flame. Then, as the remains of the Hogg-Swayne tract burned to smoking ash, lightning struck a tank belonging to Guffey and Galey and the flames traveled into the equally jammed Keith-Ward tract, destroying it.[35]

When the inferno was finally extinguished twelve days later by a providential rainstorm, only George W. Carroll's Yellowpine district, the third densely crowded area on the hill, had escaped harm. Numerous derricks and pumping units had been lost, but by this time drillers had learned to shut off valves and bank wellheads with sand to protect the wells themselves. After each fire, operators literally rose from the ashes to go on drilling, and the safety committee eventually ruled that derricks must be removed as soon as the wells came in.[36]

Explosions came from overloaded boilers or pent-up gas, and either kind could blow rig men into the air—in pieces. Gas was one of the greatest dangers in the oil field. Under pressure, it exploded or shot rocks through ten-inch well casings like cannonballs. Or it could destroy an entire operation. "One of them gas pockets would blow out, you know," Webb remembered, "and bury the hole and lose the boiler and all . . ."[37]

One blowout at Saratoga brought so much gas near the surface that it actually caused the earth to undulate. George Stoker, encountering this "waving ground," felt as though he were "walking across a carpet laid over springs." Eventually the well blew completely out, the ground rising up "like a great wave." When it sank back down, the derrick sank too, leaving only the top of the rig protruding out of the hole.[38]

Along with its explosive properties, gas could also blind or asphyxiate, presenting one of the oil field's gravest dangers. The threat of poisonous gas emissions, "as deadly as a murderer," hung over all the early fields like a noxious cloud.

> It was the fresh gas from the wells . . . that the workers dreaded. . . .
> Its effect when breathed was much like chloroform. If a person inhaled a few strong breaths of it, he would fall over unconscious; and if he lay in it and continued to breathe it, he would die as surely as if chloroformed.[39]

James Donahoe recalled that just south of the discovery well at Batson "a very poisonous gas [came in], and it killed lots of animals in the way of cattle, horses, chickens and a few men was killed . . ." Saloon owner W. E. "Bill" Bryant recalled that "those people was moving . . . with mattresses and pillows to the south end of town . . ." to get away from the gas.[40]

Treatments for poison gas were primitive. For mild eye irritations, workers applied salt solutions or raw Irish potatoes directly to the eye. Painful as the poisoning was—like "hot sand or salt" in the eyes—the salt treatment was no better. "You thought it'd kill you when you first put it on there . . .," Sam Webb remembered. George Stoker developed effective treatments for both the eyes and the respiratory system at the Saratoga field, but for some unknown reason, they did not work as quickly in Batson. He described three victims who had been "gassed" while filling water buckets:

> One of the girls and the man were lying as if dead. Not a movement, no perceptible breathing, and scarcely any pulse. But the

Oil field workers amid what is probably steam. *Courtesy Tyrrell Historical Library, Beaumont, Texas.*

> other girl was flopping around over the bed like a chicken with its head chopped off. Two men were holding her down. . . . I worked all night to keep the heart and lungs of the one girl and man going and to calm the other girl. . . . I gave all of them medicine. It was long after sun-up before any of them showed any signs of returning to consciousness. All three of them returned to normal within thirty minutes of each other.

Stoker himself almost became a victim one night; returning alone from a house call, a wave of gas hit him, and he nearly fell from his horse. He held his breath, "rode like mad," and managed to outdistance it.[41]

The workplace presented a different kind of hazard to one particular group of workers. Jim Crow segregation firmly ruled racial relations at the early Southeast Texas oil fields, and outsiders felt neither need nor inclination to tamper with the existing system. In the years following the Civil War, law and custom had created a stylized segregation in the workplace, especially where both races worked at the same trade.[42]

In the lumber industry, dominant in East Texas before petroleum, work had been segregated, the more skilled, higher-paying jobs being reserved for

A Mule team with African American drovers. These men were often caught in controversies over jobs, and at least one disagreement led to the "Little Africa" racial incident of 1902. *Courtesy Tyrrell Historical Library, Beaumont, Texas.*

white men and the lower-paying but more physically demanding and danger-ous tasks allotted to the African Americans. Even in the woods, one of the only places where both whites and blacks performed the same task, that of cut-ting timber, the races might work side by side but not together. The two men operating any given crosscut saw were either both white or both black.[43]

Segregation in the oil field was reflected in wages and types of labor. Only whites were allowed to work on derricks, no matter how arduous or danger-ous the labor, because those jobs paid the most. Black men were hired for pe-ripheral jobs—driving mule teams, building earthen tanks, stacking pipe, or digging ditches—but not for work on the rigs. "They were just treated like an-imals," Alice Slausen recalled. "[They] never got anything but the jobs that a [white] man didn't want. Scavenger work and all such jobs, that's all . . . they got to where they did use them," she added. "They needed them."[44]

Worker William Joseph Philp recalled his brother's words about black la-borers at Spindletop:

. . . now, they won't allow no nigger to do oil work. They can drive

African American half-brothers Osan Blanchette (left) and Usan Hebert, who owned a tract of land between Beaumont and Spindletop. They later donated land on which Beaumont's Hebert High School was built. *Courtesy LeVert Molett and Tyrrell Historical Library, Beaumont, Texas.*

a truck and go through there with a little lumber and anything like that, you can have nigger drivers. But you can't get out and take the brake and drill for oil. We just won't stand for it.[45]

African Americans of both sexes were permitted to cook, clean up, or perform other general work at boarding houses, restaurants, or other places of business. None were allowed to live at Spindletop; at the end of the work day, all were required to return to South Africa, or one of the other black residential neighborhoods in Beaumont. Alice Slausen recalled that each morning her father would bring his black employees to the boarding house and the livery stable, then take them home in the evening.

[African Americans] could come out there and bring lumber and bring timber and drive those mules out there to deliver material. . . . but they weren't allowed to stay out there overnight. . . . they had signs up there that said, "Nigger, don't let the sun go down on you."[46]

Ozan Blanchette and Usan Hebert, African American half-brothers who owned a tract of land that lay between Beaumont and Spindletop to the west, hitched up their wagon each day and traveled the short distance over the prairie to the oil field, going from rig to rig to clean equipment. Blanchette's granddaughter, LeVert Molett, did not recall any racial incidents but theorized that the half-brothers were so light-skinned as to be regarded by many as whites. As time went by, Blanchette and Hebert sold parcels of their land to other blacks, many of whom worked in oil-related occupations, and the area eventually became a relatively prosperous black residential area of Beaumont known as the Pear Orchard.[47]

Segregated living areas and off-limits hours did not prevent racial incidents at Spindletop. In the autumn of 1902 the local contracting firm of Callahan and Graham was building earthen tanks for oil storage in the Little Africa area. Another firm, Black and Laid, was installing tanks for the new Burt refinery. Both firms employed African American labor.[48]

On November 9, a gang of white men from Spindletop, unhappy that the blacks were working for lower wages, rode over to Little Africa to force them to leave. As James G. Callahan, the general superintendent of Callahan and Graham, told it:

> Last night about 10:30 a gang of white men invaded Little Africa
> with Indian whoops and yells. No sooner had they quit yelling than
> they commenced firing into my own and other camps. All that was
> left for every life-loving man to do was to shoulder his gun and re-
> turn the fire . . . the bullets were whizzing in the air and were going
> into our sleeping apartments . . .

Callahan sprang to the blacks' defense, telling a reporter for the *Beaumont Enterprise* that only a third of the 275 workers in the Little Africa area were African Americans and denying that any problems existed between the two races. "The trouble last night," Callahan declared, "was occasioned by a lot of Spindle Top fellows invading the settlement and making trouble where they were not the least concerned one way or the other." The only confirmed casualty on either side was a white man from Spindletop who sustained a gunshot wound.[49]

The next day the *Enterprise* printed a rebuttal signed by R. C. Grinnell, proprietor of the Log Cabin Saloon at Spindletop, and others from the hill. Swearing the wounded man was not from Spindletop but Little Africa, they accused the reporter of passing on "bogus stuff to amaze the public's mind and make newspapers sell . . . when there has been nothing of the sort going on there at all."

> It is a disgrace to the people of Spindle Top that a scandal has been started concerning a community that has been as law abiding as this from the time of the Lucas Gusher to the present day, never yet having a shooting affray or in any way causing the death of or the injury of a single man . . .[50]

Nevertheless, according to Philp, the black laborers left. "They never come back no more." Oil field worker Frank Dunn remembered them:

> They worked just like ordinary men, only they did lots of singing and going-on among themselves. But they never did bother no-body. I never could see why . . . they wanted to run them off be-cause they were handy and they did lots of real honest-to-God hard work. . . . They decided that it would be better . . . to have the nig-gers away from the field. They felt like at that time that they were taking up jobs that some white man probably would be glad to have.[51]

The Big Thicket oil towns also endured racial incidents. In Sour Lake, twenty-five black construction crew members working on a pipeline (for less money than the white laborers were getting) left for Beaumont soon after re-ceiving a warning to leave. Afterward, the *Houston Post* quoted one worker as stating that his "hide was too thin to withstand such harsh treatment." One white resident recalled that "it wasn't the real dirty element . . . that went after the Negroes. It was the hot heads of the other part. . . . And the Negroes be-haved themselves. They hadn't got bad, but people thought they had."[52]

At Batson, most of the teamsters were blacks. James Donahoe recalled that they stayed in certain "Negro quarters" north of the oil field or on a bayou about three miles from town. Employers provided them with shelter, food, and supplies. Donahoe remembered racial tension as "a little flare-up . . . at times, but they never did prove too serious."[53]

Saratoga reputedly laid down the harshest rules regarding blacks in town. Donahoe recalled,

> Now, over at Saratoga, they was very strict on them there. They didn't allow Negroes in the town of Saratoga. . . . The contractors come there with a bunch of Negroes to work and they've had a few cases of where they'd run them out, but the contractors usually

avoided that as much as they could by having their tents out away
from the townsite . . .

Even after other towns moderated their stance on African Americans, Saratoga's prohibition would continue for many years.[54]

For both whites and blacks, the dangers of the workplace presented only a part of the risks of life in the oil field. Leisure time could be hazardous, too, given the pressures of the man-killing work, the numerous saloons located right in the oil field, and the flow of cash from high-paying jobs. With the saloons came gambling and prostitution.

One estimate placed the number of saloons at Spindletop at twenty-five or thirty, which, in a population even as high as fifteen hundred, made an impressive per capita rate. "That's about the way Spindletop was," William Philp said. "It was just a saloon. . . ."[55]

Big Thicket towns had ratios at least as disproportionate. One Sour Lake resident estimated that at the peak of the oil boom, 105 saloons operated in the town. George Stoker assessed Saratoga as having "the customary excitement of work, gambling, fighting, drunkenness, pimping, and whoring that go with such places." He recalled that in Batson, saloons and restaurants opened for business in the open air just days after the discovery well came in. One estimate cited the town as having twenty-six saloons in the distance of about two city blocks—every one of them boasting dancing and gambling halls.[56]

Free-flowing alcohol made saloons natural arenas for violent encounters. Rivalry among drilling crews lent the situation a tinder-box explosivity. "In the beginning, I don't remember of [*sic*] anybody killing anyone [at Spindletop]," Curt Hamill recalled,

> but they'd fall out over different things and have fistfights. And
> after the pipe liners came in there, 'course the saloons come in
> there. . . . And those pipe liners, why, [they] was more of an Irish
> people. . . . And they would get tight and scrap amongst themselves,
> you know, and get up and shake hands and go on.[57]

Reputedly, Irish workers on the hill squared off one St. Patrick's Day into Northern and Southern Irish factions and engaged in a memorable fight.[58]

In Bill Bryant's memory, fights were more frequent than robberies. "They didn't have to highjack [the money]," he recalled, "because they was taking it fast enough with those crooked dice and crooked cards." In fact, fistfights were so common as to go nearly unnoticed. Bryant said he considered himself

Ed Cotten, Deputy Sheriff at Batson, assuming a "tough-guy" pose for the camera. *Courtesy Oral History of the Texas Oil Industry Records, CN 00357, Center for American History, University of Texas at Austin.*

fortunate because "most of it was fistfighting. None of my bunch didn't [*sic*] get killed."[59]

Bryant also recalled one of his own fights, which progressed through a forty-foot dance hall, then a saloon of about the same length:

> [W]e got down on the floor and I couldn't stay on top of him and he couldn't stay on top of me, but unfortunate [sic], I got one of my fingers in his mouth. . . . We rolled on from the dance hall through the saloon and rolled out in front of the Crosby House and there was a horse hitched to a buggy. . . . And when we rolled under him, he broke loose and run the buggy over us—caused a little excitement, the horses did, running down the street—-and the [Texas] rangers come up and arrested us both. . . . I was a little sore at him about bitin' my finger—not for fightin'—for that was just outside pastime then.

When Bryant later offered to post his opponent's bond, the latter told him he was a "good sport," and Bryant complimented him as "one of the best fighters I ever hooked in to."[60]

Fighting in oil towns was by no means limited to men. Women often fought, but rarely to the death, since someone usually separated them first. Two, Nella Dale and Grace Ashley, fought for an hour and fifteen minutes. "When they quit fighting," Bryant said later, "they didn't have on enough clothes to wipe out a twenty-two."[61]

Law enforcement in oil towns was generally either inadequate or downright incompetent. At Spindletop, an unincorporated town, enforcement of the law fell to Jefferson County officials. Sheriff Ras Landry, a colorful character with a handlebar moustache, a broad-brimmed white hat, two pearl-handled pistols, and fancy boots, apparently opted for moderate, rather than rigid, control. Landry enjoyed the reputation of allowing a situation to go so far, then "crack[ing] down." Because hauling prisoners in a buggy the four miles from the hill into Beaumont was both unwieldy and unsafe, the county eventually dispatched an extra deputy to the oil field and opened a branch jail there.[62]

Law in the Big Thicket towns of Sour Lake, Saratoga, and Batson faced an even steeper battle. For nearly a century the Big Thicket had harbored folk who, for one reason or another, wanted to be left alone, and the hold the law exercised within its shadowy reaches was tenuous, at best. With the coming of oil, law and order ranged from primitive to nonexistent in all three towns. At

Batson, women were put in a small jail building constructed of two-by-fours, with a twelve- to eighteen-inch hole close to the roof to furnish ventilation. Men were chained to trees. Later, when a flimsy jail was built, one prisoner whitewashed it, explaining that, because he spent so much time there, he thought he should clean it up.[63]

Sour Lake began its boomtown existence in a relatively orderly fashion, with only a single Justice of the Peace to enforce the law, but it soon suffered the same problems as the others. The law, as Bill Bryant recalled it, functioned only "to hold inquests and pick up dead bodies, [and] try to regulate the traffic so people could get through with boiler wagons."[64]

Prostitution, though illegal, was considered one of the mildest of offenses. When arrested, prostitutes were usually charged with vagrancy, then fined and released, creating a steady source of income for the court where they appeared. Just after the first gusher came in, Batson boasted a cluster of tents constituting the newest installation of "Ann's Place," a bordello that already operated branches in other oil fields. According to George Stoker, "She had not time to get beds for her girls, but they did not let such little inconveniences deprive them of their business." Batson and Sour Lake sported both white and black brothels. The black prostitutes were "sorta barred off to themselves," Donahoe remembered, although their customers included white men as well as black.[65]

In Saratoga, Stoker recalled the county attorney's asking a prostitute if she had any visible means of support. Receiving an affirmative answer, he demanded that she show the court.

> She did not hesitate. Bending forward from her hips as if she were
> making a bow to the county attorney and taking hold of the bottom of
> her skirts with both hands, she began to straighten up. By that time
> the judge was yelling, "Not guilty. Put down your dress. Not guilty."[66]

Lawmen sometimes even fought among themselves. Stoker recalled an episode in which a constable and his deputy, both in a drunken state, were told by a mischief-making bartender that the mayor of the town was going to arrest them for being drunk. Furious, they announced that they were going to arrest the mayor first, since he was also drunk. When the same bartender passed the news along to the mayor, he flew into a tantrum and went in search of the two. The three parties met in front of the drug store.

"In the name of the law I arrest you for being drunk," the constable shouted, staggering toward the mayor.

"You long-legged son-of-a-bitch," the mayor roared back, "I refuse to arrest."

A tug-of-war ensued—first the mayor gaining a few feet before being pulled back down the street by the constable and the deputy, then the constable and the deputy being pulled back by the mayor. A crowd gathered to bet on the outcome, but before anyone won, the contest adjourned to the nearest saloon.[67]

Periodic visits by the Texas Rangers seemed to be the only remedy for the lawlessness, as the Rangers commanded a healthy respect from even the toughs and badmen of the Big Thicket.[68] In a letter to Joseph S. Cullinan in 1903 or 1904, former Texas governor James Stephen Hogg wrote:

> Recalling our conversation on the necessity of the State taking timely action to prevent the threatened outbreaks of lawlessness around Batson, I beg to say that the Governor has ordered Captain Brooks of the Ranger force to go there to cooperate with the local officers, if necessary to this end. He is a careful, capable officer from whom much good may be expected in the performance of his duties.[69]

Another Ranger who went to Batson, Captain Bill McDonald, "convinced" the local constable, who drank as much as anyone in the town, that he needed to allow the Rangers do their job. Pointedly sending his smallest man to take the constable's guns, McDonald told the crowd that the Rangers were there to fight. "We like our job," he finished. After that duly learned lesson, the violence was mostly limited to fist fights, with very few subsequent killings.[70]

Bill Bryant became inured to violent death. "If a man got killed you'd look at him and forget it," he recalled, "because probably you'd see two more bodies the next day . . ."[71]

The undertaker stayed busy day and night. Batson laborer Plummer Barfield worked for the undertaker, who also owned the livery stable. One night, bringing home a body, Barfield was stopped by a gang of men who made him remove it from the wagon in order to load in a dead woman and a baby. They instructed him to deposit the bodies at the undertaker's, then to come back for two more bodies. On his return, Barfield discovered that the two new corpses were drunken men who had accidentally shot the woman and baby and had subsequently been lynched by the gang, a vigilante posse of "roughnecks and rig runners."[72]

Barfield built countless wooden coffins and buried many of the dead in unmarked graves, without a single mourner attending. "I pronounced a benediction over several of them," he said later. "I done the best I could. Quote a little Scripture rather than just drive off just like you was leaving a dog."[73]

The hazards of daily life in the oil field created a huge demand for doctors that remained unmet. Because money was plentiful, desperate patients were willing to pay far above a doctor's going rate. As George Stoker described it, his oil field practice consisted of "everything, from treating a toothache, to laying down the pulseless hand of a person called by sudden death from too much whiskey, pistol shots, or a fight." After a big fire in the field, he not only treated burns and injuries but many men "temporarily deranged from shock and loss of fortunes." He patched up gunshot victims, everyone from workers to gamblers to prostitutes:

> Many of these unfortunate women were young and beautiful, but it did not take long to destroy all semblance of beauty in that place of degradation. Once they entered that life, it seemed all hope left them, all power to exert themselves to leave departed. The only door that seemed open for escape was that of suicide.

As their mode of exit, most of the women chose self-administered poison, such as carbolic acid.[74]

Malnutrition, poor drainage, and a total lack of sanitation—all took their toll. Stoker treated patients suffering from malaria, rickets, and myriad other related illnesses. He deplored the primitive, squalid environment in obstetric cases. "So many of the men drank and gambled," he wrote, "that their wives and babies were often without enough to eat and wear, to say nothing of having anything ready or sanitary for the new-born life." He recalled a particularly difficult delivery:

> [O]n an old, unpainted iron bed, lay a large woman. A mop of uncombed, drab, yellow hair hung around a face tougher looking than some of the faces of the women I had seen plying their trade in the gambling houses. . . .The sheets and old quilt on the bed evidently had never been washed. Her pains were growing more frequent and harder, and her curses louder. She cursed her husband for getting her into her present condition and cursed me for not getting her out of it.

After many hours of labor, the baby was finally born. While the mother slept,

J. M. Guffey Petroleum Company employees stage a barbecue at Batson on June 7, 1906. *Courtesy Oral History of the Texas Oil Industry Records, CN 00287, Center for American History, University of Texas at Austin.*

the doctor and the drunken father rolled dice to see who would wash and dress the newborn. Stoker rolled high, won, and left thankfully, just as the mother woke up and began to curse both men all over again.[75]

Batson residents, who had to summon doctors from Liberty, Saratoga, or Beaumont, found that with childbirth, the event was often over by the time the physician arrived.[76]

Doctors learned to improvise. One young Spindletop man, who found himself serving as an informal surgical assistant to physician R. L. Cox by default, recalled,

> I've cut many a finger off. I've cut a leg off many a time, just sawed
> it off with the saw. I went in the old butcher's shop and got [the
> saw]. I've done a lot of things of that kind when Dr. Cox was in
> need of help . . . and he'd go ahead and trim it up.

Well," he added conscientiously, "sometimes with an anesthetic, most of the time not.[77]

One of the best-known health practitioners at Spindletop was not a physician, but a pharmacist who owned a drug store and ice cream parlor. Ryman Thomas provided medicine and limited medical treatment, eventually

Oil-soaked roughnecks attempting to scour off the ever-present oil. *Courtesy Texas Energy Museum, Beaumont, Texas.*

earning the nickname of "Doc." "We depended a whole lot on old man Doc Thomas, because he was pretty good," Alice Slausen remembered.[78]

In short, the quality of life in the oil fields was many times reduced to basic needs. Many oil field dwellers had neither the money nor the desire to try to make a decent place to live. George Stoker described one abode to which he was summoned:

> In one corner was an old broken cook stove, standing on pieces of brick. . . . Not a spark of fire was in it. In the center of the room stood a home-made table covered with dirty dishes, and a dish pan full of dark, greasy water. . . . Two broken chairs and a rickety packing box, on which stood an oil lamp with a smoky chimney obscuring the light it might have given, completed the furnishings.[79]

Though they must have felt in the minority, however, a fair number of decent, law-abiding citizens lived in the boomtowns. They tried hard to create a clean and orderly life in the oil field, a difficult task at best. Oil and mud made nightmares of house cleaning and washdays. Water for laundering clothes, often impregnated with sulphur, was boiled in cast-iron washpots over outdoor fires. Water was also boiled to scrub the oil-soaked workers themselves,

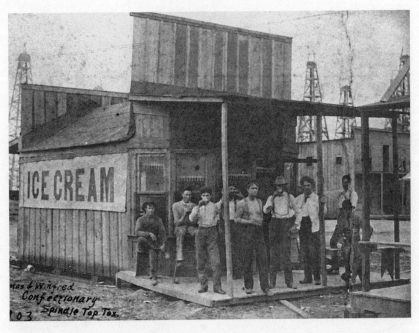

A group of "tough" oil field workers enjoying a well-earned ice cream break at the Thomas and Winfred "Confectionary." *Courtesy Texas Energy Museum, Beaumont, Texas.*

who first had to scour off most of the oil with bran, towsacks, or rough cloths before bathing in the hottest water they could bear. Women stoked their cookstoves with scraps of wood gathered from around the derricks.[80]

Alice Slausen's mother, very tidy, according to her daughter, insisted that her boarders wash up outside at the water pump before meals. Some ate in the yard or on the back porch; those who ate inside had to take off their oily shoes.[81]

Children in the oil fields survived and even thrived, their lives a blend of childhood innocence and oil field reality. They played hopscotch and jumprope, but their games of hide-and-seek were played in empty boilers. At Spindletop, Alice Slausen could "climb that derrick faster than any of them men . . . "[82]

Slausen, who had gone from a comparatively sheltered life in Houston to the pandemonium of Spindletop, reveled in the freedom of living in the oil field. She and her siblings and playmates pretended to drill for oil in the dirt and swam in the snake-infested bayous near the field. "The snakes took for . . . high ground when we kids got in there," she boasted.[83]

Slausen and her friends frequently monitored the activities of the prostitutes that came to the field.

> They'd rent buggies and hacks from Papa and they'd disappear for a while, you know, and then they'd come back. . . . later, when I got smart, well, I knew what they'd been doing. . . . We found out all about life, honey, very, very young.[84]

Their precocity extended to death as well. Slausen never forgot the horror of seeing one of her mother's boarders fall from a derrick into a hot slush pit. "It was bubbling," she remembered, tears still coursing down her cheeks at the memory more than eight decades later. "It was so hot. It just took all the skin off." Her mother pulled the man out of the pit with a stick, burning her own arms badly in the process, but he died soon after.[85]

In spite of the danger, violence, and hardship at Spindletop, many families managed to succeed in making good lives for themselves. Rising above their circumstances, the settlers created their own sedate entertainment as alternatives to saloons, gambling halls, and bordellos. In Batson, they held dances on wooden platforms, serving ice cream, soda pop, and lemonade. They did the waltz, the two-step, and the schottische, while a five-piece band (cornet, two guitars, and two violins) played the "Beaumont Rag" and other favorites. Young men chaperoned themselves, ejecting anyone who acted unsuitably or who didn't belong. "If a boy was drinkin', he was put right off the floor." At Christmas they decorated with Spanish moss, palmetto leaves, holly, and vines.[86]

Hungering for the structure and the spiritual dimension they had left behind in the more civilized world, many boomtown families tried to create their own. Oil field towns were notoriously short on churches, but the violence and vice in the oil fields attracted evangelists and religious reformers like ants to sugar.

At Spindletop, traveling ministers harangued congregations from tents. "They sure believed in preaching hell and damnation and all that kind of stuff," Alice Slausen recalled. Because the wells never shut down, Sunday was no different from any other day of the week, but service times and locations were adapted to need. One saloon keeper on Highland Avenue near the oil field allowed Sunday School to be held in his establishment Sunday mornings before he let in his usual clientele. The Reverend J. A. Smart from the First Baptist Church held services on Sunday afternoons in a store in Gladys City.[87]

In December of 1902, the Baptist Church appointed a city missionary to

Spindletop Hill from the east side, September 1902, showing the full scope of the field at the height of its production. *Courtesy Texas Energy Museum, Beaumont, Texas.*

administer its "mission at the Oil Fields" and its Riverside mission at one thousand dollars a year. By the end of 1903, the Baptist mission at Spindletop boasted fifty Sunday School attendees, weekly prayer meetings, and a total collection of $731.10, to be applied toward a mission structure. In the meantime, Methodists organized a Sunday School and church, with Brother Will Philp serving as the minister; they, and other denominations, used the small Baptist mission chapel as well.[88]

With the influx of families into Spindletop, the need arose for education of their children. The hill fell within the boundaries of the South Park School District, but the crowds of new residents quickly overloaded the one-room South Park school building. A room was added, then the district installed two teachers in a store near the school. In 1902 the district opened a school at Spindletop, employing two teachers who conducted school in still another store and also in the church building shared by the Baptists and Methodists.[89]

From time to time citizens targeted informal conjugal unions known as "sawmill marriages," often between an oil field worker and a prostitute he had bailed out of jail. (According to one Batson resident, they were so common that at times "you couldn't find a legally married man and woman living on the main street of Batson," the main street being the most lawless part of town.) Many sawmill marriages were formalized after a Good Government League was formed in town. The league instructed couples to marry or leave.[90]

The division of oil field towns into a "right" and a "wrong" side was observed by both factions. George Stoker recalled in Saratoga "a long shed on the other side of the creek, where a large colored woman fed the gamblers, whores, and pimps of the town." Others, considered more respectable— merchants, saloon men, gambling-house owners, drillers, roughnecks, contractors, lease owners—ate in a shed behind the hotel. One gently bred young woman, who prided herself on speaking to everyone, recalled being told by one woman from the "wrong" part of town, "Honey, you mustn't talk to me . . . I'm just not the right kind of person for you."[91]

Although the Big Thicket fields never produced like the Spindletop field, they served their collective purpose. Companies that had hesitated to convert their operations from coal to oil were reassured by the production at Sour Lake, Saratoga, and Batson that a large enough supply of oil did exist to justify the changeover. Spindletop, Sour Lake, Saratoga, Batson—the booms would evaporate, then move to other fields yet to be discovered. But they left their locales changed forever, with other important phases of the industry yet to move into place. In the words of contemporary oil historian Joseph Pratt:

> As the output of the Spindletop field declined, much of the capital and labor it had attracted moved on to other boom towns throughout the southwestern oil fields. But a crucial difference gave Beaumont's oil bonanza a more lasting impact: the timing of the Spindletop discovery and its location near the Gulf of Mexico encouraged the emergence of a refining complex that became a permanent connection between the region and several large, growing oil companies.[92]

And from the chaos, other individuals were emerging, a fresh cast of characters waiting in the wings to star in a new drama, this one to be played upon a world stage.

Chapter Ten

FOUNDATIONS

*"Then the insane excitement lulled; men grew calm, a new class came in on
the scene, the grafters who wished to be in at the first plucking were replaced
by heavy weights [sic] who had money to operate with, and Spindle Top was
perforated as with birdshot; pipe lines stretched out their long necks to the
sea and Beaumont took her place as the greatest producer of fuel oil in
America."*

—Beaumont Enterprise, *January 10, 1902*

AS the oil picture became a panorama, two of the main figures would fade
from center. Both Anthony Lucas and Pattillo Higgins followed their separate
dreams; neither was to play a major part in forming the global oil industry that
began to take shape in the early years of the twentieth century. From the beginning, Lucas's overriding passion had been the scientific pursuit of oil. He
had little taste for the day-to-day hustle of the oil business, and none at all for
the scams and ruthless tactics that characterized the oil booms. After he sold
his interest in the Guffey Petroleum Company back to James M. Guffey in
May of 1901, he continued to do exploration work for the company, but had
nothing further to do with the Spindletop oil field. He returned to Beaumont
that September but left again in a few weeks, ultimately moving with his family back to Washington.[1]

Higgins, while as competitive as the next man, was even more driven by
the wildcatter's insatiable need to find the next field, and the one after that.
He was still essentially a loner, and his unshakable and often abrasively expressed faith in his own vision guaranteed that he would remain that way. The
wells that the Higgins Oil and Fuel Company drilled on his thirty-three-acre
tract near the Lucas well actually proved to be more productive than the

gusher itself; Higgins probably made more money from the Spindletop field than Lucas, but, like all wildcatters, he always reinvested it in his perennial search for oil.[2]

Only one of the old players, James M. Guffey, stayed in the game just long enough to see a major company on its way. In May of 1901, he bought out Anthony Lucas and John Galey, his partners in the Guffey Petroleum Company, to form the J. M. Guffey Petroleum Company. The new company's financial backers, the Mellons, had never liked or trusted Guffey but had invested in his ventures chiefly because of their confidence in John Galey.[3]

With Galey gone, their fears were to be confirmed. Among other problems, in the heady days of June of 1901, when Spindletop oil still seemed inexhaustible, Guffey entered into a disastrous long-term contract to supply the Shell Trade and Transport Company with four and a half million barrels of oil at twenty-five cents per barrel. He did this precisely at a time when oil prices were rising rapidly; fortunately, Andrew Mellon salvaged the situation, somehow convincing Shell officials that it would be to their advantage to renegotiate a more favorable contract with J. M. Guffey Petroleum.[4]

In August of 1902, in the face of declining production at Spindletop and more trouble in the company, Mellon sent his nephew, William Larimer Mellon, down to Beaumont to investigate. Will Mellon found the company in financial chaos. Added to the early failure to secure leases on the hill was not only Guffey's near-disastrous deal with Shell Trade, but also his inexplicable sale of all mineral rights on the fifteen-acre Page tract, a heavily producing property, to the fast-growing Hogg-Swayne syndicate. There were also uncleared titles, money spent unwisely, and a general failure to exploit the company's position as the discoverer of the field. The list went on and on. Mellon recommended that the company be sold. The rub lay in that the only buyer for a company that size was Standard Oil. But Standard, still smarting from the 1900 ouster of their affiliate, the Waters-Pierce Company, in violation of Texas's antitrust laws, declined to buy, preferring to choose its own timing and circumstances. The Mellons had no choice but to stay in the oil business, expanding and vertically integrating their operations.[5]

J. M. Guffey Petroleum had already run pipelines to Port Arthur, which boasted the twin advantages of an inland situation and a ship channel to the Gulf, where oil could be picked up for shipping to the Eastern markets. It had also built a small refinery there for the same reasons, although the refinery had almost been located in another Jefferson County site, at the town of Sabine, along Sabine Pass. The exact site had been determined by a twist of

An early "tank truck." *Courtesy Tyrrell Historical Library, Beaumont, Texas.*

fate in the form of an obstructive bull. John Galey had entered into a verbal contract with the Kansas City Southern Railroad for a refinery location in Port Arthur when the KCS cancelled it, deciding not to sell land until they found out whether oil lay under it. The Port Arthur Land and Townsite Company, which was owned by KCS interests, refused to sell for the same reason.[6]

Galey informed George M. Craig, the Port Arthur land agent, that he could just as easily build his refinery at Sabine Pass. In fact, back in Pittsburgh, Guffey was already talking with Luther Kountze of the Kountze Brothers, developers of the town of Sabine, Port Arthur's biggest competitor for domination of the Sabine and Neches Rivers. Luther Kountze headed to Port Arthur to offer Galey a refinery site at Sabine, when the KCS train he was riding struck a bull. Kountze reached Port Arthur too late to contact Galey until the next day, by which time Galey's threat had caused Port Arthur townsite trustees and KCS officials to change their minds and deed him the desired Port Arthur tract.[7]

In 1902 Guffey enlarged this refinery to compete with national markets and began buying crude oil from other fields. In 1906, a pipeline was constructed to the new Glenn Pool oil field in Oklahoma, and by 1916, the refinery would become one of the three largest in the nation.[8]

In the meantime, the Mellons directed Will Mellon to take over operations, a choice fortuitous for the family interests but unwelcome to Guffey. He had frequently clashed with Will Mellon, in particular, through the years, and any time the Mellons refused funding for his proposals, he had blamed Will. Now, matters between them rapidly grew worse, and the other members of the Mellon family were eventually forced to intervene. In 1907, the Mellons reorganized J. M. Guffey Company and its affiliates, Gulf Refining Company and Gulf Pipeline Company, under the name of Gulf Oil Corporation. Guffey, still at odds with Will Mellon, protested the action. To remove Guffey, the Mellons bought his stock for two and a half million dollars. The Gulf Oil Corporation would join Standard Oil Company as one of the first titans of the world oil industry.[9]

Even before these men left the spotlight, others were moving onto center stage behind them. Just days after the Lucas well came in, the oil field and the Crosby Hotel were literally crawling with oil men and entrepreneurs. In the interaction unique to that chaotic time, their paths crossed and recrossed, they gathered, and they "cussed" and discussed. Some jumped into the business right away; others waited until the field was established. Spindletop became their proving ground, where they survived their trials by fire, sometimes all too literally. When they joined forces, each brought to the table oil expertise, business acumen, capital, or a combination thereof—not to mention a fair measure of luck, though it could be argued that they manufactured much of their own. Every step they took was significant, every decision they made set a precedent. Whether their efforts were rewarded in boardroom or field, this second wave of leaders laid the foundations for the entire modern oil industry.

The antecedents of the second giant to emerge from the Spindletop field were first set in place in 1901, at a historic meeting one night at the Crosby. Present were a group of men that included Joseph S. Cullinan, former Texas governor James Stephen Hogg, industrialist and inveterate gambler John W. "Bet-a-Million" Gates, and a New York leather executive named Arnold Schlaet. The entity that would emerge from this meeting would become the Texas Company, later known as Texaco.[10]

True to his rough-and-ready reputation, "Buckskin Joe" Cullinan had burst upon the Beaumont scene from Corsicana the morning after the Lucas Gusher came in. Al Hamill believed Cullinan to be the first oil man on the scene; with T. J. Wood and S. M. "Golden Rule" Jones, he had "knocked on the door and [come] in" while Al was eating breakfast at the Lucas home.[11]

Cullinan asked questions about the well, then went out to see it. He was

Former Texas governor James Stephen Hogg (left). Hogg's enormous size complement-
ed his larger-than-life personality. His early interest in Spindletop led to association with
J. S. Cullinan and the formation of the Texas Company, better known as Texaco. *Courtesy James S. Hogg Papers, CN 10517, Center for American History, University of Texas at
Austin.*

then in the prime of his life, a rugged-looking man around forty years of age,
muscular, with an imposing moustache, a full head of hair, and an endless supply of raw energy. Gifted with good instincts and the ability to make both
subordinates and peers believe he could effect anything, he was not afraid to
take a chance. He was bound to make his mark on his age. One historian has
called him "one of the most important figures in the American oil industry of
the early twentieth century."[12]

As it happened, in 1899 Cullinan had built a thirty-seven-thousand-bar-
rel oil tank on the Texas and New Orleans Railroad just north of the coastal
town of Sabine, around thirty-five miles southeast of Beaumont, to make

Corsicana oil available to fuel ships coming up the Sabine River from the Gulf of Mexico. Before Spindletop, however, the tank had rarely been needed.[13]

In March of 1901 Cullinan tried to interest his old company, Standard Oil, in Spindletop, but they were consistently declining overt involvement. On his own, Cullinan then formed the Texas Fuel Company, a small concern intended for the purchase and resale of Texas oil to Standard and other northern firms, and capitalized it for fifty thousand dollars. When uncontrolled production at Spindletop drove the price of oil down to a low of anywhere from three to ten cents a barrel, he quickly bought it and filled the tank at Sabine. Realizing that he needed much more storage, as well as production, transportation, and refining facilities, he began to look for sources of capital.[14]

Cullinan was to find his first money in Beaumont. Former Texas governor James Stephen Hogg, another early arrival, had come into town soon after the gusher came in and had quickly settled into the town's business and social circles, pursuing his own oil interests. He would have run into Cullinan almost immediately. Larger than life, both in personality and physique (he was said to tip the scales at some three hundred pounds), Hogg became the center of activity and attention wherever he chose to be, most notably on the gallery of the Crosby Hotel. According to one observer, "[A]ll he could get in was one of the largest chairs, and he sits there with his beard, very large in front, [a] very jolly man."[15]

Later Hogg took up residence in the more elegant Oaks Hotel, west on Calder Avenue in the Beaumont suburbs, owned by the Heywood family.[16] After a particularly heavy rainstorm, when flat terrain and lack of drainage had caused heavy street flooding, normal travel was impossible. Hogg hired a young African American man to pull him in a flat-bottomed skiff all the way to downtown Beaumont. One Beaumonter recalled the sight:

> He put a great big rocking chair in the middle of that skiff and he pulled his trousers up over his knees. And he had one of these great big umbrellas that you used to see on vegetable wagons. And it was made of red and white. And he was sitting in the rocking chair holding his umbrella to keep the sun off, it was awfully hot. . . . Well, everybody stopped, they were walking on sidewalks in water . . . they'd turn around and look at the skiff coming down the middle of Pearl. That was the only traffic on the street.[17]

Hogg's entry into the oil business involved an ingenious—and risky—plan that, although he did not realize it, would arguably shorten the life of the

Spindletop 1902, the overcrowded Hogg-Swayne tract. *Courtesy Texas Energy Museum, Beaumont, Texas.*

oil field. With former Fort Worth mayor and Texas Senate floor leader Jim Swayne and other Texas investors R. E. Brooks, A. S. Fisher, and William T. Campbell, Hogg formed a joint venture they christened the Hogg-Swayne Syndicate. On May 23, 1901, Hogg-Swayne bought surface rights to fifteen acres in the J. M. Page tract on the southeast edge of the Spindletop salt dome. The syndicate immediately spudded a well and began to sell off half its purchase in small tracts, ranging from two and a half acres to one-thirty-second of an acre in size. In turn, the buyers divided their land into even smaller tracts for resale. Many of these tracts went for a small down payment, with the balance to be paid in oil as wells came in. On June 28, the *Beaumont Age* reported "joy in the ranks of the Hogg-Swayne syndicate . . . their oil well spouted pure black oil yesterday afternoon." Needless to say, joy also reigned in the ranks of speculators who had bought land from the syndicate.[18]

The following July, in a surprise move that would prove a costly mistake, the J. M. Guffey Company relinquished to the Hogg-Swayne Syndicate the mineral rights to the fifteen-acre J. M. Page tract for $180,000—$40,000 cash and a huge $270,000 note that included additional expenses for a well already underway on the tract, the drilling contract, and the cost of clearing title to the land. Included in the deal were the existing hole and the drilling rig. The cost, totaling $310,000, gave Hogg-Swayne exclusive ownership to both surface and minerals of the tract.[19]

In light of the tract's production potential, the reasons James Guffey sold the mineral rights to the acreage remain unclear. It is possible that Guffey, perennially in financial difficulties, could not resist such a high offer. Some historians have also speculated that he feared the intrusion of Standard Oil, or

simply wanted the Texan Jim Hogg on his side. But that action, added to
Lucas's original failure to secure the additional leases in the vicinity of the first
well, would cost him control of vital areas of production on the hill.[20]

The gusher brought not only an increase in Hogg-Swayne's sales, but
also the subdivision and resale of many previously sold tracts, not to mention
"an orgy of frenzied drilling activity." Countless operators seized pieces of the
action, however small. One particular tract of one-twenty-fourth of an acre
went for fifteen thousand dollars. Developers wedged derricks into every
available space, some so close together that sections of derrick floors had to be
cut out to allow their legs to overlap. Eventually the tract held over three hundred wells.[21]

Hogg-Swayne's success inspired the minute subdivision of two other
tracts on the hill. Five acres each in the Keith-Ward tract, owned by Beaumont businessmen J. C. Ward and J. Frank Keith, and the Yellowpine tract, a
segment of Gladys City owned by George W. Carroll, became islands of
jammed-together derricks. Though each occupied a relatively small area,
these three districts, with their hundreds of wells bristling from the crest of
the mound, gave the Spindletop field its distinctive appearance (like an onion
patch, Pattillo Higgins said) and brought the average number of wells per acre
for the whole field up to twenty. The resulting overproduction "violated the
rudiments of field conservation and safety requirements" and eventually led to
a drastic drop in oil prices.[22]

For a brief, euphoric time, however, profits ran high. Hogg-Swayne
began construction on collection and storage facilities at Spindletop and ac-
quired a pipeline right-of-way to the neighboring tidewater town of Port
Arthur, just off Sabine Lake some ten miles to the south of Spindletop Hill.
They also took an option on forty acres at Port Arthur, owned by the Port
Arthur Land and Townsite Company, for a refinery location.[23]

The refinery option was obtained for the Hogg-Swayne company by an
independent agent, a "charming, penniless" Englishman named James Roche,
who had come to Beaumont to seek his fortune and had made a connection
with Hogg-Swayne. Roche proved to be a master negotiator. When he found
that the Port Arthur Land and Townsite Company was holding all its land for
possible oil sites, he informed the company's agent, George M. Craig, that if
the company was unwilling to sell, he, Roche, could easily obtain land at nearby Sabine, Port Arthur's chief rival to become the gateway to the Gulf of Mexico. Yielding, Craig countered with the offer of an option to sell the forty acres
of Port Arthur land at one hundred dollars an acre. Roche took the option,

then sold it to the Hogg-Swayne
Syndicate. Thus, for the second time,
the town of Sabine narrowly missed
being the site of a major refinery.[24]

By the fall of 1901, however,
Hogg-Swayne's producing wells and
land sales were being overset by
expansion costs and collapsed crude-
oil prices. Hogg-Swayne investors
needed a strong managerial hand to
avert financial disaster. Fortunately,
there was one very near at hand:
Hogg's friend Joseph Cullinan. He
in turn needed Hogg-Swayne's producing wells, land, and facilities. The
two interests worked out a trade. Cullinan took over management of the
Hogg-Swayne interests, and Hogg-
Swayne traded its pipeline right-of-
way and the Port Arthur refinery site
option for twenty-five thousand dol-

John Warne "Bet-A-Million" Gates,
the Chicago entrepreneur and inveterate gambler who developed Port
Arthur, Texas. He became an investor
in J. S. Cullinan's Texas Company.
*Courtesy Port Arthur Public Library, Port
Arthur, Texas.*

lars worth of stock in Texas Fuel Company, covering half of the company's
cost of capitalization.[25]

The other twenty-five thousand dollars came from German-born Arnold
Schlaet, who handled oil, carbon black, shipping, and other outside interests
for the United States Leather Company, the vast New York-based firm of
John J. and Lewis H. Lapham. Schlaet, intrigued by the business possibilities
of the new Spindletop field, came to Beaumont, met Cullinan, and saw an opportunity for the Lapham interests to profit from Cullinan's cheap oil. The
Laphams granted his request to back the Texas venture, and with Cullinan at
the helm, the Texas Fuel Company plunged into the oil business on January 2,
1902, exercising its option on the refinery site and building and purchasing
storage and pipeline facilities. Schlaet's cautious, methodical perfectionism
furnished a perfect foil for Cullinan's gambler's instincts; as unlike as the two
men were, they made a very effective team.[26]

During negotiations for the Port Arthur refinery location, Cullinan became acquainted with Chicago entrepreneur John W. "Bet-a-Million" Gates,
a majority stockholder in the Kansas City Southern Railroad and a developer

The first Texas Company Offices in Beaumont. *Courtesy Tyrrell Historical Library, Beaumont, Texas.*

of the Port Arthur Land and Townsite Company, which owned the forty-acre tract under option. Gates had come to Southeast Texas to investigate Port Arthur as a possible terminus for his railroad; when the Spindletop field had come in, he ordered the railroad completed to Port Arthur, then set about to develop the town. In early 1902 he became a major investor in Cullinan's Producers Oil Company, the producing affiliate of Texas Fuel Company.[27]

An accomplished financier and a flamboyant personality, Gates had made millions in diverse interests all over the country. He had earned his nickname by gambling in any medium, from cards to stocks to oil wells. On a train trip to Pittsburgh, went one story, a bored Gates bet his friend, barbed-wire magnate Isaac L. "Ike" Ellwood, "a million" that a raindrop of his choosing would reach the bottom of the window glass before Ellwood's. Ellwood managed to get the bet lowered to a mere thousand dollars per drop, but Gates won twenty-two thousand dollars on the bet and the nickname stuck.[28]

The success of the Texas Fuel Company created a need for a bigger company. On May 1, 1902, a new company, capitalized at three million dollars and christened the Texas Company, took over the assets of Texas Fuel. The new venture clinched its success in January 1903 by bringing in a gusher at Sour Lake on 865 acres of land on which the canny James Roche had obtained a company option. Steady production from the new oil field gave the company

Members of the drilling crew that brought in "Old Fee #3," the gusher that clinched the Texas Company's success, on January 8, 1903. Left to right: Bud Murphy, Tom Smith, R. Chance Stewart, unidentified, Ben (Bud) Coyle, Will Henry, Barney Rose, and George Cook. *Courtesy Tyrrell Historical Library, Beaumont, Texas.*

a dependable source of oil. Ironically, Roche, who had made such splendid land deals for the company, did not stay around to become part of it. He refused Cullinan's offer to take a one-eighth interest in the Sour Lake field, ultimately worth millions, taking instead his thirty thousand dollars in commission for the option and returning to England, where he eventually became a considerably less wealthy earl than he might have been.[29]

Cullinan, in choosing his major investors, had hit upon the perfect combination of local and outside capital: Hogg-Swayne, a Texas syndicate; U.S. Leather, Schlaet's East Coast firm; and Gates, whose money emanated from varied origins—the East, Chicago, and Southeast Texas. It was hardly a match made in heaven, however, since members of the Hogg-Swayne syndicate were suspicious that their interests might be subordinated to the greater wealth of Schlaet and Gates, and Schlaet in turn did not trust Gates and his gambler's reputation. They were united only in their faith in Cullinan. As his biographer has observed, what investors bought was his leadership.[30]

Fire on Spindletop Hill, September 1902, possibly the same one in which J. S. Cullinan fought the flames alongside his men for almost a week. *Courtesy Texas Energy Museum, Beaumont, Texas.*

Their feeling about Cullinan was made clear in September of 1902, when, at the request of a group of Beaumont oil men, he coordinated efforts to contain a huge fire that endangered the Spindletop field. A careless worker dropped a still-lighted cigar, quickly igniting the oil-saturated derricks and the loose petroleum contained in the earthen dikes. The entire field lay in instant danger. Cullinan, with the proviso that he be given authority to enforce his orders at gunpoint, worked alongside his men around the clock. When the fire was finally extinguished a week later, he was forced to seek bed rest, suffering from exhaustion and eye damage from gas fumes. Both Schlaet and Gates, for once in agreement, wrote him, Gates asking him to "use extreme caution for you are the irreplaceable man in our plans," Schlaet emphasizing that "the investment down there . . . will lose every attraction for us should you be disabled."[31]

As with the Texas Company, one man would make the difference in the entry of the Sun Oil Company into the major leagues of the oil industry. Like Cullinan, Pennsylvania native J. Edgar Pew was an experienced player in the

Oil man J. Edgar Pew (left), who came to Beaumont immediately after the Lucas Gusher blew in and transformed his small Pennsylvania concern, Sun Oil Company, into a Texas giant. *Courtesy Texas Oil and Gas Association, Austin, Texas.*

oil business. At the turn of the century, he worked for his uncle, Joseph Newton Pew, who served as the head of Sun Oil, a modest producing, refining, and marketing concern based in Pennsylvania. Though small, Sun Oil had managed to maintain its independence in spite of Standard Oil's domination of the industry.

When the Lucas Gusher came in, Joseph Pew sent his nephew Edgar to Beaumont to find the company a place in the field. The older man was so sure of success that he began building a refinery at Marcus Hook, Pennsylvania. Edgar Pew, reportedly arming himself with a revolver because of the lawless conditions, landed in Beaumont at the height of the boom. Resisting the temptation to jump into the wild speculation, he bided his time, in the mean-

A Lone Star and Crescent Oil Company tank. *Courtesy Texas Energy Museum, Beaumont, Texas.*

time learning all he could about the technology—and the personalities—of the Spindletop field. He also purchased a site for storage tanks and barge-loading facilities at Smith's Bluff on the Neches River south of Beaumont and began buying up Spindletop oil. On January 8, 1902, the Sun Oil Refining Company filed for a charter in the state of Texas for production, refining, and marketing of oil.[32]

Edgar Pew knew Sun's time had come in May of that year, when the Lone Star and Crescent Oil Company, once one of the most prosperous operations in the field, went into receivership. The company had signed a contract to sell ten million barrels of oil in England at the field's lowest price of three cents a barrel—just before prices rose to thirty cents. To compound the disaster, the company's wells stopped producing. But, in addition to Charley Ingalls's farmland, the company itself offered everything Pew needed: thirty-two miles of pipeline, wharves at Sabine, storage tanks, pump stations, railroad loading equipment, and transportation facilities. They formed the perfect connections to ship Spindletop oil to Sun's new Marcus Hook refinery.[33]

At the sheriff's auction in Beaumont on May 30, 1902, Pew paid one hundred thousand dollars for the Lone Star and Crescent assets, but nearly lost the sale for lack of a down payment because it was held on Decoration Day (now Memorial Day), a bank holiday. Luckily, Pew found an officer at the newly constructed Gulf National Bank, scheduled to open for the first time the next day, and obtained the money from him. Since Gulf National was backed by Standard Oil interests, it was ironic that they were responsible for financing the purchase that catapulted the Sun Oil Company from a small to a major concern.[34]

By then, Standard had conceived a purpose for building a bank in Beaumont. After missing out on the Spindletop discovery, the giant operation had decided to bide its time for a sure investment in the Texas market, in the meantime buying Texas oil from smaller producers. As Cullinan's old friend and legal counsel, Corsicana lawyer W. J. McKie, had written back in April of 1901, neither Standard nor Cullinan's Corsicana concern, J. S. Cullinan and Company, would enter the Spindletop field "unless they can enter it on conservative business lines and for the purpose of doing business in a way that is both satisfactory to themselves and to the people with whom they happen to be associated." Standard's approach was rendered more cautious by the general hostility of Texas laws toward big East Coast interests in general and Standard in particular; state statutes favored "local companies and small independent producers." In moving into the Texas market, the company wanted to attract as little attention as possible.[35]

Overproduction brought Standard its opportunity. During Spindletop's first chaotic year the Gulf refinery began construction at Port Arthur, with the Texas Company starting construction on its own facility in that town in 1902. Nonetheless, with the price of crude oil down at that time, even more local facilities were needed to avoid the expense of shipping it to refineries in the East.[36]

Standard's agent, New York financier and investor S. G. Bayne, president of the Seaboard National Bank of New York (the same bank that had financed Pew's benefactors, Gulf National Bank), recruited as planner and advance man another New Yorker, construction engineer "Colonel" George A. Burt, described variously as "a big man, colorful, with a mighty laugh," and "a bluff and blustering gentleman with a swagger like a South American general." Burt boasted a wide range of experience, including railroad construction and a stint with the French government's unsuccessful attempt at building a canal across Panama in the 1880s. He also had a way of accomplishing the impossible, such as buying a gracious home near downtown Beaumont in the midst of a severe housing shortage. He seemed equally at home in the oil field and in Beaumont's best parlors. He revealed very little information about his project—or himself, for that matter—yet managed to instill confidence and good will among enough Beaumonters to enlist a select few local investors for his company, which he named George A. Burt and Company.[37]

At the end of December 1901 Burt quietly paid the A. E. Caswell Estate forty-five thousand dollars for an eighty-nine-acre site about two miles south of downtown Beaumont, ideal for its central location near the Spindletop oil field, the town, the Neches River, and the railroad. On January 4, 1902, the *Beaumont Enterprise* excitedly scooped its rival, the *Beaumont Journal*, with the proud (if exaggerated) announcement that Beaumont was to get the "biggest refinery in the world." The newspaper was short on details, only commenting that construction would provide employment for about 750 men.[38]

After that initial announcement, the papers got precious little information, at least from Burt and Company. "I have nothing to say now—or later—to the newspapers," Burt told unhappy reporters. He maintained complete control over all information that the press received, instructing employees to say nothing and even building an eight-foot board fence around the site.[39]

To serve as his construction supervisor, he found a refinery builder and designer named Fred W. Weller, who would be assisted by his brother Dan. Burt's employees, who would build the pipelines and pumphouses, were a mix that included Mexican and German nationals and Pennsylvania Dutch. Construction began in late spring of 1902 and continued through the next year in spite of sixty-three consecutive days of rain, the resultant seas of mud, and a smallpox epidemic in the Mexican settlement. On May 1, 1903, the Burt Refinery made its initial run, refining five thousand barrels of crude a day.[40]

Then, twelve days later, the surprising announcement was made that a new company, the Security Oil Company, would take over the five-million-dollar assets of the George A. Burt Company—refinery, pipelines, ten million barrels of earthen storage tanks, and Sabine wharf facilities. The mysterious Mr. Burt left the picture as completely as if he had evaporated into thin air,

Workers at Security (later Magnolia) Refinery between 1903 and 1908. William L. McGillivray (standing), Charles H. Clark and J. H. Koster (reclining). *Courtesy Tyrrell Historical Library, Beaumont, Texas.*

although the name "Burt Refinery" stuck for years. Officers for the new Security Oil Company included New York banker Bayne, Fred Weller, and Bayne's nephew, Courtenay Marshall. Standard had been pulling the strings of the operation all along. The investors also included Standard men—Bayne, Henry Clay Folger Jr., and Anthony Lucas's old nemesis, Calvin Payne. In its own way, Standard had finally effected its entrance into Spindletop.[41]

The news came as no real surprise to either the media or the oil world. The real ownership of the Burt Refinery had been an open secret for months, at least in Beaumont. The previous December, the *Beaumont Daily Journal* had quoted the New Orleans papers as saying that the refinery was "openly believed in [Beaumont] to be a Standard Oil creation" and that it would be "the largest in the Texas field." At that point, however, Beaumonters were not terribly concerned about who built the refinery, just as long as it was in Beaumont and not Port Arthur. By the time the official announcement was made,

the Security Refinery was doing a "phenomenal" business, and no one wanted to kill the goose that laid the golden egg.[42]

The Security Refinery kept Beaumont in the oil business even after the
Spindletop field declined, and for several years Standard was allowed to enjoy
its profits unmolested. In 1906, however, state attention targeted Security's
violation of Texas antitrust laws, and after two lawsuits, in a reenactment of
the Waters-Pierce ouster, the Security Company was evicted from the state of
Texas. In 1909, the Beaumont refinery, along with the Navarro Refinery in
Corsicana, became the property of the state. That year, prominent Galveston
businessman John Sealy purchased the two facilities and created a new company, although the Standard investors—Folger, Payne, and others—essentially remained the same. In 1911 the owners formed a new, fully integrated joint
stock association they named the Magnolia Petroleum Company, which
would ultimately become part of the Mobil Oil Corporation, now Exxon/
Mobil Corporation.[43]

Standard's refinery was the second of the three enormous operations built
in Southeast Texas to handle the production from Spindletop. Gulf's refinery,
the first, began operations in 1902, and that of the Texas Company, the last,
opened in late 1903.[44]

In 1895, Standard Oil had controlled between 80 and 90 percent of the
oil from the fields in Pennsylvania, Ohio, and Indiana, either by purchasing or
owning outright. Whether its tardiness in entering the Spindletop scene cost
it the monopoly of the oil industry or whether the industry was simply out-
stripping it, the fact remained that, by 1911, it controlled only 10 percent of
the newly developed Gulf Coast area's annual crude production.[45]

The early movers and shakers at Spindletop laid the groundwork for at
least one oil company that would not grow to maturity for another sixteen
years. As oil in Beaumont progressed from boom to business after 1901, the
"center of the oil world" moved from the Crosby Hotel to an upscale, rapidly
growing neighborhood around Calder Avenue in the west end of town. Many
of the residents there were major players in the oil industry—Cullinan, Hogg,
J. Edgar Pew, Perry McFaddin, the Wiesses, and others. The central gathering place became the new three-story Oaks Hotel, where on pleasant days
guests took the air on its wraparound galleries or caught a bird's-eye view of
the town from its triple-tiered observation tower. The lobby of the Oaks was
quieter and more genteel than that of the Crosby, but it was no less the spot
where important oil deals were made. Because not only oil men but their
wives often sought lodging there, it became a center for card parties and full-

The Oaks Hotel, upscale lodgings for oil men and their wives that replaced the Crosby House. *Courtesy McFaddin-Ward House Museum, Beaumont, Texas.*

dress balls as well. Newly prosperous young couples formed a shooting club, where Mr. and Mrs. Dewey Heywood, Mr. and Mrs. Walter Sharp, Mr. and Mrs. Jim Sharp, Mr. and Mrs. Ed Prather, and others ventured forth for twice-a-week pigeon shoots, Dewey Heywood even decorating his room at the Oaks with hides from a successful deer hunt.[46]

In 1902, two young men came to live across from the Oaks in a boarding house on Calder Avenue owned by the Ervin family. One was Robert Lee Blaffer, the scion of an aristocratic New Orleans family and the manager of his father's Monongahela Coal and Coke Company distributorship. When their client, the Southern Pacific Railroad, began to convert their fuel usage from coal to oil (the first major line to do so), the company offered Blaffer the chance to supply it with Beaumont oil. Correctly reading the handwriting on the wall, he accepted, and came to Beaumont. The second was William Stamps Farish, a Natchez lawyer who had originally come to Beaumont on business for a client, then had stayed on. According to one account, the two men literally bumped into each other on Pearl Street. They became friends, then formed a partnership to engage in contract drilling, lease trading, and various other oil-related activities.[47]

In the development of their business, Blaffer and Farish became acquainted with Captain William Wiess and his young son Harry, who both lived in a gracious home across the street from the boarding house. A former riverboat pilot and the son of a Polish immigrant to the Texas Republic, William Wiess had made a comfortable fortune in lumber and other local investments. After Spindletop, he tried his hand at oil and ended up with controlling interests in the locally owned Paraffine and Reliance oil companies.[48]

William's son, Harry Carothers Wiess, who had been a teenager during the Spindletop boom, seemed as a young man to appreciate petroleum only for the speed one of its products could afford him. In August of 1908, he raced his Marion Wildcat at Beaumont's Driving Park, where automobiles went "at a greater speed than a locomotive." During the race, an inside wheel on his car collapsed just as his passenger, D. C. Proctor, leaned out "to balance the machine" on a turn. The car rolled over twice, throwing the passenger out and pinning Wiess in the wreckage. Miraculously, both men escaped serious injury, Wiess suffering only a broken arm. Within a few years, however, he graduated from Princeton and settled down to the business end of petroleum, taking over Reliance and Paraffine after his father's death.[49]

During those early years in Beaumont, Blaffer and Farish also met Tennessee native Walter Fondren, who had learned rotary skills at Corsicana and had actually been drilling a water well several miles from the Lucas well when it came in. Fondren moved to the Spindletop field after the discovery, eventually forming his own successful drilling company and becoming known as a "genius at the application of new techniques." Another of their fortuitous acquaintances, Ross Sterling, born in nearby Anahuac, Texas, was a frequent visitor to Beaumont; his connection with the oil industry originated with a chain of feed stores that supplied mule teams in the Sour Lake, Saratoga, Dayton, and Humble oil fields. He eventually went into banking and then acquired oil properties of his own in the Humble field, and in 1911 he, Fondren, and others formed a small operation they called the Humble Oil Company, after the field in which they were currently operating. Other future oil men who passed through the doors of the Oaks Hotel or the Ervin house in those early days included lawyer (and by some accounts "one of the best poker players along the Neches River") Lobel A. "Uncle Lobe" Carlton, Jesse Jones, Ed Prather, and J. Cooke Wilson, all of whom would play key roles in the development of the future Humble Oil and Refining Company.[50]

Blaffer and Farish flourished in their oil partnership ventures, and after his father's death, Harry Wiess took over management of the entire Wiess estate. By the second decade of the twentieth century, however, it became apparent that Eastern oil companies only wanted to deal with large operations that could guarantee production quantities. Accordingly, Blaffer, Farish, Wiess, and other small Beaumont producers came together to form the Independent Oil Producers Association. They soon realized, however, that one large corporation would wield more bargaining power than a confederation of small companies and independent individuals. At that point, old ties and longtime personal relationships proved strong; on March 1, 1917, Independent Oil Producers consolidated further, joining forces with Sterling and Fondren's concern, the Humble Oil Company. Sterling served as the new company's first president, with Farish as vice president and Blaffer as treasurer. Joining them in the venture and serving on the first board of directors were Wiess, Jones, and Carlton, old friends from the Spindletop boom. The company received the name of the Humble Oil and Refining Company.[51]

The original directorates of those early oil companies proved that the petroleum business during its early years was singularly egalitarian; a corporate executive and a roughneck could trade financial places with the success or failure of a single well. In early years, too, more interaction existed between the men who financed the drilling and those who performed the task. Everyone worked together, equally exposed to mud, poison-gas fumes, blowouts, fires, and general privation—and the various personalities grew to be the stuff of legend. According to one early oil field worker, "Everybody, Sharp and all of 'em lived in big tents."[52]

Brothers Walter and Jim Sharp, like their friend and colleague J. S. Cullinan, moved with ease between the worlds of the executive and the roughneck and earned the trust of both groups. They enjoyed a reputation in the industry as "perfectionists who took their drilling seriously." After drilling Pattillo Higgins's first unsuccessful well on the salt dome in 1893, they had established a successful drilling operation at Corsicana, then had reappeared at Spindletop, mainly at Hogg-Swayne, in the early days of the boom. During the chaotic summer of 1902, when pressure dropped drastically on Spindletop Hill, they developed a successful method of injecting compressed air into wells to propel oil to the surface. Although in the long term this process possibly hastened the demise of the field, their invention quickly upped field production. The Sharps were best known at Sour Lake, where in early 1903 they brought in the Texas Company's first gusher, allegedly waiting for a stormy night to complete the well so that, by daylight, the oil would have been washed away, and Texaco could thus lock in sales before crude oil prices dropped.[53]

In general, field workers liked the Sharp brothers, although they were very different.

> Walter was a tall, slim, handsome red-headed fellow; you couldn't keep from appreciating him. But Jim was kinda my type, he liked to shoot. And I think he liked to fight a little. He was different from Walter, you couldn't hardly tell they was brothers in their makeup. . . . Old Jim was snappy and fast; Walter just had a steady gait. He was permanent. And one of the best men I ever knew.[54]

Another worker recalled the two:

> I've seen Jim Sharp come in there with his pistols and shoot the door knobs off. He never drank or anything like that; he was just one of these here go-gitters. He was around everywhere, Jim Sharp was. Walter wasn't; Walter, all he ever done was chew that cigar. . . . never smoked one in his life . . . and the only gamblin' Walter Sharp'd ever do was . . . get out there and pitch dollars for the line.[55]

Others remembered Walter as having broader sporting tastes, betting anything from a nickel on how near to a crack a flipped coin would land to a hundred dollars in a greasy spoon cafe on whose square of buttered-and-sugared bread the most flies would light. Jim was recalled as one who would lend money or stand bail, while Walter would not. But Walter always looked after his men, sending food, coffee, blankets, and even a barber to the oil field. He would also give a worker a second chance—but no more.[56]

The times were rough, and the participants played that way. Tank riveter Sam Webb recalled a dispute between Jim Sharp and the Gulf Oil Company, across whose land Sharp was about to lay a pipeline. The Gulf employees stood armed with .30-30 rifles, and so did Jim Sharp's men. Before a shot was fired, Sharp's forces somehow "disarmed that bunch," Webb related. "They just got the drop on 'em, I guess."[57]

In 1902 Walter Sharp, Spindletop oil man Ed Prather, and a flamboyant inventor named Howard Hughes formed the Moonshine Oil Company, in which J. S. Cullinan was an investor. Sharp staked Hughes to his start in Sour Lake by lending him five hundred barrels of oil to fuel his boiler. Hughes, who liked fine things, had no cash, but gave Sharp a diamond stud as collateral instead. Then, using his watch for the same purpose, he obtained another five hundred barrels from a representative of the Gilbert Company. When the well came in, Hughes repaid both debts and got his jewelry back.[58]

Hughes, decked out in duster, cap, and goggles, drove a Winton automobile, complete with carbide lights and brass trim. He admonished boys who clustered admiringly around it not to touch the brass: "I worked on it," he told them, "all day yesterday." Like the Sharps, he boasted more than his share of sporting blood. Jim Sharp, scornful of Hughes's new car, reportedly won it from him in a coin toss, and, to torment him, kept it for a week or two before he returned it.[59]

Curt Hamill recalled Hughes, Walter Sharp, and others flipping silver dollars at the train station for a thousand dollars a toss. Although Al Hamill described Hughes as an "odd kind of a fellow . . . more like a playboy," and Curt found him "a little hard to get acquainted with," Curt also declared him to be "a nice man to be with." Hughes was certainly generous; on one occasion, he gave an elderly black man a large stack of silver dollars he had won. When Curt needed air compression to bring in a well but had no funds to spare, Hughes sent him pipe and equipment and never charged him for it.[60]

Curt also recalled that Hughes was "energetic and full of theories and ideas." In years after, Hughes's fame and much of his fortune derived from an invention of his, the Hughes rock bit, which revolutionized rotary drilling methods. Ultimately both Hughes and Walter Sharp became part of early Texaco management when Producers Oil, a Texaco affiliate, bought Moonshine Oil in 1905.[61]

Both Hughes and Sharp were well known for their technological contributions to the growing industry, but theirs were not the only innovations. In those early days, technology evolved constantly from sheer necessity to meet instant, unimagined needs. Though overproduction ruined many early concerns, the sheer number of wells drilled served as a training ground for innumerable infant companies and inexperienced workers who became the oil field's boll weevils, hard tails, swivel necks, roustabouts, and roughnecks, and who later formed the core of the oil business. Just as the Hamills had done at Spindletop, they constantly improvised, learning as they went. As Al Hamill commented, each well was different.[62]

Training for most laborers arriving at the oil field was strictly "on the job." In the wake of the boom, workers stayed in short supply, although men poured into the fields looking for work, seeking the high pay they had heard was there. Drillers looked for men who had garnered some experience, at least, with farm machinery. One early oil crew headed up its rotary drilling team with a man whose only experience had been in cable drilling. The pump man on that rig was a steamboat engineer from the steamboat *Belle of Austin*.

The rest of the crew was "a bunch of fellows from the piney woods of Texas, who had been lured from their home by a promise of $3 per day for 12 hours of hard work. But $3 a day in 1902 was a lot of money."[63] In spite of their lack of experience, the workers learned quickly, formulating methods and tools on the spur of the moment to serve a specific purpose. Al Hamill recalled:

> Well, inventions then, they just kind of happened so. If you'd need a tool, you'd think about it, you'd rig it up and go to the machine shop and have it made. Never think anything about patenting it. . . . They just developed up as necessity demanded, you see.[64]

According to Curt, the oil business required a combination of "perseverence and . . . horse sense." In Al's memory, the man who originated an idea seldom got credit for it. The Hamills' first primitive manufacture of drilling mud for the Lucas well led to Jim Sharp's "mud mixer," a machine which was forthwith copied extensively by other drillers in the Spindletop field. Even the prototype for the Hughes bit was possibly developed by a Sour Lake machinist named Johnny Wynn, although Hughes was the one who perfected and patented it.[65]

As Lucas and Higgins had proved, scientific methods of locating oil at the turn of the twentieth century often proved to be little more accurate than were psychics, or boys with x-ray eyes, or wiggle sticks. Especially along the Gulf Coast, "there was no geology," as Curt Hamill put it. Even the most successful men utilized a combination of instinct and common sense. Al Hamill recalled John Galey's saying that the best method of finding oil was to use "Professor Drill." As one historian has observed, the whole Spindletop story was one of "astute geological hunches by nonprofessionals and lack of intuition on the part of more expert scientists."[66]

Detecting the presence of oil once the well was nearing completion was also chancy. Drillers knew they were getting into oil sand when it began to "soften up" and oil began to "show on the ditch." Early drillers sounded more like chefs testing a new recipe than men after oil: according to worker Claude Deer, "We'd smell it [the sand], feel of it and taste it, put it on the boiler and heat it up, or dry it out, and see how it looked." "Those days," Curt Hamill recalled, "we had to see rainbows on water. We hadn't even begun to take cores yet. So we had to discover, find our oil sand, through rainbows coming out with our returns."[67]

Derrick floors were scrubbed clean so a "rainbow," or oil sheen, would show as it came out of the well. But the method was useless if the crude oil

The *Cardium*, the first oil tanker to sail into Port Arthur, left with 60,000 barrels of Guffey oil. *Courtesy Tyrrell Historical Library, Beaumont, Texas.*

used to lubricate the rig's machinery dripped down onto the floor. In an incident that perhaps illustrates as well as any the instant technology as well as the interchangeability of executives with roughnecks in those defining days, Pittsburgh financier Will Mellon was present one day when a careless worker allowed crude oil to drip onto a freshly scoured derrick floor, making it impossible to spot any oil from the well. In his ire at the workman, Mellon invented on the spot a method of thickening lubricating oil by boiling it, then applying it from a long-necked container for more accurate and less wasteful use.[68]

Refining technology was primitive as well, the early "shell" stills, or distilling units, being "unscientific but economic." Quality control depended greatly on the skills of expert stillmen. One Fred Driehs, a "towering German with a Hohenzollern moustache, a barrel chest and broad shoulders" who was among the first stillmen at the Security Refinery, was said to be able to gauge the quality of the refined oil by smelling and feeling it.[69]

As producing and refining facilities developed, the oil market grew with remarkable speed. Once the supply was assured, oil's long-touted advantages over other fuel sources became fact. Three barrels of oil at twenty cents each produced as much energy as a $3.50 ton of coal, and occupied much less space. Besides, oil was cleaner-burning and less labor-intensive, and it could be manipulated under pressure.

Adjustment to the new fuel was relatively simple and of short duration. Even as early as June of 1901, the first locomotive in the South to convert from coal to oil pulled the private car of an official of the Gulf, Colorado and Santa Fe Railroad from Cleburne, Texas, to Beaumont. Curt Hamill recalled his first ride on an oil-burning locomotive, going from Beaumont to Sabine Pass and back. The crude oil was full of "flies and bugs" that had to be filtered out, and the engineer "swore all the way down [that] the darn poor railroad had sent a man out to burn water, but on coming back, with the oil cleaned up, he said he wished they'd put an oil burner on every damn engine they had." Among early converters were sugar-cane planters in Louisiana and Mississippi, using petroleum to fuel their boilers. In November 1901 the *Cardium*, the first oil tanker to sail into Port Arthur, departed with sixty thousand barrels of the Guffey Company's desulphurized oil from Spindletop. And this was only the beginning.[70]

The oil business grew by leaps and bounds to meet its soon-to-be-global market, and perforce, oil technology kept up. In fact, the technologies themselves would evolve into huge worldwide industries—seismology, drilling fluids, special tools, firefighting equipment, and more—a long way from the days of Cullinan beating the flames alongside his men, Jim Sharp, protecting oil property with pistols, and Curt Hamill, looking for rainbows on water.

Chapter Eleven

SPINDLETOP: A RETROSPECTIVE

"Your new husband is going to have to learn a new profession. We've just left the Liquid Fuel Age and entered the Atomic Age. That's where energy will come from from now on. . . . But not right this minute."
—*Texas oilman Michel T. Halbouty to his bride, on learning of the United States' use of atomic weaponry against Japan*[1]

BY 1903, the capricious oil and gas pressure of the hill had finally spent itself, and Spindletop became a pumper field. By that time, the Gulf Coast's prairies and salt domes were studded with drilling efforts, fanning out from Spindletop to spread rapidly to the rest of the state and across the Sabine River into southwestern Louisiana. The Gulf Coast would never again be regarded as a region devoid of petroleum products; the Lucas Gusher, brought in where it was considered to be a geological impossibility, had reshaped geological thought.

The Spindletop field would be surrounded by discoveries, not only at Sour Lake, Saratoga, and Batson, but Humble in 1904 and Goose Creek in 1908. Then, southwest down the coastline, fields would be brought in at West Columbia, Barbers Hill, Hull, High Island, and others, and more fields would come in in other parts of the state: the Red River Uplift fields in North Texas, the Panhandle and Permian Basin fields, the Mexia fault, and the East Texas field, the greatest oil field the world had ever known. In August of 1901, just seven months after the Lucas Gusher had come in, the *New York Journal* had written: "Texas has found her glory. It is OIL. . . ." The prophetic words would come true a thousandfold. Although extensive fields would eventually be discovered in neighboring states, then in the rest of the country, it was Texas whose image was irrevocably changed, both in its own eyes and in those of the rest of the world. Texas would soon become an icon for Big Oil. By 1905, more than a quarter of the crude pumped in the country came from the Lone Star State.[2]

As a result of the Texas boom, the hub of the country's oil production moved from the eastern part of the United States to the southwestern, and the new giants engendered at Spindletop—Gulf, Texaco, Sun, Humble, and the many other associated concerns—recast the industry with a new set of players who rose to global dominance. On the eve of World War II, there would be forty-six oil fields operating within a hundred-mile radius of Spindletop alone, with 2,440 producing wells.[3]

The town of Beaumont, jerked from its previous course and precipitately thrust into another, enjoyed a brief golden age, the problems that would surface because of its too-rapid, uncharted development still in the future. With Galveston's star in eclipse after the Great Storm of 1900, hope flared briefly in city fathers' breasts that Beaumont would become the premier city of the Gulf Coast. Texas oil production would gradually move westward toward Houston, however, and Old Sam's namesake town, more populous and more centrally located, with finance and statewide rail connections already in place, would forge ahead with plans for its deepwater port to take its place as the "primary regional metropolis." But the fact remained that the event of Spindletop took away the physical, economic, and social image of Beaumont as a lumber, rice, and cattle town and redefined it in oil.[4]

Beaumont would remain a large refining center; a proliferation of plants would range outward from Spindletop, making the upper Gulf Coast the eventual site of the largest concentration of refineries in the world.[5]

> By the end of 1917 there were twenty-six refineries in Texas, valued at $48,950,000, with an estimated daily capacity of 225,000 barrels. Gulf, Texas, and Magnolia owned about 70 per cent of the Texas refinery capacity, located mostly in the Port Arthur–Beaumont area.[6]

Those three great refineries spawned at Spindletop—Gulf, Texaco, and Magnolia (later a part of Mobil)—would still be operating at the turn of the millennium. Mobil would eventually merge with Exxon (formerly Humble) to form Exxon-Mobil, the largest oil company in the world, and ironically, in a move rife with history, the successors to the first two Spindletop-born companies, Gulf (later Chevron) and Texaco, would merge in October of 2000, only a little less than a century after their birth. Their progenitors—Guffey, Galey, Lucas, Cullinan, Hogg, and the others—would be probably proud, if not astounded.

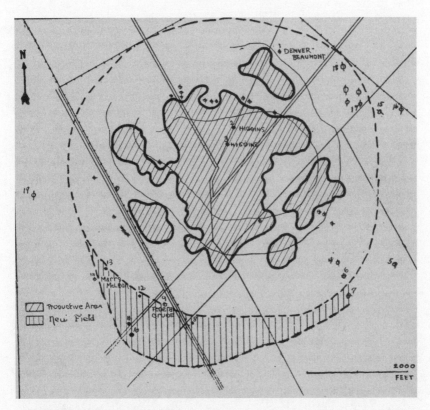

Map showing production area of the new Spindletop oil field, brought in in 1925 on the flanks of Spindletop Hill. The discovery well, the McFaddin #2, drilled by Marrs McLean and Frank Yount, was, like the Lucas Gusher, brought in on McFaddin-Wiess-Kyle land. *Courtesy Tyrrell Historical Library, Beaumont, Texas.*

The settlements on the hill—Spindletop, Gladys City, and Little Africa— lost their boomtown character and became merely places for oil field workers to live, though life there was never easy. "Spindletop kids" had a reputation for being tough. "The boys and girls from around Spindletop way were a rough-and-ready type," one Beaumont writer reported. "[when they came to school] they marched down Highland Avenue in several groups of fifteen or twenty. . . . Every pupil on the campus knew when the Spindletop gangs arrived."[7]

After the Spindletop field had played itself out, the hill was thought by most authorities to be drained. They were wrong. It was the pioneers—Galey, Lucas, and Higgins—whose earlier predictions of more oil under Spindletop Hill would prove to be true. On November 13, 1925, in an encore that would not be its last surprise, the hill hosted a brand-new field, this time on its flanks.

Tanks, derrick, and crew of the Rio Bravo Oil Company, circa 1926. Rio Bravo was one of the smaller companies that gained a foothold in the second Spindletop field, dominated almost totally by Frank Yount and Marrs McLean. *Courtesy Jo Ann Stiles.*

The discovery well, the McFaddin No. 2, was, like its predecessor, brought in on the same 3,850-acre tract of McFaddin-Wiess-Kyle land, on the flank of the dome several hundred feet to the southeast of the site of the old Lucas Gusher.

It was brought in by two more visionaries in a reprise of the Higgins-Lucas roles: Marrs McLean, a sometime High Island melon-farmer-turned-drilling-promoter, and his Calder Avenue neighbor, Miles Frank Yount, the guiding genius of the local Yount-Lee oil company, whose stockholders included former Texas Company oil men E. F. Woodward and brothers Thomas P. and William E. Lee; Yount's son-in-law, Talbot Rothwell; and a young Beaumont grocery salesman named Harry Phelan. This time, no gushers blew in wild; the wells were controlled from the outset. This time, the town of Beaumont saw no frenzied land speculation; Yount and McLean already controlled most of the producing areas of the hill, and most of the remainder was leased out by major oil companies. This time, Beaumont was not caught in the state of flat-footed reaction that had afflicted it before; much of the money stayed in town to foster another boom in the local economy.[8]

The hill saw none of the pandemonium that had accompanied the first boom; derricks (now made of steel), mess halls, bunk houses, and offices sprang up, but without the company of tents, shanties, saloons, or brothels.

The granite obelisk marking the original site of the Lucas Gusher, ready to be unveiled at the Spindletop 40th Anniversary Celebration, January 10, 1941. Local oil man Scott Myers helped find the original site by locating the sunken timbers that had held the gate valve assembly used to cap the well and the remains of the protruding drill pipe that had been cut off at ground level. *Courtesy Tyrrell Historical Library, Beaumont, Texas.*

Since 1901, the oil industry had matured into big business. There was no frantic search for a market; in the twenty-four-year interim, America—and the world—had become hungry for oil. The new Spindletop field, which would prove larger than the first one, would flow over fifty-nine million barrels of oil in its first five years of production.[9]

The town of Beaumont eventually began to acquire some historical perspective on its unique and colorful past. In 1941, the fortieth anniversary of the advent of the Lucas Gusher, officials decided to celebrate. There was one problem. In the chaos on the hill subsequent to the boom, the actual physical site of the gusher had been lost.

A hasty convocation of old-timers, headed by Gulf Oil Corporation's Marion Brock, spearheaded the effort to find the well's location. Independent oil operator Scott Myers, who had been born at Spindletop, marked what he

From left: Al, Curt, and Jim Hamill, Mrs. Anthony FitzGerald Lucas, and Anthony F.G. Lucas after the unveiling of the Lucas Gusher monument at the Spindletop 40th Anniversary Celebration in 1941. *Courtesy Allen William Hamill Jr., Houston, Texas.*

believed to be the spot, and the committee erected a pink Texas-granite obelisk to commemorate the gusher. The marker read:

> On this spot, on the tenth day of the twentieth century, a new era of civilization began. At ten-thirty on the morning of January 10, 1901, the first great oil well in the world, the Anthony F. Lucas Gusher, blew in, making an estimated 100,000 barrels of oil per day from a depth of 1,160 feet. Lucas supervised the drilling by J. G. and A. W. Hamill for J. M. Guffey and J. H. Galey on the Mc-Faddin-Wiess-Kyle lease. The well produced 800,000 barrels in the nine days it ran wild.
>
> –Erected in July 1941 by the Lucas Gusher Monument Association, J. Cooke Wilson, President; Stephen W. Pipkin, Vice-President; Scott W. Myers, Secretary; and Marion E. Brock, Treasurer.

The name of Pattillo Higgins was not inscribed on the marker.[10]

In 1951, Spindletop's fiftieth anniversary celebration was chaired by John

The Hamill brothers, Curt (second from left), Jim (center), and Al (right), reenacting spudding in the Lucas #1, October 9–11, 1941, in Beaumont, at the Texas Mid-Continent Oil and Gas Association Old-Timers' Convention. *Courtesy Tyrrell Historical Library, Beaumont, Texas.*

W. Newton, the plant manager of the Magnolia Refinery. Big plans were set in motion more than two years in advance, and the celebration was carried out on a grand scale.[11]

Initially, a slogan contest for the celebration was held. The winner, "Spindletop—Where Oil Became an Industry," was patently wrong; oil had been very big business before 1901, but the slogan itself was catchy.[12]

The celebration began with a broadcast on Thursday, January 4, 1951, of Gulf Oil Corporation's national radio and television show, "We, the People," featuring Al Hamill, who recounted the drilling of the Lucas Gusher. Other special events included a "Spindletop Revue," performed by the Melody Maids, Beaumont's renowned girls' singing group, with music composed by their director, Eloise Milam, and Sunday morning, January 7, DuPont's national radio show, "The Cavalcade of America," broadcast from the Beaumont City Auditorium, starring Robert Cummings and Teresa Wright in the roles of Anthony and Caroline Lucas.[13]

Spindletop 50th Anniversary Celebration, old- and new-style derricks in Beaumont's Sunset Park, with the new Crosby Hotel in the background. *Courtesy Tyrrell Historical Library, Beaumont, Texas.*

Stellar guests flocked by the hundreds into town: then-governor of Texas Allan Shivers, Attorney General Price Daniel, Houston independent oil producer Glenn McCarthy, geologist Everette DeGolyer, and Houston petroleum geologist and Beaumont native son Michel Halbouty. National figures on the scene included John G. Pew, president of Sun Oil Company; Charles E. Wilson, the president of General Motors Corporation; Walter S. Carpenter Jr., the chairman of the board of E. I. DuPont de Nemours and Company; and B. Brewster Jennings, president of Socony-Vacuum Oil Company.[14]

Wednesday, January 10, 1951, dawned clear and cold, a fresh wind blowing from the north—weather almost identical to that of that other January day, fifty years before. Area schools were dismissed for the day. At exactly 10:30 A.M., refinery and locomotive whistles and automobile horns sounded all over town to commemorate the exact moment the gusher blew in, and a squadron of jets flew over Pearl Street, then out over Spindletop Hill. At noon, in an act that surely made several shades smile, David Rockefeller, grandson of that former specter of every Texas schoolchild's nightmares, old John D. Rockefeller, addressed a Beaumont Rotary Club luncheon attended by nearly five hundred members and guests. That afternoon, a gargantuan "Parade of Progress" rolled through the streets of Beaumont. Three guests of honor led the parade: Anthony FitzGerald Lucas, son of the by-then-deceased Captain; seventy-five-year-old Al Hamill, his genial face beaming; and eighty-nine-year-old Pattillo Higgins, resembling nothing so much as an elderly bird of prey, a rusty smile occasionally parting his thin lips. (Peck Byrd and Jim Hamill were dead, and Curt Hamill was ill in San Antonio, unable to attend.) The parade was viewed by approximately seventy-five thousand people. For a few hours, the town, the nation, and the world paused to remember.[15]

Old Spindletop Hill held another surprise. In the 1950s and '60s, it was gutted for more of its hoarded treasure, mined extensively by the Texas Gulf Sulphur Company for the substance that had first piqued Anthony Lucas's interest in Southeast Texas—sulphur.[16]

With the passage of time, the successive casts of principals exited the scene. Time-honored Captain George Washington O'Brien died in 1909, but at the turn of the millenium, his descendants still operated the historic Gladys City Company.[17]

George Washington Carroll, that passionate advocate of faith and morality, became through his lumber and oil interests one of Beaumont's wealthiest men. In the kindness of his spacious heart, he finally succeeded in giving most of it away, notably to the First Baptist Church of Beaumont and to Baylor University, Texas's largest Baptist college. He died in 1935, universally beloved but in modest circumstances, in a small room in the Beaumont YMCA building his money had helped to construct.[18]

The McFaddin, Wiess, and Kyle families, the landowners on whose property the Lucas Gusher was drilled, continued to reap the benefits of the various mineral treasures unearthed on Spindletop Hill through the years. Harry Carothers Wiess became chief executive officer of the Humble Oil and Refining Company in 1933, serving in that capacity for fourteen years before his death in Houston in 1948. Although Perry McFaddin's interests were diversified with farming, ranching, oil, and real estate, he remained "a cattleman, born and bred" throughout the remainder of his life, daily riding horseback with his ranch hands well into his old age. He died at his home in Beaumont on November 5, 1935.[19]

Buckskin Joe Cullinan served as president of the Texas Company, later known as Texaco, until 1913, building the foundation for the global corporate giant it would later become. In 1913, he resigned under pressure because of the company's temporary economic reverses, growing differences with Arnold

John Galey (right) with his nephew in one of the gasoline-powered automobiles his wildcatting skills helped to fuel. Note canine passenger perched on his own homemade running-board seat, embellished with his name, "Sambo." *Courtesy Drew Patterson and Center for American History, University of Texas at Austin.*

Schlaet, and his strong belief that the corporate offices of Texaco should be kept in Texas. After his resignation, the company moved its corporate offices to New York, and Cullinan died in Palo Alto, California, on March 11, 1937.[20]

"Colonel" James McClurg Guffey, whose genius at finding money for wildcat oil ventures was equaled only by his poor management skills, dived headlong into a West Virginia coal mining venture after the Mellons had maneuvered him out of the Gulf Oil Corporation. The venture failed, and it was his old friend and partner John Galey who bailed him out. Guffey's assets then went into the hands of receivers.[21]

Galey, Guffey's "lucky old oil hound," continued doing what he knew how to do best—looking for oil anywhere and everywhere, always sinking what money he made into new ventures. Forever in search of the "peculiar excitement" of discovering what lay beneath the surface of the earth, he regarded financial matters as irrelevant details, and he disdained such mundane activities as record-keeping.[22]

According to his grandson, John H. Galey II, the senior Galey's personal papers long ago disappeared, stored either in an old rolltop desk in a Pittsburgh warehouse (the contents forfeit because the bill wasn't paid) or in a London storage building later destroyed in World War II by German bombs. The Standard Oil Company representative who negotiated Standard's buyout of Guffey and Galey's Neodesha, Kansas, operations reported in horror: "I found Guffey and Galey's leases and other papers hurled into old wooden barrels and into other queer places." Spindletop probably represented the height of Galey's fortunes. He had conducted numerous mining and oil prospecting ventures through the years, during the 1880s opening a silver mine in Arizona, about forty miles from Tombstone. The boomtown that grew up around the mine, named "Galeyville" after him, boasted its share of saloons, outlaws, gunfights, and murders, as well as a local sheriff whose avocation was cattle rustling. (Galeyville no longer exists; in timber-poor Arizona, it was dismantled to furnish lumber for another town.)[23]

Ironically, or perhaps appropriately, Galey's final wildcat effort was financed by Al Hamill, who had once drilled wells for him. The old wildcatter died in 1918, bankrupt. James Guffey, who attended his old friend's funeral, told Galey's wife, "We are burying the best man I have ever known."[24]

Many of the greatest fields in the country were brought into production by Galey's efforts, and he was widely considered to be one of the best wildcatters of the century. As William Larimer Mellon said of him, "his amazing power to scent a hidden pool of oil underground transcended the power of other men with or without the benefit of a geologist's education."[25]

The men who brought in and capped the Lucas Gusher—Al, Curt, and Jim Hamill—remained drillers of oil wells, staying in oil production all their lives. Their innovations at Spindletop, spawned from sheer necessity—the flushing of sand from the hole to facilitate drilling, the back-pressure valve to prevent sand from heaving up into the drill pipe, the drilling mud, the Christmas-tree valve assembly the brothers hastily designed to cap the raging Lucas well, and others—these prototypes revolutionized the technology of the oil industry. For the Hamill brothers, they were all in a day's work.

Curt soon left his brothers' company to drill with another company on Spindletop Hill. For a time, Al and Jim continued to work together, then they split and contracted separately. When the Kiser-Kelly well, drilled about a mile north of the Lucas Gusher, came in dry in late May of 1901, the Hamills moved on to other fields, including Sour Lake, Batson Prairie, and Humble, then others in Texas and Louisiana.[26]

Drillers par excellence as they were, the Hamills enjoyed considerable economic success without becoming involved—or going broke, like many of their contemporaries—in other phases of the industry. No one ever accused the Hamill brothers of lacking good common sense.

At least one member of the Hamill crew had a personal reason for staying

Allen William Hamill Jr. (left) with his father, Al, who was visiting his son in Texas. Allen Hamill Jr., also in the oil business, was helpful in the writing of this book. *Courtesy Allen William Hamill Jr., Houston, Texas.*

in touch with Southeast Texas. In 1910 Al married a young woman from Beaumont named Evelyn Edwards, having finally convinced her after nearly ten years, as he told it, "that maybe an oilman wasn't such a bad one to live with."[27]

Jim Hamill died in 1947, at the age of seventy-nine. Al and Evelyn ended up in Tulsa, Oklahoma, where Al died at the age of eighty in 1956. Curt retired to Kerrville in March of 1952; he and Eva both suffered from throat trouble, which he blamed on the "sulphuric gas" they encountered at the Spindletop, Sour Lake, and Batson Prairie oil fields. Curt would be the last brother left, living to the age of one hundred and dying in the 1970s. Until the day he died, he kept the old twenty-gallon wash pot that Eva Hamill had used to boil the oil out of the crew's clothing at Spindletop.[28]

"I feel life's been very kind to me," Al remarked in a 1952 interview. "We've been very fortunate." In the spring of 2000, the Hamills returned some of their good fortune to the place where it all began. The Hamill Foundation of Houston, founded by Curt's son Claude Hamill, made a generous donation to the Spindletop Centennial celebration, held January 10, 2001, at the Spindletop/Gladys City Boomtown Museum in Beaumont, near the oil field. In an appropriate measure, the gift was used to fund construction of a replica of the Lucas Gusher, which "blew in" at the celebration with a thundering, 150-foot spray of *water*, to the cheers of an assembled crowd of thousands, including former president of the United States George Herbert Walker Bush.[29]

Pattillo Higgins, in the tradition of the true wildcatter, continued to explore the Texas oil fields for the next fifty years, characteristically making important finds but then withdrawing before the big payoffs, leaving the companies who came after him to reap the lion's share of the profit. During his long lifetime, he made—and lost—several fortunes.[30]

Higgins remained a dogmatic, unreconstructed maverick all his life, true to his own inner dictates. At the age of forty-five, in the face of scandal, he married his eighteen-year-old adopted daughter, Annie Johns of San Antonio. Annie bore him three children: sons Pattillo "Pat" Higgins Jr. and Jack, and their only daughter Gladys, presumably named after one or both of the Gladyses in Higgins's earlier life. In 1919, following, as always, his hunches for another potential field, the family moved to San Antonio, where Pattillo Higgins died on June 5, 1955. He is buried in Mission Burial Park in San Antonio.[31]

His great-nephew Robert McDaniel reported in his biography of Higgins that the Beaumont wildcatter left three instructions in his personal papers for whoever might write the story of Spindletop:

> In the first place, he said to make the account factual and not to use
> any "bullfrog" poetry. Second, he said not to say anything that
> would make him appear to be an idle dreamer who never accom-
> plished anything practical. And finally, he said to give Lucas credit
> for what he accomplished at Spindletop.[32]

Pattillo Higgins (left) and Al Hamill at the Spindletop 50th Anniversary Celebration. *Courtesy Tyrrell Historical Library, Beaumont, Texas.*

It was Anthony Lucas above all who received the majority of credit for discovery of the field. For several years after the gusher blew in, he continued to be lionized all over the world. He was met by crowds wherever he went, and any land he examined, regardless of where it was located, immediately skyrocketed in price. Newspapers everywhere followed every move of the "Oil King of the World," as he was popularly known. A plethora of songs and poems were written about the new hero and his discovery, one published under the title, "The Lucas Geyser March Song," by Frederick C. King and Fannie Lamb:

> You talk about your Klondike rush and gold in frozen soil,
> But it don't compare with Beaumont rush when Lucas he struck oil.
> So if you want a lease for oil you must be an early riser
> To get a whack at our Cracker Jack, the Famous Beaumont Geyser.[33]

After selling his interest in Guffey Petroleum Company back to Guffey, Lucas continued to drill for that company for a limited time. In 1902, he accepted an offer to prospect for oil in Mexico for the Mexican Eagle Oil Company, Ltd., and Sir Wheetman Pearson, later Lord Cowdray, who held large oil interests there. While there, he located two oil fields near Coatza-coalcos.[34]

In February of 1904, Lucas made a final visit to Beaumont to tour the

The "Lucas Geyser March Song," by Frederick C. King and Beaumonter Fannie Lamb. One of many songs and poems written in honor of Spindletop's new hero, Anthony Lucas, and his discovery. *Courtesy Tyrrell Historical Library, Beaumont, Texas.*

Anthony Lucas in later life. This photograph appeared in *The Oil Weekly*, October 6, 1941. *Courtesy Allen William Hamill Jr., Houston, Texas.*

site of his spectacular success. The field had produced three and a half million barrels of oil in the discovery year, 1901; in 1902, seventeen and a half million barrels; in 1903, only a little over eight and a half million. At the time of the Captain's visit, Spindletop's pumper production was down to little more than ten thousand barrels a day. "The cow was milked too hard," he observed sadly, "and moreover, she was not milked intelligently."[35]

In 1905 Lucas returned to Washington, where he spent the rest of his life as a consulting engineer, traveling all over the world—Algeria, North Africa, Russia, Rumania, Galicia, and other locations— as well as to numerous oil fields in the United States. When the country entered World War I, he joined actively in the quest for minerals to be utilized in the war effort.[36]

He and Carrie maintained a cordial relationship with Al and Evelyn Hamill until his death, exchanging periodic Christmas cards and other personal correspondence. In a letter dated December 28, 1919, Lucas confided to Al that he had endured a spell of poor health of an unspecified nature and had lost some thirty pounds, but that he was feeling better. Al's reply, dated January 10, 1920, expressed gratitude for the Captain's improved health. "I feel that this is an appropriate day to answer your nice letter," he wrote further, "for as you well remember, it is just nineteen years ago today that our real excitement began on Spindletop."[37]

Anthony Lucas died at his Washington home on September 2, 1921, only a little over twenty years after the discovery that had turned the tide of history and, against his own nature, had made him famous. He is buried in the Rock Creek Cemetery in Washington, D.C. It is his tombstone that perhaps speaks most eloquently of this very private man. It reads, presumably at his direction: "Anthony Francis Lucas, of Illyrian parentage." Proud of his ancient roots, he wanted to be remembered for them if for nothing else. His will, dated July 27, 1921, only a little over six weeks before he died, provides funds "in aid of Montenegrin orphans of the late war" and for orphanages in

Spalato and Lesina, "including the Little Island of Saint Clement near the said Island of Lesina, where my grandfather was born . . . "[38]

A memorial article described him as having

> An energetic, magnetic personality . . . noted for his persistence, in-
> dustry, endurance, and courage. He was sincere, honest, firm
> against all obstacles, backing his judgment with his own hard work
> along any course which he had determined to correct. Those who
> numbered him among their friends found him a congenial, hos-
> pitable host with a keen sense of humor, besides being a veritable
> storehouse of information gleaned from his experiences in many
> countries.[39]

He garnered professional honors both during his lifetime and posthu-
mously, including his appointment in 1913 as the first chairman of the special
committee on petroleum and gas for the American Institute of Mining and
Metallurgical Engineers. In 1936, the Petroleum Division of that organization established the Anthony F. Lucas Gold Medal to recognize "distinguished achievement in improving the technique and practice of finding and
producing petroleum."[40]

Curiously, in all of the Captain's later interviews and accounts of the
events leading to the discovery at Spindletop, he never mentioned Pattillo
Higgins at all.

The question of which man, Lucas or Higgins, was the more instrumental in the Spindletop discovery is still being debated a century later. Curt
Hamill commented:

> Mr. Higgins, according to my idea, is the real man that found Beau-
> mont or the Spindletop Oil Field, but it was developed by Captain
> Lucas. And I have never understood why Mr. Higgins has not
> gained more popularity through the early days and even up till now
> (1952).[41]

In the words of Lucas's friend and fellow oil man Everette DeGolyer,

> Both men [Higgins and Lucas] are entitled to credit. Higgins, for
> his unwavering faith in the direct indications on the mound and for
> his perseverance in promoting the entire enterprise. Lucas, if for
> nothing else, for his promotional and technical ability and his
> tenacity in carrying the enterprise to a successful conclusion. We
> prefer to follow the good old oil country rule of giving credit to the

man whose decision was directly responsible for drilling the discovery well: Lucas.[42]

Lucas's son, Anthony FitzGerald "Tony" Lucas, served as a lieutenant in the United States Army during World War I and went to France in June of 1917 with the Sixteenth Regiment of Infantry. His battalion marched in Paris in that year's July 4 celebrations. At the Spindletop fiftieth anniversary celebration, Tony Lucas, by then sixty-two, was greeted by standing ovations wherever he went. As one historian put it, "the name had a magic appeal."[43]

Caroline FitzGerald Lucas, arguably the real heroine of Spindletop Hill, supported her husband in his every endeavor for all her days. She died on November 9, 1932, and lies buried beside him in Rock Creek Cemetery. In his words, "she urged the risk and the sacrifice."[44]

Dr. George Parker Stoker, the young oil field medico who found himself hooked on the boomtown excitement, was finally brought to his senses by a funeral service for a Saratoga prostitute. The pimps, gamblers, saloon men and "girls" who were her mourners wanted to honor her memory fittingly, but no one knew a hymn, and they had forgotten how to pray. Finally, one elderly saloon man suggested they sing the following song, which everyone seemed to know:

We were born into this world
All naked and bare.
We go through it with sorrow and care;
When we die we are going no one knows where,
But if we are rounders here,
We will be rounders there.

It was then that Stoker decided to return to his respectable roots in the East, in a place where he could, at least, be buried "in decency and order."[45]

Litigation over the Spindletop field had begun in 1898, when George W. Carroll sued Pattillo Higgins for his interest in the Gladys City Oil, Gas, and Manufacturing Company. It continued on through the discovery and beyond, with the suits and countersuits among the principals, Lucas, Higgins, and Carroll, setting a litigious precedent that endures today. Spindletop created an entire new world of legal problems and precedents over surface and mineral rights, safety, "rule of capture," and countless other issues.[46]

The most famous and flamboyant legal controversy of all involved the William Pelham Humphries survey, the 3,850-acre tract Anthony Lucas

Michel T. Halbouty (left) and James A. "Jimmy" Clark. Halbouty, eminent petroleum geologist and engineer and one of the last of the legendary Texas oil men, and Clark, author and historian, wrote *Spindletop*, a story of the discovery, in 1952. *Courtesy Gittings
Studio, Houston, Texas.*

leased from the McFaddin-Wiess-Kyle Beaumont Pasture Company in 1900,
on which the discovery wells for both the 1901 and the 1925 Spindletop
booms were located. To this day, hope seems to spring eternal in the breasts of
the alleged heirs of the original owners, even though the courts have repeatedly found throughout the years that, in 1901, the land was unquestionably
owned by the McFaddin family and their associates and heirs. As historians
James A. Clark and Michel Halbouty have put it, "Legal controversy over the
William Pelham Humphries survey has become an institution, like the hill itself." But that is another story, better told elsewhere.[47]

The successive aftershocks of the discovery at Spindletop, which Joseph
Pratt has called a "departure of history," spread in ever-growing waves
throughout the state and the nation to mark the twentieth century as the century of oil.[48] In the words of historian C. A. Warner,

> It is indeed doubtful whether any other single event in the history
> of the petroleum industry in the United States has ever had a signif-
> icance comparable to that of the Lucas gusher. Unexpected and un-
> prepared for, it announced to the world in no uncertain manner
> that oil in tremendous quantities and at relatively shallow depths

Abandoned Lucas Gusher monument base, 1982. Photograph by John H. Walker. *Courtesy Tyrrell Historical Library, Beaumont, Texas.*

was present on the coastal plain in a state considered by many to be incapable of large production.[49]

Heraclitus wrote that nothing endures but change, and to realize it, we have only to look at the undreamed-of changes in the hundred years since the gusher came in. Those first changeovers from coal to oil as a fuel source were only the beginning. Petroleum and related petrochemicals have permeated daily life worldwide, generating countless products and by-products from asphalt to jet fuel, toys to telephones, lunch boxes to Christmas ornaments. Oil has changed our way of life, our very way of looking at things. It has altered the way we fight wars, the way we play, the way we get from one place to another. It has redefined our necessities and given us luxuries we never imagined. It has changed our economy. It has shrunk the globe. As Daniel Yergin puts it, "ours is a century in which every facet of our civilization has been transformed by the modern and mesmerizing alchemy of petroleum." And the vast quantity of oil found at Spindletop brought these changes within the realm of possibility.[50]

Not all of the changes have brought pat solutions. In this age of complexity, we cherish fewer icons, and definite answers sometimes seem farther

To commemorate the one hundredth anniversary, January 10, 2001, of the discovery well of the Spindletop oil field, the site of the Lucas Gusher was marked with a new flagpole, seen here in the distance. *Photograph by Brian Sattler.*

away than they ever were. Since Spindletop's semicentennial celebration in 1951, when petroleum still reigned as lion rampant, the state and the nation have confronted an increasingly complex world, where, with increasing frequency, global events govern local conditions. As Texas oil historian Roger Olien has pointed out, with the exception of the still-thriving petrochemical industry, "at a rate governed by international prices and technology, the . . . petroleum industry in Texas [is] inching down the road from Spindletop."[51]

In the last quarter of the twentieth century, around the time of Spindletop's seventy-fifth anniversary, the balance of power in the political economy of petroleum shifted to the Middle East. In the early 1980s, after the fall of the government of Iran half a world away, the petroleum industry, and Texas oil and gas in particular, faced the possibility of the Götterdämmerung of the oil industry as we have known it. And in the wake of new environmental awareness, the petroleum industry itself, once regarded as the embodiment of the American spirit of enterprise and the fount of all things positive, is in many quarters finding itself regarded as one of society's prime villains.[52]

Besides, who knows what new technology or energy source will accord petroleum an honorable retirement? In the intervening century, atomic energy, unimagined in 1901, has literally burst upon the scene, and another as-yet-un-dreamed-of source of energy may be only as far away as tomorrow's sunrise. Older sources of energy, left at the altar at the dawn of the Petroleum Centu-ry, are again being courted; on the cusp of the millenium, several automobile manufacturers have produced cars powered by a combination of gasoline and electricity. As the centennial anniversary of the Lucas Gusher was observed just ten days into the new millenium, the future is in some ways more unpre-dictable than it ever was. But knowledge of the past fortifies us with the capa-bility to face the future.

In the meantime, oil will continue to permeate every aspect of our lives, from minute to global, for a long time to come. After all, as recently as the 1990s, when Middle Eastern strongman Saddam Hussein invaded Kuwait to pirate its oil reserves, oil still meant worldwide wealth and power. And as M. A. Adelman has observed, "No mineral, including oil, will ever be exhausted. . . . How much oil is still in the ground when extraction stops, and how much was there before extraction began, are unknown and unknowable. The amount extracted from first to last depends on cost and price."[53]

Over the last three years of the twentieth century and the beginning of the twenty-first, a new group of wildcatters is taking a chance on Spindletop. Four independent oilmen from Dallas—Bill Whaling, Leo Newport, J. C. Gentry, and Alan Balser, known in the industry as the Four Horsemen—began reexamining salt domes on the Gulf Coast in the mid-1990s. Of the sixty-four domes they examined, three, including Spindletop, held special promise for additional production. The original group then sold the idea to Herbert Hunt and his company, Petro-Hunt, L.L.C., who brought addition-al investors into the deal, and Centennial Oil and Gas Investments, Ltd., was born. In March of 2001, a three-dimensional seismic survey, a Spindletop first, was shot of a fifty-seven-square-mile area around Spindletop Hill to ob-tain a comprehensive view of the structure of the dome, perhaps producing new strikes, especially of natural gas, at a depth of from four thousand to six-teen thousand feet. All partners agreed that the centennial celebration of the original Spindletop discovery was instrumental in drawing interest to this new operation. The fascination of the search, this time using modern technology to increase knowledge of the hill, is a never-ending element in the saga of the oil industry. Shades of Anthony Lucas, Pattillo Higgins, and the Hamills! Who knows? Perhaps old Spindletop Hill will produce again.[54]

In the final analysis, however, the tale of Spindletop will be told by those individuals who played a part in the discovery, whether they brought in wells, founded giant companies, made their fortunes speculating, or wrestled with the cantankerous equipment; whether they fought fires, survived injury, illness, or saloon brawls, or minded children in the shadows of derricks, or under the greasy spray of wells run amok. It will be told by those who waited, hoped, and prayed for a show of oil—or a husband or father to come safely home. It was they who linked dream to reality. They did their jobs, and they changed the world. They deserve—and have found—their place in history.

A century after it hosted such momentous events, the old hill is quiet once again. The remains of the oil field were dozed down in the 1950s, when the sulphur-mining operations were begun. The flanks are now covered in vegetation—myrtle, willow, and the interloper Chinese tallows—so that the slope of the hill is now barely discernible to the human eye. Yet, if those who travel the old road up to the crest look back, they can see the rise in the ground.

The crater created by the sulphur-mining effort now disfigures the summit of the dome, and gradual subsidence and the ubiquitous tallows have further altered the look of the terrain. Yet the hill still boasts life. Its interior has been hollowed out, and the resulting caverns are now used to store natural gas. Here and there, in an eerie reprise of a sound formerly common in these parts, old pumpjacks—the "donkeys" of the oil fields—nod, creak, and strain to pull out the last dregs of oil from the hill's inner recesses for an independent stripper operation. Stained gray tanks, pine or cypress , some dating from the early glory days, haunt the landscape. Scattered by the thousands over the ground lie sulphur-laced rocks, so alien to the Southeast Texas marshes and plains.

The old monument base, abandoned in the 1950s when the granite obelisk was first moved, lies on the very edge of the rain-filled crater. It is canted with the increasing slant of the land, which is gradually subsiding into the water.

New surveys have established the site of the old Lucas Gusher beyond a doubt. As it happened, that day back in the 1930s, Scott Myers had been right. The base lies within five feet of the original well site. A new bronze marker now pinpoints the exact spot where, in that one history-changing, watershed moment, the world suddenly became a different place.

Across the top of the hill, the shifting Gulf winds whistle through the marsh grass, still—and always—carrying the perennial, all-pervasive scent of oil.

SELECTED BIBLIOGRAPHY

I. Books

Abernethy, Francis E., editor. *Tales From the Big Thicket.* Austin: University of Texas Press, 1966.

Adelman, Morris Albert. *The Genie Out of the Bottle: World Oil Since 1970.* Cambridge: MIT Press, 1995.

Advantages and Conditions of Port Arthur Today. Beaumont: Oil Exchange and Board of Trade, 1901.

Asbury, Ray. *The South Park Story 1891–1971 and the Founding of Lamar University 1923–1941.* Fort Worth: Evans Press, 1972.

Ashford, Gerald. *Spanish Texas Yesterday and Today.* Austin: Pemberton Press, 1971.

Beaumont: A Guide to the City and Its Environs. Federal Writers' Project of the Work Projects Administration in the State of Texas. American Guide Series. Houston: Anson Jones Press, 1938.

Block, W. T. *Sour Lake, Texas: From Mudbaths to Millionaires, 1835–1909.* Liberty, Texas: Atascosito Historical Society, 1994.

Boatright, Mody, and William Owens. *Tales from the Derrick Floor: A People's History of the Oil Industry.* Lincoln: University of Nebraska Press, 1970.

Brantly, J. E. *History of Oil Well Drilling.* Houston: Gulf Publishing Company, a product of the Energy Research Education Foundation, 1971.

Cassell's Spanish Dictionary. Edgar Allison Peers et al., editors. New York: Funk and Wagnalls Company, 1960.

Chernow, Ron. *Titan: The Life of John D. Rockefeller, Sr.* New York: Random House, 1999.

Clark, James A., and Michel T. Halbouty. *Spindletop.* New York: Random House, 1952.

DeSoto Chronicles, The: The Expedition of Hernando deSoto to North America in 1539–1543. Tuscaloosa: University of Alabama Press, 1993.

Donahue, Jack. *Wildcatter: The Story of Michel T. Halbouty and the Search for Oil.* New York: McGraw-Hill, 1979.

Estep, W. R. *And God Gave the Increase: The Centennial History of the First Baptist Church of Beaumont, Texas, 1872–1972.* Beaumont: First Baptist Church, 1972.

Foy, Jessica, and Judith Linsley. *The McFaddin-Ward House.* Austin: Texas State Historical Association, 1992.

Franks, Kenny, and Paul Lambert. *Early California Oil: A Photographic History, 1865–1940.* College Station: Texas A&M University Press, 1985.

Goodwyn, Lawrence. *Texas Oil, American Dreams: A Study of the Texas Independent Producers and Royalty Owners Association.* Austin: Texas State Historical Association for the Center for American History, 1996.

Gould, Lewis L. *Progressives and Prohibitionists: Texas Democrats in the Wilson Era.* Austin: University of Texas Press, 1973.

Hamill, Curtis G. *We Drilled Spindletop!* Houston: privately published, 1957.

James, Marquis. *The Texaco Story: The First Fifty Years, 1902–1952.* New York: The Texas Company, 1953.

Jenson, Vernon. *Lumber and Labor.* New York and Toronto: Farrar and Rinehart, 1945.

Johnson, Thelma, et al. *The Spindletop Oil Field: A History of Its Discovery and Development.* Beaumont: privately published by George W. Norvell, 1927.

King, John O. *Joseph Stephen Cullinan: A Study of Leadership in the Texas Petroleum Industry, 1897–1937.* Nashville: Vanderbilt University Press, 1970.

Knight and Sutton Directory of the City of Beaumont, 1900. Published by the *Beaumont Enterprise,* 1900.

Knowles, Ruth Sheldon. *The Greatest Gamblers: The Epic of American Oil Exploration.* New York: McGraw-Hill, 1959.

Langenkamp, R. D. *Handbook of Oil Industry Terms and Phrases.* 2nd edition. Tulsa: PPC Books, a division of Petroleum Publishing Company, 1977.

Larson, Erik. *Isaac's Storm.* New York: Crown Publishers, 1999.

Larson, Henrietta M., and Kenneth Wiggins Porter. *A History of the Humble*

Oil and Refining Company. New York: Harper & Brothers, 1959.

Lewis, Theodore H., editor. *Spanish Expeditions in the Southern United States, 1528–1543: Narrative of the Expedition of Hernando de Soto by the Gentleman of Elvas.* New York: Barnes & Noble, 1907.

Linsley, Judith Walker, and Ellen Walker Rienstra. *Beaumont: A Chronicle of Promise.* Woodland Hills, California: Windsor Publications, 1982, 2nd edition, 1987.

McBeth, Reid Sayers. *Pioneering the Gulf Coast: A Story of the Life and Accomplishments of Capt. Anthony F. Lucas.* Privately published, 1917. Tyrrell Historical Library, Beaumont, Texas.

McDaniel, Robert W., with Henry C. Dethloff. *Pattillo Higgins and the Search for Texas Oil.* College Station: Texas A&M University Press, 1989.

Mellon, William Larimer, and Boyden Sparks, collaborator. *Judge Mellon's Sons.* Privately printed, 1948.

Olmsted, Frederick Law. *A Journey Through Texas.* New York: Dix, Edwards & Company, 1857.

Owen, Edgar W. *Trek of the Oil Finders.* Tulsa: The American Association of Petroleum Geologists, 1975.

Parker, George. *Oil Field Medico.* Dallas: Banks and Upshaw, 1948.

Penn, W. E. *The Life and Labors of Major W. E. Penn.* St. Louis: C. B. Woolard Printing Company, 1896.

Pomeroy, C. David, Jr. *Pasadena: The Early Years.* Pasadena, Texas: Pomerosa Press, 1993.

Port Arthur. Federal Writers' Project of the Work Projects Administration in the State of Texas. American Guide Series. Houston: Anson Jones Press, 1940.

Pratt, John Stricklin. *The Road to Spindletop: Economic Changes in Texas, 1875–1901.* Dallas: SMU Press, 1955.

Pratt, Joseph A. *The Growth of a Refining Region.* Greenwich, Conn.: JAI Press, 1980.

Rioux, Terry Lee. *G. W. Carroll: Southern Capitalist and Dedicated Beaumont Baptist.* Austin: Eakin Press, 2001.

Rister, Carl Coke. *Oil! Titan of the Southwest.* Norman: University of Oklahoma Press, 1949.

Robertson, Robert J. *Her Majesty's Texans: Two English Immigrants in Reconstruction Texas.* College Station: Texas A&M University Press, 1998.

Rundell, Walter, Jr. *Early Texas Oil.* College Station: Texas A&M University Press, 1977.

Sanders, Christine Moor. *Captain George Washington O'Brien and the History of the Gladys City Oil Company at Spindletop.* Woodville, Texas: privately printed, 1992.

Seale, William. *Texas In Our Time.* Dallas: Hendrick-Long Publishing Company, 1972.

Varner, John Grier, and Jeannette Johnson Varner, editors. *The Florida of the Inca.* Austin: University of Texas Press, 1951.

Walker, John H., and Gwendolyn Wingate. *Beaumont: A Pictorial History.* Virginia Beach: Donning Publishing Company, 1983.

Warner, Charles A. *Texas Oil and Gas Since 1543.* Houston: Gulf Publishing Company, 1939.

Williamson, Harold F., and Arnold R. Daum. *The American Petroleum Industry, 1859–1899: The Age of Illumination.* Evanston: Northwestern University Press, 1959.

Yergin, Daniel. *The Prize: The Epic Quest for Oil, Money, and Power.* New York: Simon & Schuster, 1991.

II. ARTICLES

"A Biography of Captain Anthony Francis Lucas, 1855–1921," Washington, D.C., December 14, 1944. Typescript, no author given. Center for American History, University of Texas, Austin, Texas.

"The Birth of a Great Discoverer." *American Croatian Historical Review,* July, 1946. Beaumont/Spindletop vertical files. Tyrrell Historical Library, Beaumont, Texas.

Bruffey, E. C. "Captain Lucas, Oil King of the World, Tells How He Won Success and Fame," article dated Jan. 1902, in Lucas Scrapbook (CAH).

Bruseth, James E. "The Moscoso Expedition." *The New Handbook of Texas.* Ron Tyler et al., editors. Austin: Texas State Historical Association, 1996. Volume IV, 851–852.

Cashen, Alice. "Boom-Town Tales." *Tales from the Big Thicket.* Francis E. Abernethy, editor. Austin: University of Texas Press, 1966, 143–144.

DeGolyer, Everette. "Anthony F. Lucas and Spindletop." Reprinted from the *Southwest Review.* Dallas, Southern Methodist University, Fall, 1945. Copy in "Biography . . . Lucas," Spindletop 50th Anniversary Collection file. Texas Energy Museum Collection, Beaumont, Texas.

Etienne-Gray, Tracé. "Pattillo Higgins." *The New Handbook of Texas.* Ron Tyler et al., editors. Austin: Texas State Historical Association, 1996. Volume III, 595–596.

Geiser, Samuel Wood. "Benjamin Taylor Kavanaugh and the Discovery of

East Texas Oil." Undated copy of *Field and Laboratory* in the possession of Jo Ann Stiles, Lamar University, Beaumont, Texas.

———. "Dr. John Allen Veatch." *Southwestern Historical Quarterly*, 46 (Oct., 1941), 169–173.

Gerland, Jonathan K. "Sawdust City: Beaumont, Texas, on the Eve of the Petroleum Age." *Texas Gulf Historical and Biographical Record*, 2 (Nov., 1996), 21–47.

———. "The Spindletop Letters of Anthony F. Lucas to Pattillo Higgins, 1899," *Texas Gulf Historical and Biographical Record*, 34, no. 1 (1998), 77–91.

Hamill, Allen W. "The Lucas Gusher." Typed, unpublished article in the Beaumont/Spindletop/Diaries and Memories file, vertical files. Tyrrell Historical Library, Beaumont, Texas.

House, Boyce. "Spindletop." *Southwestern Historical Quarterly*, 50 (July, 1946), 36–43.

Jeffries, Charlie. "Reminiscences of Sour Lake." *Southwestern Historical Quarterly*, 50 (July, 1946), 32–33.

Linsley, Judith Walker, and Ellen Walker Rienstra. "George Washington Carroll (1855–1935)." *The New Handbook of Texas*. Ron Tyler et al., editors. Austin: Texas State Historical Association, 1996. Volume I, 990.

———. "George Washington O'Brien (1833–1909)." *The New Handbook of Texas*. Ron Tyler et al., editors. Austin: Texas State Historical Association, 1996. Volume IV, 1098–1099.

Lucas, Anthony F. "The Great Oil Well Near Beaumont, Texas." *Transactions* of the American Institute of Mining Engineers, 31 (1902), 362–374.

O'Brien, Chilton. "John Allen Veatch: Early Gulf Coast Surveyor." *Texas Gulf Historical and Biographical Record*, 18 (Nov., 1982), 38–41.

Olien, Roger M. "The Oil and Gas Industry." *The New Handbook of Texas*. Ron Tyler et al., editors. Austin: Texas State Historical Association, 1996. Volume IV, 1119–1128.

Pratt, Joseph A. "Spindletop: Fueling the Nation." Paper given at Beaumont History Conference, Beaumont, Texas, January 8, 2000.

Rickard, T. A. "Anthony F. Lucas, and the Beaumont Gusher, an Interview." *Mining and Scientific Press* (Dec. 22, 1917), 897–894.

Rioux, Terry Lee. "Biographical Sketch of George Washington Carroll." *The Texas Gulf Historical and Biographical Record*, 34 (Nov., 1998), 2–19.

Smith, D. Ryan. "Spindletop's 50th Anniversary Celebration." *The Texas Gulf Historical and Biographical Record*, 32 (Nov., 1996), 61–72.

Stiles, Jo Ann. "A Venture Into Oil: The Cartwright Company." *The Texas Gulf Historical and Biographical Record*, 34 (Nov., 1998), 57–65.

Wagner, Paul. "Spindletop's History-Making Comeback Lacks Human Background of Old." *National Petroleum News* (Sept. 22, 1926), 73, 75, 76, 78.

Weddle, Robert. "Luis De Moscoso Alvarado." *The New Handbook of Texas*. Ron Tyler et al., editors. Austin: Texas State Historical Association, 1996. Volume IV, 851.

Wooster, Robert. "Anthony Francis Lucas." *The New Handbook of Texas*. Ron Tyler et al., editors. Austin: Texas State Historical Association, 1996. Volume IV, 325–326.

III. NEWSPAPERS AND MAGAZINES

Beaumont Age, February 1–June 28, 1901.

Beaumont Enterprise, July 18, 1899–January 10, 1999.

Beaumont Journal, March 23, 1895–January 10, 1969.

DuPont Magazine, 1959.

Galveston Daily News, March 9, 1978–February 19, 1901.

Houston Post, April 21, 1901–October 4, 1901.

National Oil Reporter, June 27–October 10, 1901.

New York Journal, August 18, 1901.

New York Times, January 13–24, 1901.

Oil Investors' Journal, May 24, 1902.

IV. THESES

Martin, Everette Armstrong. "A History of the Spindletop Oil Field." Master's thesis. University of Texas, Austin, Texas, 1934.

Rioux, Terry Lee. "George Washington Carroll: A Biography." Master's thesis. Lamar University, Beaumont, Texas, 2000; a 2001 publication of Eakin Press, Austin, Texas.

Simons, Vivian Yvetta. "The Prohibition Movement in Beaumont, Texas, 1835–1919." Master's thesis. Lamar University, 1963.

Trevey, Marilyn Dianne Stodgehill. "The Social and Economic Impact of the Spindletop Oil Boom on Beaumont in 1901." Master's thesis. Lamar University, 1974.

V. LETTERS

Shane K. Bernard, Historian and Curator, McIlhenny Company Archives (Archives@TABASCO.com), e-mail to Jo Ann Stiles, Lamar University, Beaumont, Texas, Dec. 4, 5, 7, 2001.

George M. Craig to T. J. Donoghue of the Texas Company, April 10, 1937. In possession of James W. McManus, Craig's grandson.

John H. Galey II, Neosho, Missouri, to Jo Ann Stiles, Lamar University, Beaumont, Texas, March 25, 2000. Copy in possession of JAS.

Nathan Gilbert, Beaumont, Texas, to G. W. Cochran, Cairo, Illinois, October 6, 1865. Copy in possession of Jo Ann Stiles, Lamar University, Beaumont, Texas.

James S. Hogg to J. S. Cullinan at Beaumont, January 22, 1903. Copy in Center for American History, University of Texas, Austin, Texas, 3K9, folder 5 (Miscellaneous Manuscript Letters).

W. J. McKie to Matthew Cartwright of Terrell, Texas, April 2, 1901. Copy in possession of Jo Ann Stiles. Lamar Univerisity, Beaumont, Texas, and the Cartwright Collection, Center for American History, University of Texas, Austin, Texas.

VI. COLLECTIONS

Caldwell Diary, J. L. Caldwell Family Papers, box 2. McFaddin-Ward Historic House Museum, Beaumont, Texas.

Cartwright Family Papers. Center for American History, University of Texas, Austin, Texas.

Center for American History Photographic Collections, University of Texas, Austin, Texas.

Hogg Collection, Ima. Center for American History, University of Texas, Austin, Texas.

Lucas Scrapbook, Anthony F. Pioneers in Texas Oil Collection. Center for American History, University of Texas, Austin, Texas.

Osborne Collection, Jackson Broocks. Tyrrell Historical Library, Beaumont, Texas.

Texas Oil and Gas Association Collection, Austin, Texas.

VII. INTERVIEWS

Barfield, Plummer. Interview with William A. Owens, Sour Lake, Texas, tape #25, August 1, 1952. Pioneers in Texas Oil Collection. Center for American History, University of Texas, Austin, Texas.

Bryant, W. E. "Bill." Interview with William A. Owens, Sour Lake, Texas, tape #27, July 29, 1952. Pioneers in Texas Oil Collection. Center for American History, University of Texas, Austin, Texas.

Carper, Mary Dale. Interview by Jo Ann Stiles, Lamar University, Beaumont, Texas, April 1997.

Chaney, Earl. Untranscribed interview by Roger Dimmick, undated, tape recording in Texas Energy Museum Files, Beaumont, Texas.

Coe, B. A. Interview with Judith Linsley, Kountze, Texas, September 7, 2000.

Daniels, V. B. Interview with William A. Owens, Sour Lake, Texas, tape #22, July 3, 1952. Pioneers in Texas Oil Collection. Center for American History, University of Texas, Austin, Texas.

Deer, Claude. Interview with William A. Owens, Spindletop, Texas, tape #8, July 7, 1952. Pioneers in Texas Oil Collection. Center for American History, University of Texas, Austin, Texas.

Donahoe, James. Interview with William A. Owens, Batson, Texas, tapes #22 and #23, August 1, 1952, and #24, August 3, 1952. Pioneers in Texas Oil Collection. Center for American History, University of Texas, Austin, Texas.

Dowell, Dale. Telephone interview with Jo Ann Stiles, Beaumont, Texas, April 25, 2001. Office interview, November 2001.

Fehl, W. B. Untranscribed interview by unidentified person. Texas Energy Museum, Beaumont, Texas.

Galey, Tom. Interview with Ellen Rienstra and Judith Linsley, Beaumont, Texas, January 10, 2001.

Gentry, James C. , and Alan Balser. Interviews by phone, e-mail, and in person with Jo Ann Stiles, January 2001.

Gerland, Jonathan K. Telephone interview with Judith Linsley, May 23, 2000.

Hamill, Allen William. Interview with William A. Owens, Tulsa, Oklahoma, tapes #84, 85, September 2, 1952. Pioneers in Texas Oil Collection. Center for American History, University of Texas, Austin, Texas.

Hamill, Allen William, Jr. Interview with Jo Ann Stiles, Houston, Texas, November 17, 2000, and February 3, 2001.

Hamill, Curtis G. Interview with William A. Owens, Kerrville, Texas, tapes #16, 17, 18, July 17, 1952. Pioneers in Texas Oil Collection. Center for American History, University of Texas, Austin, Texas.

Henry, Willie. Interview in San Antonio, Texas, January 15, 1952. Pioneers in Texas Oil Collection. Center for American History, University of Texas, Austin, Texas.

Hudson, W. M. Interview with William A. Owens, tape #80, September 18, 1952. Pioneers in Texas Oil Collection. Center for American History, University of Texas, Austin, Texas.

Hunt, Herbert, and other officials of Petro-Hunt. Interviews with John Burnett and Wayne Bell of National Public Radio, December 2000.

Lucas, Joe. Interview with Ellen Rienstra and Jo Ann Stiles, March 6, 2001.

Molett, LeVert. Telephone interview with Judith Walker Linsley, Beaumont, Texas, February 23, 2000, and July 21, 2000.

Myers, Edna Wherry. Interview with Jo Ann Stiles, Beaumont, Texas, April, 1997.

Paramore, Harry. Interview with William A. Owens, Beaumont, Texas, tape #7, July 7, 1952. Pioneers in Texas Oil Collection. Center for American History, University of Texas, Austin, Texas.

Pelt, Arnold, Petroleum Well Services. Interview with Judith Linsley, Kountze, Texas, September 7, 2000.

Simmons, Bud. Interview with Suzy Wilson, August 5, 1981. Unpublished school project in possession of Jo Ann Stiles, Lamar University, Beaumont, Texas.

Singleton, Dillard. Untranscribed interview by unidentified person, Texas Energy Museum, Beaumont, Texas.

Slausen, Ethel Alice. Interview by Jo Ann Stiles, Beaumont, Texas, tape #60, June 14, 1989, and #61, July 20, 1989. McFaddin-Ward Historic House Museum, Beaumont, Texas.

Stell, Bill. Telephone interview by Jo Ann Stiles, May 15, 2000, July 20, 2000, and July 25, 2000.

Webb, Sam W. Interview with William A. Owens, Fort Worth, Texas, tape #76, September, 1952. Pioneers in Texas Oil Collection. Center for American History, University of Texas, Austin, Texas.

Webb, Mrs. Sam W. Interview with William A. Owens, Fort Worth, Texas, tape #76, September, 1952. Pioneers in Texas Oil Collection, Center for American History, University of Texas, Austin, Texas.

Wheat, John S. Untranscribed interview March 7, 1977. Texas Energy Museum, Beaumont, Texas.

Wilson, Rosine McFaddin. Interview with Ellen Rienstra, Beaumont, Texas, September 24, 2000.

VIII. Miscellaneous Sources

Beaumont City Council Minutes, 1898. Tyrrell Historical Library, Beaumont, Texas.

Blain, Sally Coburn, Memoirs, transcribed by Mary Fort Blain. In the private collection of Scott Blain, Beaumont, Texas.

First Baptist Church of Beaumont, Texas, Church Minutes, December 19, 1902, and December 31, 1903.

First Methodist Church of Beaumont, Texas, Church Records, Sermon May 22, 1904, "Christian Citizenship," by the Rev. B. A. Godbey.

Hice, C. B. *Spindle Top Guide and Directory.* Beaumont: Undated, but probably 1903.

Higgins, Pattillo. *The True History of the Beaumont Oil Fields: A Prospectus*. Beaumont: Printed by Pattillo Higgins, 1902.

Jefferson County Deed Records. Jefferson County Courthouse, Beaumont, Texas.

1900 United States Census, Jefferson County, Precinct 4.

Prieur, W. L., Jr., Clerk of Courts, Corporation Court, Norfolk, Virginia, from letters dated June 22, 1945, and April 4, 1946 (cited by *American Croatian Historical Review*, July, 1946, in Spindletop vertical files, Tyrrell Historical Library, Beaumont, Texas).

NOTES

Prologue

1. James A. Clark and Michel T. Halbouty, *Spindletop* (New York: Random House, 1952), 191–192.

2. Carl C. Rister, *Oil! Titan of the Southwest* (Norman: University of Oklahoma Press, 1949), 64, citing R.T. Hill, "The Beaumont Oil Field, With Notes on Other Oil Fields of the Texas Region," reprinted from the *Journal of the Franklin Institute* (Aug.–Oct., 1902), 27.

3. Daniel Yergin, *The Prize: The Epic Quest for Oil, Money, and Power* (New York: Simon and Schuster, 1991), 79

4. Ibid., 80.

5. Ibid., 12.

Chapter One

1. Christine Sanders, *Captain George W. O'Brien and the History of the Gladys City Company* (Woodville, Tex.: privately printed, 1992), 12.

2. Edgar A. Owen, *Trek of the Oil Finders* (Tulsa: American Association of Petroleum Geologists, 1975), 1, 11–12; Yergin, *The Prize*, 27–28.

3. Ibid., 1–3.

4. Daniel Yergin, *The Prize*, 24; Harold F. Williamson and Arnold R. Daum, *The American Petroleum Industry, 1859–1899: The Age of Illumination* (Evanston: Northwestern University Press, 1959), 8.

5. Owen, *Trek of the Oil Finders*, 8; Williamson and Daum, *The American Petroleum Industry*, 8–12.

6. John Grier Varner and Jeanette Johnson Varner (eds.), *The Florida of the Inca* (Austin: University of Texas Press, 1951), xxi–xxii; Theodore H. Lewis (ed.), *Spanish Expeditions in the Southern United States, 1528–1543: Narrative of the Expedition of Hernando deSoto by the Gentleman of Elvas* (New York: Barnes & Noble, 1907), 129; James

E. Bruseth, "The Moscoso Expedition," *The New Handbook of Texas*, ed. Ron Tyler et al. (Austin: Texas State Historical Society, 1996), IV, 852–853; Gerald Ashford, *Spanish Texas Yesterday and Today* (Austin: Pemberton Press, 1971), 39; Robert Weddle, "Luis De Moscoso Alvarado," *The New Handbook of Texas*, IV, 851.

7. Lewis, *Spanish Expeditions in the Southern United States*, 246 (quotation), 250.

8. Ibid., 246 (1st, 3rd, and 4th quotations); *The DeSoto Chronicles: The Expedition of Hernando deSoto to North America in 1539–1543* (Tuscaloosa: University of Alabama Press, 1993), 527 (2nd quotation).

9. Charles A. Warner, *Texas Oil and Gas Since 1543* (Houston: Gulf Publishing Co., 1939), 1.

10. Ibid., 2.

11. Owen, *Trek of the Oil Finders*, 191.

12. Ibid., 2.

13. Samuel Wood Geiser, "Dr. John Allen Veatch," *Southwestern Historical Quarterly*, 46 (Oct., 1942), 170–171; Chilton O'Brien, "John Allen Veatch: Early Gulf Coast Surveyor," *The Texas Gulf Historical and Biographical Record*, 18 (Nov., 1982), 38–41.

14. O'Brien, "John Allen Veatch: Early Gulf Coast Surveyor," 40.

15. Geiser, "Dr. John Allen Veatch," 171 (1st quotation), 172 (2nd quotation).

16. Frederick Law Olmsted, *A Journey through Texas* (Austin: University of Texas Press, 1978), 375–376.

17. Warner, *Texas Oil and Gas Since 1543*, 3.

18. Yergin, *The Prize*, 23.

19. Williamson and Daum, *The American Petroleum Industry*, 29.

20. Yergin, *The Prize*, 23; Owen, *Trek of the Oil Finders*, 9; Williamson and Daum, *The American Petroleum Industry*, 45.

21. Yergin, *The Prize*, 25–28; Owen, *Trek of the Oil Finders*, 11; Williamson and Daum, *The American Petroleum Industry*, 63–81.

22. Yergin, *The Prize*, 32–33; Owen, *Trek of the Oil Finders*, 12.

23. Yergin, *The Prize*, 33, 56 (quotation); Owen, *Trek of the Oil Finders*, 12.

24. J. A. Nations to Matthew Cartwright, Beaumont, Tex., June 12, 1868, Cartwright Family Papers (Center for American History, University of Texas, Austin, cited hereafter as CAH); Edgar Allison Peers et al. (eds.), *Cassell's Spanish Dictionary* (New York: Funk and Wagnalls Co., 1960), 138, 212.

25. Undated article by Milton Turner, "Primary Quest of Sulphur Led to Spindletop Discovery" (quotation), undated article ca. 1950, *Beaumont Enterprise*, in the possession of Frank Bonura of Beaumont, and in files of Terry Rioux and Jo Ann Stiles, Lamar University, Beaumont, Tex.; Boyce House, "Spindletop," *Southwestern Historical Quarterly*, 50 (July, 1946), 42.

26. *Galveston Daily News*, Mar. 9, 1878.

27. Ibid.

28. Judith Walker Linsley and Ellen Walker Rienstra, *Beaumont: A Chronicle of Promise* (Woodland Hills: Windsor Publications, 1982), 64 (quotation), citing *Beaumont News-Beacon* article, 1873.

29. W. T. Block, "Spindle Top Once Isolated Plague Victims," *Beaumont Enterprise*, Jan. 9, 1999; *Beaumont Enterprise*, May 27, 1934; [Beaumont] *Sunday Enterprise and Journal*, Feb. 26, 1978; Robert W. McDaniel with Henry C. Dethloff, *Pattillo Higgins and the Search for Texas Oil* (College Station: Texas A&M University Press, 1989), 31.

30. Christine Moor Sanders, *Captain George Washington O'Brien and the History of the Gladys City Company at Spindletop* (Woodville, Tex.: Privately printed, 1992), 8–9; Linsley and Rienstra, *Beaumont*, 49.

31. Sanders, *Captain George Washington O'Brien*, 9; Linsley and Rienstra, *Beaumont*, 51.

32. Ron Chernow, *Titan: The Life of John D. Rockefeller, Sr.* (New York: Random House, Vintage Books Edition, 1999), xiv.

33. Yergin, *The Prize*, 39–55.

34. Sanders, *Captain George Washington O'Brien*, 12.

35. Walter Rundell, Jr., *Early Texas Oil* (College Station: Texas A&M University Press, 1977), 17.

36. Warner, *Texas Oil and Gas Since 1543*, 7.

37. Ibid., 8.

38. Nathan Gilbert, Beaumont, Tex., to G. W. Cochran, Cairo, Ill., Oct. 6, 1865 (quotation), copy in possession of Jo Ann Stiles.

39. Warner, *Texas Oil and Gas Since 1543*, 9 (quotation); William Seale, *Texas In Our Time* (Dallas: Hendrick-Long Publishing Co., 1972), 59, 70.

40. Warner, *Texas Oil and Gas Since 1543*, 6; Rundell, *Early Texas Oil*, 18.

41. *Flake's Daily Galveston Bulletin*, July 11, 1866; Linsley and Rienstra, *Beaumont*, 55.

42. Samuel Wood Geiser, "Benjamin Taylor Kavanaugh, and the Discovery of East Texas Oil," *Field and Laboratory* (date and year missing, copy in possession of Jo Ann Stiles), 50.

43. Cartwright Family Papers (CAH).

44. *Beaumont Journal*, undated article ca. 1935–36, in possession of Jo Ann Stiles.

45. *Beaumont Lumberman*, Jan. 18, 1878 (quotation); House, "Spindletop," 37; Everette Armstrong Martin, "A History of the Spindletop Oil Field" (unpub. Master's thesis, University of Texas, 1934; copy at THL), 7.

46. Sanders, *Captain George Washington O'Brien*, 12.

47. *Galveston Tri-Weekly News*, Feb. 22, 1867.

48. *Beaumont Journal*, May 16, 1901, citing 1878 *Beaumont Lumberman* article.

49. Warner, *Texas Oil and Gas Since 1543*, 12–17.

50. Ibid., 17 (quotation); John O. King, *Joseph Stephen Cullinan: A Study of Leadership in the Texas Petroleum Industry, 1897–1937* (Nashville: Vanderbilt University Press, 1970), 9.

51. Warner, *Texas Oil and Gas Since 1543*, 24.

52. Ibid., 25.

53. Ibid., 26; McDaniel and Dethloff, *Pattillo Higgins*, 60; Lawrence Goodwyn,

Texas Oil, American Dreams: A Study of the Texas Independent Producers and Royalty Owners Association (Austin: Texas State Historical Association for the Center for American History, 1996), 14; William Larimer Mellon and Boyden Sparkes, Collaborator, *Judge Mellon's Sons* (privately printed, 1948), 282.

54. Allen William Hamill interview with William A. Owens, "Spindletop, The Lucas Gusher," Tulsa, Okla., Sept. 2, 1952, tape #84, pp. 1–7, Pioneers in Texas Oil Collection (CAH); Curtis G. Hamill interview with William A. Owens, "The Lucas Gusher, Spindletop," Kerrville, Tex., July 17, 1952, tape #16, pp. 1–6, Pioneers in Texas Oil Collection (CAH).

55. Yergin, *The Prize*, 92, 93 (quotation); Warner, *Texas Oil and Gas Since 1543*, 26–38.

56. Warner, *Texas Oil and Gas Since 1543*, 29; Rundell, *Early Texas Oil*, 25; R. D. Langenkamp, *Handbook of Oil Industry Terms and Phrases* (Tulsa: PPC Books, a division of Petroleum Publishing Co., 1977), 141.

57. Yergin, *The Prize*, 56; Williamson and Daum, *The American Petroleum Industry*, vii.

Chapter Two

1. Robert W. McDaniel and Henry C. Dethloff, *Pattillo Higgins and the Search for Texas Oil* (College Station: Texas A&M University Press, 1989), 40.

2. Ibid.

3. McDaniel and Dethloff, *Pattillo Higgins*, 4–9.

4. Ibid.

5. Ibid.

6. Ibid.

7. *Beaumont Enterprise*, Jan. 29, 1898 (quotation); Linsley and Rienstra, *Beaumont*, 57–63.

8. *Beaumont: A guide to the City and Its Environs*, Federal Writers Project of the Work Projects Administration in the State of Texas (Houston: Anson Jones Press, 1938), 89; Linsley and Rienstra, *Beaumont*, 40 (quotation), 62.

9. Robert J. Robertson, *Her Majesty's Texans: Two English Immigrants in Reconstruction Texas* (College Station: A&M University Press, 1998), 44–56, 64–65, 68–69.

10. Linsley and Rienstra, *Beaumont*, 57, 62, 64.

11. *Beaumont: A Guide*, 89; Linsley and Rienstra, *Beaumont*, 62–63 (quotation).

12. McDaniel and Dethloff, *Pattillo Higgins*, 9.

13. Ibid., 15.

14. *Beaumont Enterprise*, Oct. 1, 1881.

15. McDaniel and Dethloff, *Pattillo Higgins*, 16.

16. Ibid., 19.

17. Ibid., 17–19.

18. Linsley and Rienstra, *Beaumont*, 59–60, 73.

19. "Beaumont's Destiny is Linked With a $50 Gift and a Baptist Revival," *Beaumont Enterprise*, Mar. 6, 1927, copy donated to CAH by Pattillo Higgins on July 21, 1952.

20. Ibid. (quotation); McDaniel and Dethloff, *Pattillo Higgins*, 19–21.

21. Judith Walker Linsley and Ellen Walker Rienstra, "George Washington Carroll, 1855-1935," *The New Handbook of Texas*, I, 990; McDaniel and Dethloff, *Pattillo Higgins*, 21; Terry Lee Rioux, "A Biographical Sketch of George Washington Carroll," *Texas Gulf Historical and Biographical Record*, 34 (Nov., 1998), 12–13.

22. "Beaumont's Destiny," *Beaumont Enterprise*, Mar. 6, 1927.

23. Ibid.

24. Tracé Etienne-Gray, "Pattillo Higgins," *The New Handbook of Texas*, III, 595-596; "Beaumont's Destiny," *Beaumont Enterprise*, Mar. 6, 1927; McDaniel and Dethloff, *Pattillo Higgins*, 23 (quotation), 24; Clark and Halbouty, *Spindletop*, 9; W. E. Penn, *The Life and Labors of Major W. E. Penn* (St. Louis: C. B. Woolward Printing Co., 1896), 138–139.

25. W. R. Estep, *And God Gave the Increase: The Centennial History of the First Baptist Church of Beaumont, Texas, 1872-1972* (Beaumont: First Baptist Church, 1972), 50, 68 (quotation).

26. McDaniel and Dethloff, *Pattillo Higgins*, 33.

27. Rioux, "Biographical Sketch of George Washington Carroll," 6; Tracé Etienne-Gray, "Pattillo Higgins," *The New Handbook of Texas*, III, 595-596; McDaniel and Dethloff, *Pattillo Higgins*, 25–26.

28. McDaniel and Dethloff, *Pattillo Higgins*, 27.

29. Ibid., 27.

30. Ibid., 26–28.

31. Ibid., 35 (quotation); Clark and Halbouty, *Spindletop*, 7.

32. McDaniel and Dethloff, *Pattillo Higgins*, 13 (quotation), 31. This account holds that Robert Higgins remembered that there was petroleum floating in globules on the water of one of the springs, and that it was used by Confederate soldiers to grease their axles. In an interview published in the *Kansas City Star*, April 21, 1901, Higgins purportedly said that he had noticed "indications of oil in a surface well, which was being cleaned." Pioneers in Texas Oil Collection, Anthony F. Lucas Scrapbook (CAH), (cited hereafter as Lucas Scrapbook). In an interview in 1927, however, Pattillo Higgins "stated positively that no oil seepage was in evidence" on Sour Spring Mound, or Spindletop Hill, as it was by then called. The interviewers go on to say that "in this contention he is supported by all witnesses whom we have interviewed on the point." Thelma Johnson, et al., *The Spindletop Oil Field: A History of Its Discovery and Development* (Beaumont: Privately published, 1927, by George W. Norvell), 6.

Chapter Three

1. Pattillo Higgins, *The True History of the Beaumont Oil Fields: A Prospectus* (Beaumont: printed by Pattillo Higgins, 1902), 60 (original booklet in files at TEM).

2. McDaniel and Dethloff, *Pattillo Higgins*, 31–32.

3. Clark and Halbouty, *Spindletop*, 8.

4. McDaniel and Dethloff, *Pattillo Higgins*, 38.

5. Ibid., 33.

6. Ibid., 35.

7. Ibid., 37.

8. Ibid., 35.

9. Undated article by Milton Turner, "Primary Quest of Sulphur Led to Spindletop Discovery," from *Beaumont Enterprise*, in the possession of Bonura's grandson, Frank Bonura of Beaumont. Frank Bonura, a native of Sicily who immigrated to Beaumont in the 1880s, also claimed to have curbed the springs with cypress planks that he hauled with his wagon, pulled by his "lame white horse," from a Pine Street shingle mill to the hill, with the object of opening a health spa. When Anthony Lucas first came to Beaumont, he contacted Bonura on the recommendation of mutual friends in New Orleans for help in situating himself in town. Bonura had worked in the sulphur mines in Sicily in his youth, and he and Lucas had shared a common interest in the product that first had interested Lucas in Sour Spring Mound. Lucas, fluent in Italian, was able to converse with Bonura in his native Italian language, and the two men soon became friends. Ibid.

10. McDaniel and Dethloff, *Pattillo Higgins*, 33.

11. Owen, *Trek of the Oil Finders*, 191 (quotation); Clark and Halbouty, *Spindletop*, 8, 132.

12. McDaniel and Dethloff, *Pattillo Higgins*, 34.

13. Clark and Halbouty, *Spindletop*, 8–9.

14. McDaniel and Dethloff, *Pattillo Higgins*, 40–42, 43 (quotation).

15. Terry Lee Rioux, "George Washington Carroll: A Biography" (Master's thesis, Lamar University, Beaumont, Tex.; publication pending by Eakin Press, Austin, Tex.), 37 (quotation); Everette Armstrong Martin, "A History of the Spindletop Oil Field," (unpub. Master's thesis, University of Texas, Austin, 1934), 10.

16. McDaniel and Dethloff, *Pattillo Higgins*, 40, 41 (quotation).

17. Clark and Halbouty, *Spindletop*, 10.

18. Martin, "A History of the Spindletop Oil Field," 11.

19. Rioux, "Biographical Sketch of George Washington Carroll," 6.

20. *Neches Valley News* (Beaumont) and *The Beaumont News-Beacon*.

21. Sanders, *Captain George Washington O'Brien*, 15, citing Jefferson County Court Records, vol. 4, p. 561.

22. Sanders, *Captain George Washington O'Brien*, 18.

23. Clark and Halbouty, *Spindletop*, 12–13; Sanders, *Captain George Washington O'Brien*, 18; Martin, "A History of the Spindletop Oil Field," 12.

24. Sanders, *Captain George Washington O'Brien*, 18.

25. *Beaumont Enterprise*, Jan. 12, 1901.

26. Sanders, *Captain George Washington O'Brien*, 18, 20; Martin, "A History of the Spindletop Oil Field," 12–13, citing Minute Book of Gladys City Oil, Gas, and Manufacturing Company, 1–7. Sanders notes that the amount of capital stock on the stock certificates was printed as $200,000, but the actual amount was $54,000—an overstatement of capitalization.

27. Sanders, *Captain George Washington O'Brien*, 20; McDaniel and Dethloff, *Pattillo Higgins*, 42.

28. McDaniel and Dethloff, *Pattillo Higgins*, 38 (quotation), 39–40; Sanders, *Cap-*

tain George Washington O'Brien, 20.

29. Martin, "A History of the Spindletop Oil Field," 13–14.

30. McDaniel and Dethloff, *Pattillo Higgins,* 42.

31. Clark and Halbouty, *Spindletop,* 16–17.

32. McDaniel and Dethloff, *Pattillo Higgins,* 43; Pattillo Higgins, *The True History of the Beaumont Oil Fields,* 62 (1st quotation); Clark and Halbouty, *Spindletop,* 15–16. Rioux, "Biographical Sketch of George Washington Carroll," 7 (2nd quotation).

33. McDaniel and Dethloff, *Pattillo Higgins,* 44.

34. Clark and Halbouty, *Spindletop,* 16; Sanders, *Captain George Washington O'Brien,* 22; Martin, "A History of the Spindletop Oil Field," 14.

35. Clark and Halbouty, *Spindletop,* 17; McDaniel and Dethloff, *Pattillo Higgins,* 48.

36. Clark and Halbouty, *Spindletop,* 18; McDaniel and Dethloff, *Pattillo Higgins,* 44; Warner, *Texas Oil Since 1543,* 20–21.

37. Clark and Halbouty, *Spindletop,* 18; McDaniel and Dethloff, *Pattillo Higgins,* 44; Warner, *Texas Oil Since 1543,* 20–21.

38. McDaniel and Dethloff, *Pattillo Higgins,* 45.

39. Ibid., 46.

40. Sanders, *Captain George Washington O'Brien,* 20.

41. McDaniel and Dethloff, *Pattillo Higgins,* 47. The article appeared in the April 1894 *American Geologist.*

42. Clark and Halbouty, *Spindletop,* 25.

43. *Beaumont Journal,* Mar. 23, 1895.

44. McDaniel and Dethloff, *Pattillo Higgins,* 46, 47 (quotation), 48–49.

45. Ibid., 47.

46. Martin, "A History of the Spindletop Oil Field," 15; Clark and Halbouty, *Spindletop,* 20.

47. Clark and Halbouty, *Spindletop,* 20.

48. McDaniel and Dethloff, *Pattillo Higgins,* 48.

49. Clark and Halbouty, *Spindletop,* 20–21.

50. McDaniel and Dethloff, *Pattillo Higgins,* 48–49.

51. Rioux, "George Washington Carroll: A Biography," 63, citing George W. Carroll vs. Pattillo Higgins No. 2052, District Court, Jefferson County, Tex., May 23, 1898, box 28, file 10, Jefferson County Collection (Sam Houston Regional Library, Liberty, Tex.); *Kansas City Star,* Apr. 21, 1901 (quotation), Lucas Scrapbook; McDaniel and Dethloff, *Pattillo Higgins,* 50, 54.

52. Sanders, *Captain George Washington O'Brien,* 22, citing Gladys City Company Records and Jefferson County Court Records, vol. 12, p. 433; Martin, "A History of the Spindletop Oil Field," 17, citing a personal interview with Beaumont City Engineer L. F. Daniell, who drew Higgins's plat for Gladys City.

53. McDaniel and Dethloff, *Pattillo Higgins,* 54.

54. Copy in the Jackson Broocks Osborne Collection (Tyrrell Historical Library, Beaumont, Tex.; cited hereafter as THL).

Chapter Four

1. Anthony Lucas to Pattillo Higgins, June 7, 1899, Jackson Broocks Osborne Manuscript Collection (THL; cited hereafter as Osborne Collection). The following Lucas-Higgins letters in the Osborne Collection have been transcribed in an article by Jonathan Gerland, "The Spindletop Letters of Anthony F. Lucas to Pattillo Higgins, 1899," *Texas Gulf Historical and Biographical Record*, 34 (Nov., 1998), 77–91. Several words in the transcription are open to debate, and the authors suggest a comparison with the originals.

2. "A Biography of Captain Anthony Francis Lucas, 1855–1921," unpub. memorial article dated Dec. 14, 1944, Washington, D.C. (CAH), 1 (quotation); Robert Wooster, "Anthony Francis Lucas," *The New Handbook of Texas*, IV, 325–326. "Antonio Francesco" is the Italian version of Lucas's first name, the Slavic equivalent being "Anton Frantisek." His name has appeared in Croatian publications as "Anton Lucic." Lucas's cultural heritage included both the Slavic and Italian traditions. "The Birth of a Great Discoverer," *American-Croatian Historical Review* (July, 1946), no author mentioned, vertical files (THL), 4.

3. T. A. Rickard, "Anthony F. Lucas, and the Beaumont Gusher, an Interview," *Mining and Scientific Press*, Dec. 22, 1917, p. 887, and "The Birth of a Great Discoverer," 4. Montenegro, on the Balkan peninsula, is part of the old kingdom of Illyria, dating to the fourth century B.C. Originally influenced by the Greek culture, it was conquered by Rome in 167 B.C.

4. *Kansas City Star,* Apr. 21, 1901 (quotation), and *St. Louis Post Dispatch*, May 5, 1901, Lucas Scrapbook.

5. In post–World War I global realignments, Dalmatia, an old province of Croatia, was given to the newly formed republic of Yugoslavia, and Trieste was given to Italy.

6. Rickard, "Anthony F. Lucas, and the Beaumont Gusher," 887 (quotation); Reid Sayers McBeth, *Pioneering the Gulf Coast: A Story of the Life and Accomplishments of Capt. Anthony F. Lucas* (Privately published, 1917; copy at THL), 6. Martin, in his 1934 thesis, *A History of the Spindletop Oil Field*, reports that "Lucas is supposed to have dictated *Pioneering the Gulf Coast* . . . to [Reid Sayers] McBeth and to have printed the book at private expense. Only a few copies were put into circulation, and one of these was given to Mrs. Frank T. Higgins of Beaumont by Lucas" (p. 19). Al Hamill refers to the picture "in [Lucas's] book" (presumably the work by McBeth) that Lucas drew of the valve assembly used to close the Lucas Gusher. Allen W. Hamill interview with William A. Owens, Sept. 2, 1952, Tulsa, Okla. Pioneers in Texas Oil Collection (CAH), tape #84, p. 29. Also, in a letter from Tulsa, Oklahoma, to Anthony FitzGerald Lucas in Washington, D.C., dated July 8, 1940, Al Hamill writes, "I have checked your father's book, *Pioneering the Gulf Coast.* . . ." He also speaks of trying to contact "Mr. McB." [Reid Sayers McBeth, the book's author]. (Letter in possession of estate of Al's son, Allen Hamill, Houston, Tex.; copy in possession of Jo Ann Stiles.)

7. Everette DeGolyer, "Anthony F. Lucas and Spindletop," reprinted from the *Southwest Review* (Dallas, Southern Methodist University, Fall, 1945); "Biography . . . Lucas," Spindletop 50th Anniversary Collection file (Texas Energy Museum Collection, Beaumont, Tex.; cited hereafter as TEM), 1; McBeth, *Pioneering the Gulf Coast*, 7; W. L. Prieur Jr., Clerk of Courts, Corporation Court, Norfolk, Virginia, from letters dated June 22, 1945, and Apr. 4, 1946 (cited by *American-Croatian Historical Review*, July, 1946), vertical files (THL); *Galveston Daily News*, Feb. 28, 1901.

8. Rickard, "Anthony F. Lucas, and the Beaumont Gusher," 888–889; "The Birth of a Great Discoverer," 5; McBeth, *Pioneering the Gulf Coast*, 7.

9. Rickard, "Anthony F. Lucas, and the Beaumont Gusher," 888; "The Birth of a Great Discoverer," 5; McBeth, *Pioneering the Gulf Coast*, 7.

10. "The Birth of a Great Discoverer," 5; Rickard, "Anthony F. Lucas, and the Beaumont Gusher," 887 (quotations); McBeth, *Pioneering the Gulf Coast*, 7.

11. Rickard, "Anthony F. Lucas, and the Beaumont Gusher," 887 (quotations); McBeth, *Pioneering the Gulf Coast*, 8; Prieur, from letters dated June 22, 1945, and Apr. 4, 1946, Norfolk Corp. Court; "The Birth of a Great Discoverer," 5.

12. "Biography . . . Lucas," 2; *Kansas City Star*, Apr. 21, 1901; Rickard, "Anthony F. Lucas, and the Beaumont Gusher," 888; McBeth, *Pioneering the Gulf Coast*, 8; E. C. Bruffey, "Captain Lucas, Oil King of the World, Tells How He Won Success and Fame," unidentified newspaper dated January 1902, Lucas Scrapbook.

13. McBeth, *Pioneering the Gulf Coast*, 8; *Kansas City Star*, Apr. 21, 1901; Bruffey, "Captain Lucas, Oil King of the World."

14. *Washington Evening Star*, Sept. 21, 1901 (1st quotation), Lucas Scrapbook; "The Real Captain A. F. Lucas," written for *The Sunny South*, undated but probably about May 31, 1901 (2nd quotation), ibid.; article in unidentified Macon, Ga., newspaper dated Jan. 20, 1902 (3rd quotation), ibid.

15. Rickard, "Anthony F. Lucas, and the Beaumont Gusher," 888.

16. *Kansas City Star*, Apr. 21, 1901, and article in unidentified Hartselle, Ala., newspaper dated May 29, 1902, Lucas Scrapbook; Rickard, "Anthony F. Lucas, and the Beaumont Gusher," 888; DeGolyer, "Anthony F. Lucas and Spindletop," 84.

17. DeGolyer, "Anthony F. Lucas and Spindletop," 84; Clark and Halbouty, *Spindletop*, 281; McDaniel and Dethloff, *Pattillo Higgins*, 58.

18. McBeth, *Pioneering the Gulf Coast*, 53 (quotation), 54–56. The McIlhenny family is a branch of the Avery family. Email to Jo Ann Stiles from Shane K. Bernard, Archives@Tabasco.com, historian and curator, McIlhenny Co. Archives, Dec. 4, 5, 7, 2001.

19. DeGolyer, "Anthony F. Lucas and Spindletop," 84; Rickard, "Anthony F. Lucas, and the Beaumont Gusher," 888.

20. Rickard, "Anthony F. Lucas, and the Beaumont Gusher," 888.

21. Ibid., 888; McBeth, *Pioneering the Gulf Coast*, 57.

22. Rickard, "Anthony F. Lucas, and the Beaumont Gusher," 889.

23. Ibid., 889. McBeth gives different figures stating that the amount for the title was $40,000 in bonds and $10,000 in cash. McBeth, *Pioneering the Gulf Coast*, 59. W. P. H., Rachel and William McFaddin to A. F. Lucas, Mar. 9, 1898 (quotation), (McFaddin-Ward House Archives; cited hereafter as MWH). Under the terms of the lease, Lucas had two years in which to begin drilling operations or the lease would expire. He apparently did not drill, since there is no mention of it in later records.

24. McDaniel and Dethloff, *Pattillo Higgins*, 57; Owen, *Trek of the Oil Finders*, 15.

25. Anthony Lucas to Pattillo Higgins, June 7, 1899, Osborne Collection.

26. *Kansas City Star*, Apr. 21, 1901, Lucas Scrapbook. Higgins says he was asked for and made a report. Lucas said he learned of oil near Beaumont, from reports of the U.S. Geological Survey. Lucas to Higgins, May 4, 1899, Osborne Collection.

27. Lucas to Higgins, May 4, 1899, Osborne Collection. In his letter Lucas asks Higgins for a copy of his report "if it was made one," as if he had never seen it. A bit of a mystery still exists; Lucas and Higgins continued to maneuver around each other throughout their correspondence.

28. Ibid., May 11, 1899.

29. Ibid., June 22, 1899.

30. Ibid., May 21, 1899.

31. Ibid., May 29, 1899.

32. Ibid., May 11, 1899.

33. Ibid., June 7, 1899. The phrase "broad gage (or gauge) man" was one used to describe a person's approach to reform in the progressive era.

34. *Kansas City Star*, Apr. 21, 1901 (1st quotation); A. Hamill interview with Owens, Sept. 2, 1952 (2nd quotation), Tulsa, Okla., tape #84, p. 21; Bruffey, "Captain Lucas, Oil King of the World"; Clark and Halbouty, *Spindletop*, 64; *National Oil Reporter*, New York, June 27, 1901, vol. 1, #2; "The Real Captain A. F. Lucas," written for *The Sunny South* [May 31, 1901] (3rd quotation); *Sunday States*, June 16, 1901, Lucas Scrapbook; *National Oil Reporter*, N. Y., June 27, 1901, Vol. 2, ibid.

35. McBeth, *Pioneering the Gulf Coast*, 72; Rickard, "Anthony F. Lucas, and the Beaumont Gusher," 890 (quotation).

36. McDaniel and Dethloff, *Pattillo Higgins*, 57.

37. Jefferson County Court Records, vol. 25, p. 497, filed July 25, 1899.

38. Lucas to Higgins, June 22, 1899, Osborne Collection.

39. Ibid. (quotation). Attorney Dale Dowell stated that a 20 or 25 percent interest in the option would require Higgins to put up that part of the purchase price. Dowell also said that the contract was obviously not drawn up by an attorney, because it did not include a physical description of the land, but, according to Dowell, that was just the way it was done in 1899–1900. Dale Dowell, telephone interview with Jo Ann Stiles, Beaumont, Tex., Apr. 26, 2001; Dale Dowell interview with Jo Ann Stiles, Nov. 2001, at his office, Beaumont, Texas.

40. Lucas to Higgins, June 24, 28, 1899, Osborne Collection.

41. Jefferson County Deed Records, vol. 30, p. 136, filed Oct. 14, 1899, original copy in Osborne Collection; McDaniel and Dethloff, *Pattillo Higgins*, 57.

42. Lucas to Higgins, July 23, Aug. 4, 1899, Osborne Collection.

43. *Beaumont Journal*, Sept. 22, 1899; Memoirs of Sally Coburn Blain, transcribed by Mary Fort Blain, in the private collection of Scott Blain, Beaumont, Tex.

44. "Gladys City: Mineralogist Lucas Again in the City," *Beaumont Journal*, Sept. 22, 1899 (also in Lucas Scrapbook, undated, but placed next to article dated July 25, 1899).

45. Ibid.; 1900 United States Census; *Beaumont Journal*, Jan. 5, 1901.The house still stands on Highland Avenue a century later, now surrounded by tall shade trees. Ms. Benard was born in Louisiana, according to the census.

46. *Beaumont Enterprise*, Oct. 21, 1899.

47. Ibid., Aug. 26, 1899 (quotation); *Beaumont Journal*, Jan. 2, 1900.

48. Clark and Halbouty, *Spindletop*, 31; J. E. Brantly, *History of Oil Well Drilling*

(Houston: Gulf Publishing Co., a product of the Energy Research Education Foundation, 1971), 223. Some sources state that the well was spudded that June (McDaniel and Dethloff, *Pattillo Higgins*, 57), but Lucas's last letter to Higgins concluding preliminary preparations to drill was dated from Lafayette August 4, 1899; hence, drilling operations commenced sometime after that date.

49. *Beaumont Semi-Weekly Journal*, Dec. 29, 1899.

50. Ibid.

51. *Beaumont Journal*, Jan. 2, 1900.

52. Clark and Halbouty, *Spindletop*, 32.

Chapter Five

1. A. Hamill interview with Wm. A. Owens, Sept. 2, 1952, Tulsa, Oklahoma, tape #84, p. 8.

2. *Kansas City Star*, Sunday, Apr. 21, 1901, Lucas Scrapbook; *Beaumont Enterprise*, Oct. 5, 1941, Memorial Edition; unidentified newspaper, dated May 14, 1901, article titled "The Lucas Gusher and Its Romance" (quotation), headed "Special to the Press," Lucas Scrapbook.

3. *Beaumont Enterprise*, Jan. 10, 1901; ibid., Oct. 5, 1941 (quotation), Memorial Edition; Clark and Halbouty, *Spindletop*, 41.

4. "Oil in Texas: A Report of the Industry in the State from Government Reports," from the *Beaumont Enterprise* or *Beaumont Journal*, Lucas Scrapbook. Lucas penciled the date, 1900. The article was based on the 1898 Annual Report for the U.S. Geological Survey. In 1897 Texas produced 65,975 barrels of oil and in 1898 536,070 barrels, a 727.5 percent gain. The reporter predicted big strikes and made note of the drilling in Beaumont.

5. McBeth, *Pioneering the Gulf Coast*, 12 (1st and 2nd quotations); Rickard, "Anthony F. Lucas, and the Beaumont Gusher," 887–889, 890 (3rd quotation), 891–894.

6. Chernow, *Titan*, 431; Lewis L. Gould, *Progressives and Prohibitionists: Texas Democrats in the Wilson Era* (Austin: University of Texas Press, 1973), 18; McDaniel and Dethloff, *Pattillo Higgins*, 59; McBeth, *Pioneering the Gulf Coast*, 13; Rickard, "Anthony F. Lucas, and the Beaumont Gusher," 890. Baumé is a hydrometer scale measuring the weight of liquids in relation to that of water, indicating specific gravity in degrees.

7. Rickard, "Anthony F. Lucas, and the Beaumont Gusher," 890–891; McBeth, *Pioneering the Gulf Coast*, 13–14.

8. Rickard, "Anthony F. Lucas, and the Beaumont Gusher," 891.

9. Ibid.

10. McBeth, *Pioneering the Gulf Coast*, 14 (quotation).

11. Rickard, "Anthony F. Lucas, and the Beaumont Gusher," 891; Goodwyn, *Texas Oil, American Dreams*, 12–13; McBeth, *Pioneering the Gulf Coast*, 13–14; Clark and Halbouty, *Spindletop*, 58–60.

12. Rickard, "Anthony F. Lucas, and the Beaumont Gusher," 891.

13. Ibid.

14. The dome was at the time being mined by German-born chemist and inventor Herman Frasch. Rickard, "Anthony F. Lucas, and the Beaumont Gusher," 891.

15. DeGolyer, "Anthony F. Lucas and Spindletop," 85.

16. Rickard, "Anthony F. Lucas, and the Beaumont Gusher," 891 (quotation); Mc-Beth, *Pioneering the Gulf Coast*, 14–15.

17. Clark and Halbouty, *Spindletop*, 36 (quotation). In a later interview, Curt Hamill states that J. S. Cullinan was the one who instructed Lucas to contact Galey. C. Hamill interview with Owens, July 17, 1952, Kerrville, Tex., tape #16, p. 7.

18. John H. Galey (II), letter to Jo Ann Stiles, Mar. 25, 2000, in possession of Jo Ann Stiles; Mellon and Sparkes, *Judge Mellon's Sons*, 149.

19. Mellon and Sparkes, *Judge Mellon's Sons*, 150.

20. Clark and Halbouty, *Spindletop*, 38, 129; Mellon and Sparkes, *Judge Mellon's Sons*, 261.

21. Joseph A. Pratt, *The Growth of a Refining Region* (Greenwich, Conn.: JAI Press, 1980), 36.

22. Mellon and Sparkes, *Judge Mellon's Sons*, 148.

23. Ruth Sheldon Knowles, *The Greatest Gamblers: The Epic of American Oil Exploration* (New York: McGraw-Hill, 1959), 30; Clark and Halbouty, *Spindletop*, 40.

24. Clark and Halbouty, *Spindletop*, 38–41; Goodwyn, *Texas Oil, American Dreams*, 14–16; McDaniel and Dethloff, *Pattillo Higgins*, 60–64.

25. Jefferson County Deed Records, vol. 35, p. 176.

26. McDaniel and Dethloff, *Pattillo Higgins*, 61–62; *Kansas City Star*, Sunday, Apr. 21, 1901 (quotation), Lucas Scrapbook.

27. Jefferson County Deed Records, vol. 34, p. 488; *Beaumont Journal*, Jan. 11,1901. Missing from these leases were the 33 acres owned by Higgins on the south flank of the dome, which he had received as part of a settlement made after Carroll had sued him in 1898 for half the money he, Carroll, had originally provided to buy Gladys City land. Higgins dropped out of the company in this settlement as well. Rioux, "George Washington Carroll: A Biography," 63.

28. A. Hamill interview with Owens, Sept. 2, 1952, Tulsa, Okla., tape # 84, p. 7; C. Hamill interview with Owens, July 17, 1952, Kerrville, Tex., tape #16, pp. 6–7; Curtis G. Hamill, *We Drilled Spindletop!* (Houston: privately published, 1957; copy at THL), 11–12.

29. C. Hamill interview with Owens, July 17, 1952, Kerrville, Tex., tape #16, p. 16.

30. In cable tool drilling, a tool dresser is the worker who restores the correct gauge to worn drill bits by heating them and hammering them out on an anvil with a twelve-pound sledge. A. Hamill interview with William A. Owens, Sept. 2, 1952, Tulsa, Okla., tape #85, p. 5.

31. A. Hamill interview with Owens, Sept. 2, 1952, Tulsa, Okla., tape #85, p. 5 (quotation); Hamill, *We Drilled Spindletop!*, 4.

32. Hamill, *We Drilled Spindletop!*, 4.

33. C. Hamill interview with Owens, July 17, 1952, Kerrville, Tex., tape #16, p. 4.

34. A. Hamill interview with Owens, Sept. 2, 1952, Tulsa, Okla., tape #84, p. 7.

35. Ibid., 8 (quotation); C. Hamill interview with Owens, July 17, 1952, Kerrville, Tex., tape #16, p. 8.

36. A. Hamill interview with Owens, Sept. 2, 1952, Tulsa, Okla., tape #84, p. 11.

37. C. Hamill interview with Owens, July 17, 1952, Kerrville, Tex., tape #16, p. 8; C. Hamill, *We Drilled Spindletop!*, 10 (quotation); McDaniel and Dethloff, *Pattillo Higgins*, 62. As Al Hamill told it, Galey decided on "any place there," pointing generally to the springs for the location of the well. A. Hamill interview with Owens, Sept. 2, 1952, Tulsa, Okla., tape #84, pp. 10–11.

38. A. Hamill interview with Owens, Sept. 2, 1952, Tulsa, Okla., tape #85, pp. 10–11.

39. Ibid., 11.

40. Ibid., 12.

41. "Slabs" are trimmings from the outsides of logs when they are squared to be cut into lumber.

42. McBeth, *Pioneering the Gulf Coast*, 18 (quotation); Clark and Halbouty, *Spindletop*, 41–42; A. Hamill interview with Owens, Sept. 2, 1952, Tulsa, Okla., tape #85, p. 9.

43. McBeth, *Pioneering the Gulf Coast*, 18.

44. A. Hamill interview with Owens, Sept. 2, 1952, Tulsa, Okla., tape #84, p. 10; C. Hamill, *We Drilled Spindletop!*, 9.

45. C. Hamill interview with Owens, July 17, 1952, Kerrville, Tex., tape #16, p. 8.

46. A. Hamill interview with Owens, Sept. 2, 1952, Tulsa, Okla., tape #84, p. 34.

47. C. Hamill, *We Drilled Spindletop!*, 14 (2nd quotation); C. Hamill interview with Owens, July 17, 1952, Kerrville, Tex., tape #16, p. 9 (1st quotation).

48. C. Hamill, *We Drilled Spindletop!*, 14.

49. C. Hamill interview with Owens, July 17, 1952, Kerrville, Tex., tape #18, p. 2.

50. A. Hamill interview with Owens, Sept. 2, 1952, Tulsa, Okla., tape #84, pp. 10–11; C. Hamill interview with Owens, July 17, 1952, Kerrville, Tex., tape #16, p. 10.

51. C. Hamill interview with Owens, July 17, 1952, Kerrville, Tex., tape #16, pp. 9, 10 (quotation), 18; Langenkamp, *Handbook of Oil Industry*, 73.

52. A. Hamill interview with Owens, Sept. 2, 1952, Tulsa, Okla., tape #84, p. 11.

53. C. Hamill, *We Drilled Spindletop!*, 17–18.

54. A. Hamill interview with Owens, Sept. 2, 1952, Tulsa, Okla., tape #84, pp. 11–12; C. Hamill interview with Owens, July 17, 1952, Kerrville, Tex., tape #16, p. 11. Curt Hamill described their equipment as a Feren and Treft 25-horsepower boiler, an Oilwell Supply engine, Wolf gear, a Chapman rotary, and two 8x10 Smith-Vaile pumps set up just outside the derrick floor. He couldn't remember the brand of the draw works. C. Hamill interview with Owens, July 17, 1952, Kerrville, Tex., tape #16, pp. 10–11. The pipe was provided by the F. W. Heitmann Company of Houston, the first exclusive iron dealers in Texas and, by 1900, already in the business for more than 35 years. The Heitmann Company also claimed to be the first oil-well supplies distributor in Texas in an ad in the *Beaumont Enterprise*, Oct. 5, 1941, in honor of the dedication of the Lucas Gusher Memorial. On February 5, 1919, Anthony Lucas wired Al Hamill: "Wire makeup of rotary that drilled Spindletop." Al's notation of his reply, penned in his hand across the bottom of the telegram, read: "Rotary made by American Well Works of Aurora, Illinois. A. W. Hamill." Telegram in possession of estate of Allen W. Hamill Jr., Houston, Tex.

55. C. Hamill interview with Owens, July 17, 1952, Kerrville, Tex., tape #16, p. 11.

Chapter Six

1. Dillard Singleton, undated, untranscribed interview with unidentified interviewer, probably in the mid-1970s (TEM).

2. *Beaumont Journal*, Oct. 26, 1900; C. Hamill interview with Owens, July 17, 1952, Kerrville, Tex., tape #16, p. 12; *Beaumont Enterprise*, Jan. 11, 1901 (quotation).

3. *Beaumont Journal*, Oct. 26, 1900.

4. *Galveston Daily News*, Dec. 27, 1900.

5. *Beaumont Journal*, Oct. 23, 1900.

6. Erik Larson, *Isaac's Storm* (New York: Crown Publishers, 1999), 15–16.

7. C. David Pomeroy Jr., *Pasadena: The Early Years* (Pasadena, Tex.: Pomerosa Press, 1993), 75–76; Larson, *Isaac's Storm*, 244; Linsley and Rienstra, *Beaumont*, 76.

8. The casing originally consisted of 12-inch pipe, then was replaced by 10-inch pipe. After three joints of 10-inch pipe, they switched to 8-inch casing, and by the time they reached the rock cap, and the oil underneath it, they were using 6-inch casing. What they used inside that casing varied, but it was usually either 4-inch or 6-inch pipe to hold the drill bit and deliver water to wash out the hole.

9. A. Hamill interview with Owens, Sept. 2, 1952, Tulsa, Okla., tape #84, p. 12 (quotation); C. Hamill interview with Owens, July 17, 1952, Kerrville, Tex., tape #16, pp. 12–13.

10. A. Hamill interview with Owens, Sept. 2, 1952, Tulsa, Okla., tape #84, p. 16 (1st quotation); McDaniel and Dethloff, *Pattillo Higgins*, 63 (2nd quotation).

11. C. Hamill interview with Owens, July 17, 1952, Kerrville, Tex., tape #16, p. 12.

12. A. Hamill interview with Owens, Sept. 2, 1952, Tulsa, Okla., tape #84, p. 12. As Lucas explained it in "The Great Oil Well near Beaumont, Tex.," the paper he read before the American Institute of Mining Engineers in Richmond, Virginia, in February, 1901 (*Transactions*, New York: Published by the Institute, 1902), XXXI, 362–374) the plan was to use pipe of 12, 10, 8, 6, and 4-inch diameter, telescoped one into the other, diminishing in size as the hole was drilled deeper. Some of the larger pipe would serve as casing for the smaller sizes when the soft sand formations needed to be cased off and prevented from caving into the hole.

13. When discussing this particular problem in drilling the Lucas well, Al stated that in Corsicana, when the holes caved in, they would use a shoe on the bottom of the drill pipe. Presumably, he used the same method with the Lucas well. A. Hamill interview with Owens, Sept. 2, 1952, Tulsa, Okla., tape #84, p. 12; Brantly, *History of Oil Well Drilling*, 232.

14. Allen W. Hamill, "The Lucas Gusher," unpub. and undated typescript in Spindletop Diaries and Memories folder, Vertical Files (THL), 2.

15. Brantly, *History of Oil Well Drilling*, 2; Clark and Halbouty, *Spindletop*, 45; C. Hamill interview with Owens, July 17, 1952, Kerrville, Tex., tape #16, p. 13; A. Hamill interview with Owens, Sept. 2, 1952, Tulsa, Okla., tape #84, pp. 12 (quotation), 13. Curt, when questioned years later, said he had never heard of anyone's using the drive-block device before. He believed the idea developed on their drilling rig, perhaps from Captain Lucas. In his recollections, Al claimed to have had the idea. It was probably a combination of both. A cathead is a spool-shaped hub on a winch shaft, around which

a rope is wound for pulling and hoisting. The draw works is the collective name for all of the machinery used on a rig. Langenkamp, *Handbook of Oil Industry,* 26, 47.

16. A. Hamill interview with Owens, Sept. 2, 1952, Tulsa, Okla., tape #84, pp. 12–13; A. Hamill, "The Lucas Gusher," 2; C. Hamill interview with Owens, July 17, 1952, Kerrville, Tex., tape #16, p. 13; C. Hamill, *We Drilled Spindletop!,* 19–21; Brantly, *History of Oil Well Drilling,* 233.

17. McBeth, *Pioneering the Gulf Coast,* 19; Rickard, "Anthony F. Lucas, and the Beaumont Gusher," 892.

18. Rickard, "Anthony F. Lucas, and the Beaumont Gusher," 892; McBeth, *Pioneering the Gulf Coast,* 19; Brantly, *History of Oil Well Drilling,* 233; Rickard, "Anthony F. Lucas, and the Beaumont Gusher," 892; McBeth, *Pioneering the Gulf Coast,* 19.

19. McBeth, *Pioneering the Gulf Coast,* 19–20; Rickard, "Anthony F. Lucas, and the Beaumont Gusher," 892.

20. C. Hamill, *We Drilled Spindletop!,* 20; McBeth, *Pioneering the Gulf Coast,* 19–20, Rickard, "Anthony F. Lucas, and the Beaumont Gusher," 892 (quotation); Brantly, *History of Oil Well Drilling,* 232–233. Curt Hamill told a slightly different story, without mentioning Lucas at all. As he related it, "we whittled a piece of wood off a soap box with a pocket knife and trimmed it where it would go inside a 4-inch collar. We cut a hole in the middle of the piece of wood and made a flap to cover the hole from the sole of a boot. We tacked the flap over the hole. We put the device at the top of the first joint of pipe above the drilling bit." Curt said it helped until the drilling reached "about 200 feet," while Lucas maintained that his was used at around 300 feet. It is probable that both parties gave slightly different versions of the same thing. C. Hamill, *We Drilled Spindletop!,* 19–20.

21. A. Hamill, "The Lucas Gusher," 2. According to Al, they didn't have an accurate method of keeping depth measurements; they simply measured by "averaging up [our joints] at around twenty feet apiece."

22. Al called this formation "gumbo," Curt called it "shale or gumbo," and Lucas's revised well log calls it "marle." A. Hamill, interview with Owens, Sept. 2, 1952, Tulsa, Okla., tape #84, p. 13; C. Hamill interview with Owens, July 17, 1952, Kerrville, Tex., tape #16, p. 13; McBeth, *Pioneering the Gulf Coast,* 23. To explain the difference between Al's and Curt's "shale and gumbo" descriptions, oil field worker and valve man Bill Stell observed, "when gumbo is dry, it is as hard as rock . . . or shale, and when one drills into it, it can shatter like shale." He further observes that "blue clay" is the same thing as gumbo, and that "gray clay" is close. Telephone interview with Jo Ann Stiles, May 2000.

23. A. Hamill, interview with Owens, Sept. 2, 1952, Tulsa, Okla., tape #84, p. 13 (quotations). Brantly, in *History of Oil Well Drilling* (p. 233), writes that it was at this depth, 645 feet, after the gas blowout, that sand heaved 100 feet up into the pipe, and Lucas accordingly invented the check valve. Lucas himself, in a 1917 interview, stated that he invented the valve when the drilling had reached approximately 300 feet. Rickard, "Anthony F. Lucas, and the Beaumont Gusher," 892. In his 1952 interview with William A. Owens, Curt Hamill mentioned the gas blowout as having occurred "after having our sand troubles." C. Hamill interview with Owens, July 17, 1952, Kerrville, Tex., tape #16, p. 23.

24. A. Hamill, interview with Owens, Sept. 2, 1952, Tulsa, Okla., tape #84, pp.

13–14 (quotations); Brantly, *History of Oil Well Drilling*, 234. According to Bill Stell, the major damage in these blowouts resulted from acid in the soil and from sand. The gas might be impossible to avoid, but the continuous drilling prevented it from building up in the hole, and the sand damage could be reduced. Telephone interview of Bill Stell by Jo Ann Stiles, July 20, 2000; oral interview of Bill Stell by Jo Ann Stiles, July 25, 2000.

25. A. Hamill interview with Owens, Sept. 2, 1952, Tulsa, Okla., tape #85, p. 3 (1st quotation), and tape #84, p. 34 (2nd and 3rd quotations).

26. C. Hamill interview with Owens, July 17, 1952, Kerrville, Tex., tape #16, p. 14.

27. A depth for this sand formation was given as "640—maybe 700 feet" in Curt Hamill's interview conducted in the 1950s. It does not match the second revision of the log, but that was also constructed after the fact. The log shows a sand at about 540 feet, but it is not identified as a water sand. Take your own best guess. C. Hamill interview with Owens, July 17, 1952, Kerrville, Tex., tape #16, p. 14.

28. The jet is a small engine used to force water down into the hole, then back up again to clear the pipe. It also maintains pressure. Langenkamp, *Handbook of Oil Industry*, 8.

29. Willie Henry, affadavit, Jan. 15, 1952 (quotation), Pioneers in Texas Oil Collection (CAH). Henry was also, in the words of a contemporary, "a pretty fair muleskinner because he done all the fancy driving . . . had the best team. [You] usually could tell [their ability] by the team they drove." Plummer Barfield, interview with William A. Owens, Aug. 1, 1952, Sour Lake Texas, tape #25, p. 10, Pioneers in Texas Oil Collection (CAH). The Reverend John Chaney's name is spelled "Cheney" in some sources.

30. C. Hamill, *We Drilled Spindletop!*, 22.

31. C. Hamill interview with Owens, July 17, 1952, Kerrville, Tex., tape #16, p. 15; C. Hamill, *We Drilled Spindletop!*, 22 (quotation).

32. A Fresno is a type of horse-drawn, earth-moving or -cutting scoop with curved runners, or supports, on the sides and a single long handle used to guide the scoop blade into the earth or the material being moved. Langenkamp, *Handbook of Oil Industry*, 66.

33. Several sources state that the Hamill crew used heavy mud in the drilling process in the *upper* part of the hole on the Lucas well. Curt Hamill's account indicates that they used it much lower in the hole. Brantly, *History of Oil Well Drilling*, 241; Clark and Halbouty, *Spindletop*, 44–45; C. Hamill interview with Owens, July 17, 1952, Kerrville, Tex., tape #16, p. 14; C. Hamill, *We Drilled Spindletop!*, 22 (quotations). Brantly notes that mud was a regular byproduct of the rotary drilling process in the well itself; therefore, the Hamills were used to seeing mud in connection with drilling. They themselves claimed to have had no prior knowledge of mud actively pumped into wells. Brantly mentions a Chapman patent (No. 409,272) in 1889 that covered the use of mud-laden fluid and a New Orleans water-well driller who used it before 1900. The Hamills claimed to be the first (to their knowledge) actually to pump mud into the ground to aid in drilling for oil. Al actually claimed that they discovered it at the Lucas well by accident! C. Hamill interview with Owens, July 17, 1952, Kerrville, Tex., tape #16, pp. 14–23; C. Hamill, *We Drilled Spindletop!*, 24; A. Hamill interview with Owens, Sept. 2, 1952, Tulsa, Okla., tape #84, pp. 29–30. Because of the hard formations, wells

being drilled in Corsicana, the Hamills' former field of operations, did not require drilling mud to be added. Brantly offers no evidence that drilling mud had been added in oil-well drilling anywhere before Spindletop. It seems to have been the first. Brantly, *History of Oil Well Drilling*, 241. A little different story appeared in the *Oil and Gas Journal* in an ad for Mission Petroleum Company, whose officers included two of Walter Sharp's sons. Their version claimed that Sharp was the first to use it at Corsicana, when the Hamills were drilling for him. *Oil and Gas Journal*, Golden Anniversary Issue (May, 1951), 274.

34. C. Hamill interview with Owens, July 17, 1952, Kerrville, Tex., tape #16, p. 18; C. Hamill, *We Drilled Spindletop!*, 22 (quotation), 23–24.

35. Rosine McFaddin Wilson, Perry McFaddin's granddaughter, interview with Ellen Rienstra, Sept. 24, 2000; C. Hamill, *We Drilled Spindletop!*, 23.

36. C. Hamill, *We Drilled Spindletop!*, 24 (quotations); C. Hamill interview with Owens, July 17, 1952, Kerrville, Tex., tape #16, pp. 19–21.

37. According to Curt, one of the offshoots of their invention was Jim Sharp's development of the first mud mixer to be used in the Spindletop field. He came up with the idea right after the big strike, and its use spread rapidly. He credited the Hamills, Peck Byrd, and the Reverend Chaney with giving him the idea. C. Hamill interview with Owens, July 17, 1952, Kerrville, Tex., tape #16, pp. 20–22.

38. C. Hamill, *We Drilled Spindletop!*, 22–27; C. Hamill interview with Owens, July 17, 1952, Kerrville, Tex., tape #16, p. 21; McBeth, *Pioneering the Gulf Coast*, 20–21; Driller's Log, McBeth, *Pioneering the Gulf Coast*, 23; "The Most Excited Town on Earth," *Kansas City Star*, typescript, 227, Lucas Scrapbook; Bruffey, "Captain Lucas, Oil King of the World" (quotation).

39. C. Hamill, *We Drilled Spindletop!*, 24 (1st quotation); A. Hamill interview with Owens, Sept. 2, 1952, Tulsa, Okla., tape #84, pp. 14 (2nd–5th quotations), 15.

40. Brantly states that the bottom of the oil sand lay at 880 feet (Brantly, *History of Oil Well Drilling*, 234), as did Al Hamill (A. Hamill, "The Lucas Gusher," 3 [quotations]).

41. A. Hamill interview with Owens, Sept. 2, 1952, Tulsa, Okla., tape #84, p. 15 (quotations). In 1903, Frank Hill of Union Oil Company in Lompoc, California, claimed to have first used cement to stabilize a deep-hole drilling job. Kenny Franks and Paul Lambert, *Early California Oil: A Photographic History, 1865–1940* (College Station: Texas A&M University Press, 1985), 22.

42. According to Al, Lucas "was pretty Scotch in a way." Al believed the reason Lucas told them to place the joint of six-inch pipe on the bottom of the string of four-inch was that the Captain was afraid that if they used all their six-inch in this well, Guffey and Galey wouldn't back another well for him. A. Hamill interview with Owens, Sept. 2, 1952, Tulsa, Okla., tape #84, p. 16. A bailer is a bucket-like piece of equipment used in cable-tool drilling to remove mud and rock cuttings from the bore hole. Langenkamp, *Handbook of Oil Industry*, 10.

43. A. Hamill interview with Owens, Sept. 2, 1952, Tulsa, Okla., tape #84, pp. 16 (quotation), 17.

44. C. Hamill, *We Drilled Spindletop!*, 25.

45. Rickard, "Anthony F. Lucas, and the Beaumont Gusher," 892; C. Hamill, *We Drilled Spindletop!*, 25.

46. A. Hamill interview with Owens, Sept. 2, 1952, Tulsa, Okla., tape #84, p. 17. Al never explained why it was so difficult, but a possible explanation could be that the mud they put in the hole, with all of its roots and debris, created quite a challenge when a six-inch pipe was pulled through an eight-inch pipe to the surface, especially since it was following the smaller, four-inch pipe up through the hole.

47. *Beaumont Journal*, Dec. 21, 1900.

48. C. Hamill, *We Drilled Spindletop!*, 24–27; C. Hamill interview with Owens, July 17, 1952, Kerrville, Tex., tape #16, pp. 20–21; A. Hamill interview with Owens, Sept. 2, 1952, Tulsa, Okla., tape #84, pp. 14–17; A. Hamill, "The Lucas Gusher," 3.

49. The Pittsburgh, Gulf and Kansas City Railroad. By October 1900 it had become the Kansas City Southern. *Beaumont Journal*, Oct. 29, 1900.

50. C. Hamill, *We Drilled Spindletop!*, 27.

51. Ibid. According to Lucas's revised drilling log, printed in McBeth, *Pioneering the Gulf Coast*, 22, they drilled into the pocket of gas before they reached the sulphur layer.

52. McBeth, *Pioneering the Gulf Coast*, 21; A. Hamill, "The Lucas Gusher," 3.

53. A. Hamill interview with Owens, Sept. 2, 1952, Tulsa, Okla., tape #84, p. 18 (quotation). A seemingly unsolvable mystery exists over the correct depths of the strata in this well. When Lucas addressed his professional society, the American Institute of Mining Engineers, in Richmond in February of 1901, he did not present a well log. When the resulting paper, "The Great Oil Well Near Beaumont," was printed in the *Transactions* of the American Institute of Mining Engineers (New York: Published by the Institute, 1902), XXXI, 362–374, he added a well log, which he stated was the "complete record of the boring of the well, which I could not furnish at the time this paper was read . . ." (p. 373). In the *National Oil Reporter* of October 10, 1901, this log was presented again, indicating the depths of the various strata and a total depth of 1,160 feet.

Later, a revised log was printed in *Pioneering the Gulf Coast*, by Reid Sayers McBeth (supposedly written at Lucas's dictation), giving a total depth of 1,139 feet (p. 23). In the first log, the "heaving sands" (or quicksand) are not mentioned; Lucas simply refers to various layers of sand. In the revised log he lists "quick sand" on upper levels of the well, to about 400 feet, but lists the lower levels as just "sand." Both James A. Clark and Michel T. Halbouty in *Spindletop* and J. E. Brantly in *History of Oil Well Drilling* claim that drilling mud was developed on these upper levels in the well. Curt Hamill disagrees; it is this lower level that he claims necessitated drilling mud.

Al Hamill disagrees on another very important point. He claims that the well had 51 joints of 20-foot pipe sections hanging in it when it blew out, making it a total of 1,020 feet deep. According to him, on December 24, 1900, the drilling crew had landed the six-inch casing in a hard formation below the first oil sand at 880 feet; when they began drilling again in January, they drilled another 140 feet past the point where the six-inch casing had stopped, totaling 1,020 feet, at which point they struck oil. Hamill was not sure why Lucas used another depth. A. Hamill, "The Lucas Gusher," 3; Clark and Halbouty, *Spindletop*, 62; Brantly, *History of Oil Well Drilling*, 237.

A third log was made up by Alexander Deussen, a noted Gulf Coast geologist, using the Lucas log but making variations in the last five strata near the bottom of the hole, which was noted as 1,139 feet. The Gulf Oil Corporation released the log in 1967, and it was published by the Texas Bureau of Economic Geology in *Geology and*

Underground Waters of the Southeast part of the Texas Coastal Plain. A fourth, columnar log, copyright 1901 by the Beaumont Engineering Company, used the depths of the strata noted in Captain Lucas's first log almost to the bottom of the hole, but made slight variations in the bottom two layers of the hole. The final depth noted in this log was 1,160 feet.

Everyone agrees that making a log at this juncture in oil field history was not a scientific process, but a combination of instinct, analysis of well cuttings, which, when brought out by the circulating pump, were always badly mixed, and knowing the "feel" of the equipment—largely a matter of guesswork. Did the Hamills make the guesses? Did Lucas? There is no final answer. A well 1,000 feet to the north of the Lucas well came in at 1092 feet.

Brantly made the best study of the development of well logs on the Texas Gulf Coast in 1901. Using the existing accounts from Lucas and the Hamills and the memories of three men who worked in these early fields, as well as *Spindletop*, by Clark and Halbouty, Brantly concludes that it was impossible to tell how and when the Lucas gusher log was drawn and later revised. Brantly states that normally, drillers made the log; there was usually no geologist around, or particularly welcome, but Lucas, a mining engineer, was an exception. Brantly, *History of Oil Well Drilling*, 237–243. Perhaps the last word should be that of Lucas: "The hydraulic system of boring [drilling] . . . proved admirably adapted for penetrating the heavy quicksands; but quite unsatisfactory as to the accuracy of the record which it permitted of the strata traversed in boring . . ." Lucas, "The Great Oil Well near Beaumont, Texas," last paragraph.

54. *Deed Records of Jefferson County*, vol. 35. In his interview, Al Hamill stated that Louis Mayer's Drygoods Store was the location of Captain Lucas's "headquarters up when he was hanging around town." A. Hamill interview with Owens, Sept. 2, 1952, Tulsa, Okla., tape #84, pp. 20–21.

55. Clark and Halbouty, *Spindletop*, 52; McDaniel and Dethloff, *Pattillo Higgins*, 64.

56. Ramos, "Eyewitness to History," *Beaumont Enterprise-Journal*, Sept. 16, 1973, Aug. 11, 1974.

57. A. Hamill interview with Owens, Sept. 2, 1952, Tulsa, Okla., tape #84, pp. 18–20.

58. Ramos, "Eyewitness to History," *Beaumont Enterprise-Journal*, Sept. 16, 1973, Aug. 11, 1974; C. Hamill, *We Drilled Spindletop!*, 28–29 (quotations). In the *Beaumont Journal* of January 11, 1901, the day after the discovery, Curt was quoted as saying that he was near the top of the derrick when the pipe began to move up out of the well, but the beginning was so gradual that he had plenty of time to climb down, and was on the ground at a safe distance when the pipe shot out. In Anthony Lucas's paper, "The Great Oil Well Near Beaumont, Texas," read to the American Institute of Mining Engineers in Richmond in February 1901, he says, "Mr. Hamill was on the top of the 60-foot derrick when the pipe began to move; but the beginning was so gradual that, warned by the outflow of the water, he had ample time to climb down and retire to a safe distance before the pipe was shot into the air." Lucas, who was not present when the well came in, was apparently quoting the newspaper article directly.

59. A. Hamill interview with Owens, Sept. 2, 1952, Tulsa, Okla., tape #84, p. 18. The traveling block is the large heavy-duty block hanging in the derrick, to which the hook is attached. The traveling block supports the drill column and "travels" up and

down as it hoists the pipe out of the hole or lowers it in. Langenkamp, *Handbook of Oil Industry*, 180.

60. C. Hamill, *We Drilled Spindletop!*, 28.

61. Lucas, "The Great Oil Well Near Beaumont, Texas," 252.

62. A. Hamill interview with Owens, Sept. 2, 1952, Tulsa, Okla., tape #84, p. 18.

63. Ibid., 20.

64. Ibid., 19–20.

65. C. Hamill interview with Owens, July 17, 1952, Kerrville, Tex., tape #16, p. 25 (quotation); Ramos, "Eyewitness to History," *Beaumont Enterprise-Journal*, Sept. 16, 1973, Aug. 11, 1974.

66. Ramos, "Eyewitness to History," *Beaumont Enterprise-Journal*, Sept. 16, 1973, Aug. 11, 1974.

67. Ibid.

68. A. Hamill interview with Owens, Sept. 2, 1952, Tulsa, Okla., tape #84, p. 20.

69. Ibid (quotation). Another version places Lucas in the French Market when he got the news. He supposedly borrowed a horse from Jim Blain, the owner, and rode the horse to the well. (Memoirs of Sally Coburn Blain, transcribed by Mary Fort Blain, in the private collection of Scott Blain, Beaumont, Tex.) In at least one contemporary newspaper account, Lucas is quoted as claiming he was present at the well when it blew in, which, by all firsthand accounts, he was not. It is possible that the reporter misunderstood or misquoted him. "The Most Excited Town on Earth," *Kansas City Star*, Sunday, Apr. 21, 1901, typescript, pp. 220–221, Lucas Scrapbook.

70. A. Hamill interview with Owens, Sept. 2, 1952, Tulsa, Okla., tape #84, p. 21.

71. C. Hamill interview with Owens, July 17, 1952, Kerrville, Tex., tape #16, p. 27 (quotation); C. Hamill, *We Drilled Spindletop!*, 29.

72. A. Hamill interview with Owens, Sept. 2, 1952, Tulsa, Okla., tape #84, p. 25; Clark and Halbouty, *Spindletop*, 63–64. According to Galey family lore, the family was actually in Florida when the news of the gusher came. John Galey was headed out the door of his house, holding his young son by the hand. "Mr. Galey," someone from inside the house called, "Beaumont is on the phone." He whirled back in to the house so fast that his son hit his nose on the door. "All I ever got out of Spindletop," the boy would say later, "was a broken nose." Tom Galey, John Galey's grandson, interview with Ellen Rienstra and Judith Linsley, Jan. 10, 2001, Beaumont, Tex..

73. *Beaumont Enterprise*, Apr. 10, 1901, Oct. 5 , 1941 (quotation), Memorial Edition. Victor Aubey, the teacher at the school (the Common School District that would later become the South Park School at 3866 Port Arthur Road, now Martin Luther King, Jr., Parkway), stayed at his school that day, even though the 40–50 students he usually taught were hard to find. *Beaumont Enterprise*, Jan. 11, 1951, p. 4; Mary Dale Carper, interview with Jo Ann Stiles, Apr. 1997, Fannett, Tex..

74. *Atlanta Constitution*, May 31, 1901, and unnamed newspaper dated Tuesday evening, May 14, 1901, both in Lucas Scrapbook.

Chapter Seven

1. St. Louis *Globe-Democrat*, Mar. 17, 1901, Lucas Scrapbook.

2. Dillard Singleton, undated, untranscribed interview (ca. mid-1970s) with unidentified interviewer (TEM).

3. C. Hamill interview with Owens, July 17, 1952, Kerrville, Tex., tape #16, p. 27 (1st quotation); Barfield interview with Owens, Aug. 1, 1952, tape #25, p. 2; "William Perry Herring McFaddin of Beaumont," *Beaumont Enterprise*, Feb. 20, 1927 (2nd quotation); Mody Boatright and William A. Owens, *Tales from the Derrick Floor: A People's History of the Oil Industry* (Lincoln: University of Nebraska Press, 1970), 22 (3rd quotation), 23.

4. *Beaumont Enterprise-Journal*, Aug. 8, 1971.

5. W. B. Fehl, undated, untranscribed interview with unidentified interviewer (TEM).

6. *Beaumont Journal*, Jan. 10, 1901.

7. C. Hamill interview with Owens, July 17, 1952, Kerrville, Tex., tape #16, pp. 28–29.

8. Ibid., 29.

9. "The Most Excited Town on Earth," *Kansas City Star*, Apr. 21, 1901, transcription, pp. 220–221, Lucas Scrapbook.

10. Clark and Halbouty, *Spindletop*, 68.

11. *Beaumont Journal*, Jan. 10, 1901 (2nd quotation); *Galveston Daily News*, Jan. 11, 1901 (1st quotation).

12. *Beaumont Journal*, Jan. 10, 1901 (1st–3rd quotations); *Beaumont Enterprise*, Jan. 10, 1901 (4th and 5th quotations).

13. *Beaumont Journal*, Jan. 10, 1969.

14. *Beaumont Journal*, Jan. 8, 9, 10 (quotations), 1901; *Oil Investors' Journal*, 1 (May 24, 1902), 13. Trost would go on to photograph the Beatty and Heywood gushers. "The 'gusher photographer' seems to have a special talent for this kind of work," the *Oil Investors' Journal* reported. "Others have tried to obtain the results shown in his photographs but without success." The *Oil Investors' Journal* went on to report that one of Trost's hobbies was raising fine horses. He owned ". . . one of the handsomest stallions in Texas, and . . . blooded stock in Missouri" (p. 13).

15. A. Hamill, "The Lucas Gusher," 4.

16. Clark and Halbouty, *Spindletop*, 62; Brantly, *History of Oil Well Drilling*, 237; *National Oil Reporter*, Oct. 10, 1901; McBeth, *Pioneering the Gulf Coast*, 23.

17. Warner, *Texas Oil and Gas Since 1543*, 36.

18. Rickard, "Anthony F. Lucas, and the Beaumont Gusher," 891.

19. *New York Times*, Jan. 13 (2nd quotation), 17 (3rd quotation), 1901; *Galveston Daily News*, Jan. 11, 1901 (1st quotation); *Lloyd's Weekly Newspaper*, Jan. 20, 1901, quoted in *Beaumont Age*, Feb. 1, 1901 (4th quotation); *American Lumberman*, undated, quoted in *Beaumont Age*, Feb. 15, 1901 (5th quotation). (Some copies of *The Beaumont Age* are located on microfilm in the Beaumont Public Library, Beaumont, Tex., and at the Lamar University Mary and John Gray Library, Beaumont, Tex.)

20. *Beaumont Journal*, Jan. 15, 1901 (quotations). In other sources, Lucas is represented as a teetotaler. Clark and Halbouty, *Spindletop*, 64; *National Oil Reporter*, June 27, 1901, Lucas Scrapbook. The latter reference even carries the magazine's voucher that "The facts herewith presented are absolutely correct, as we have received them directly from Captain Lucas himself."

21. *Cleveland Press*, May 14, 1901 (1st quotation), Lucas Scrapbook; *Galveston*

Daily News, Jan. 11, 1901 (2nd quotation).

22. McDaniel and Dethloff, *Pattillo Higgins,* 66.

23. Ibid., 47.

24. Barfield interview with Owens, Aug. 1, 1952, Sour Lake, Tex., tape #25, pp. 3–4; *Knight & Sutton Directory of the City of Beaumont, 1900* (Beaumont: *Beaumont Enterprise, 1900);* Clark and Halbouty, *Spindletop,* 81; *Beaumont Journal,* Jan. 15 (2nd quotation), 16 (1st quotation), 1901; *Galveston Daily News,* Jan. 13, 1901.

25. *Galveston Daily News,* Jan. 15, 1901; *New York Times,* Jan. 17, 1901; *Beaumont Enterprise,* Jan. 12, 1901 (quotations).

26. J. L. Caldwell Diary, Caldwell Family Papers, box 2 (MWH).

27. Ibid.

28. *Galveston Daily News,* Jan. 16, 1901.

29. *Beaumont Enterprise,* Jan. 14, 1901 (quotation).

30. George Parker, *Oil Field Medico* (Dallas: Banks, Upshaw and Co., 1948), 3; Clark and Halbouty, *Spindletop,* 85.

31. Boatright and Owens, *Tales from the Derrick Floor,* 65–66 (quotation); Clark and Halbouty, *Spindletop,* 84–85.

32. Clark and Halbouty, *Spindletop,* 81; *Beaumont Journal,* Jan. 16, 1901; *Galveston Daily News,* Jan. 16, 1901.

33. *Galveston Daily News,* Jan. 21, 1901 (quotation); *Knight & Sutton Directory of the City of Beaumont, 1900* (Beaumont Enterprise, 1900), 144, 149–150, 155–156.

34. Rioux, "George Washington Carroll: A Biography," 74 (2nd quotation); *Beaumont Enterprise,* Jan. 11, 1901 (1st and 3rd quotations).

35. *Beaumont Enterprise,* Jan. 11, 14, 1901.

36. Johnson et al., *The Spindletop Oil Field,* 9.

37. Bruffey, "Captain Lucas, Oil King of the World." Some possibly fanciful contemporary newspaper accounts declare that Carrie Lucas rushed up to her husband with what was variously called "a great glass of liquor" or a "cordial" in her hand and exhorted him, "You work; I'll pray." *The Sunny South* (2nd quotation), undated but probably about May 31, 1901, in Lucas Scrapbook; Bruffey, *Captain Lucas, Oil King of the World* (1st and 3rd quotations).

38. Boatright and Owens, *Tales from the Derrick Floor,* 42–44; *Beaumont Enterprise,* Apr. 9, 1901; Clark and Halbouty, *Spindletop,* 63; Warner, *Texas Oil and Gas Since 1543,* 37 (quotation). Before the advent of the Lucas well, the largest gusher the world had ever seen was the Drooja "fountain" in Baku, Russia, a well that flowed 48,000 barrels a day.

39. Rickard, "Anthony F. Lucas, and the Beaumont Gusher," 892.

40. A. Hamill, "The Lucas Gusher," 4; A. Hamill interview with Owens, Sept. 2, 1952, Tulsa, Okla., tape #84, p. 25 (quotations).

41. A. Hamill interview with Owens, Sept. 2, 1952, Tulsa, Okla., tape #84, pp. 25–28; C. Hamill interview with Owens, July 17, 1952, Kerrville, Tex., tape #16, p. 32; ibid., tape #17, p. 1.

42. A. Hamill interview with Owens, Sept. 2, 1952, Tulsa, Okla., tape #84, p. 26.

43. Boatright and Owens, *Tales from the Derrick Floor,* 45; A. Hamill interview with

Owens, Sept. 2, 1952, Tulsa, Okla., tape #84, p. 28 (quotations).

44. A. Hamill interview with Owens, Sept. 2, 1952, Tulsa, Okla., tape #84, pp. 27, 28 (quotation).

45. Rickard, "Anthony F. Lucas, and the Beaumont Gusher," 892; A. Hamill interview with Owens, Sept. 2, 1952, Tulsa, Okla., tape #84, pp. 26, 27 (quotations), 28; "Harnessing the Gusher,"*Galveston Daily News*, Jan. 20, 1901; Clark and Halbouty, *Spindletop*, 67.

46. Clark and Halbouty, *Spindletop*, 64–69; Boatright and Owens, *Tales from the Derrick Floor*, 45; *Galveston Daily News*, Jan. 20, Feb. 28 (quotation), 1901; A. Hamill interview with Owens, Sept. 2, 1952, Tulsa, Okla., tape #84, pp. 25–27; A. Hamill, "The Lucas Gusher," 4; C. Hamill, *We Drilled Spindletop!*, 31–32.

47. *Galveston Daily News*, Jan. 21, 1901.

48. Undated, unsigned article, probably reprinted from Beaumont newspaper, Lucas Scrapbook.

49. *Beaumont Enterprise*, Jan. 10, 1901.

50. *Galveston Daily News*, Jan. 11 (1st and 2nd quotations), 13 (3rd quotation), 1901; Happy Jack, "All About the New Oil Field," *Bradford [Pennsylvania] Record*, Jan. 27, 1901 (4th and 5th quotations), Lucas Scrapbook.

51. *Beaumont Journal*, Jan. 16, 1901.

52. *Galveston Daily News*, Jan. 17, 1901.

53. *Houston Post* quoted in the *Beaumont Journal*, Jan. 18, 1901 (1st quotation); *Galveston Daily News*, Jan. 17, 1901; *Beaumont Age*, Feb. 1, 1901 (3rd quotation); Clark and Halbouty, *Spindletop*, 133.

54. Undated, unidentified article, transcription, p. 72, Lucas Scrapbook; *Beaumont Journal*, Dec. 26, 1900.

55. Clark and Halbouty, *Spindletop*, 58–59, 70; McDaniel and Dethloff, *Pattillo Higgins*, 68–69; *Beaumont Journal*, Jan. 14, 1901; Map, "Cleveland Land, 'Spindle-Top' Heights, Showing All Gushers Struck Up to Date on the Hill," Sept. 2, 1901" (MWH).

56. A. Hamill interview with Owens, Sept. 2, 1952, Tulsa, Okla., tape #85, pp. 24–27.

57. Clark and Halbouty, *Spindletop*, 157–159.

58. *Beaumont Journal*, Jan. 11, 1901 (1st quotation), Lucas Scrapbook; *New York Times*, Jan. 13 (2nd quotation), 17 (3rd quotation), 1901; Happy Jack, undated article, *Bradford [Pennsylvania] Record*, Jan. 21, 1901 (4th quotation), transcription, p. 186, Lucas Scrapbook.

59. Clark and Halbouty, *Spindletop*, 70–75.

60. *Beaumont Enterprise*, July 18, 1899 (quotation); Chernow, *Titan*, 431.

61. *New York Times*, Jan. 22, 26, 1901 (quotation); *Galveston Daily News*, Jan. 21, 1901.

62. *New York Times*, Jan. 15, 1901.

63. Caldwell Diary; *Beaumont Journal*, Feb. 1, 1901; *Beaumont Age*, Feb. 1, 15, 1901; Clark and Halbouty, *Spindletop*, 72.

64. Clark and Halbouty, *Spindletop*, 72; *Beaumont Enterprise or Journal*, dated, probably incorrectly, Mar. 23, 1901 (quotations), Lucas Scrapbook; *Houston Post*, Apr. 21, 1901.

65. Clark and Halbouty, *Spindletop*, 75, 159; *Beaumont Journal*, June 24, 1901; *Beaumont Age*, June 28, 1901; *Houston Post*, Apr. 21, 1901.

66. When the field first became known as Spindletop, it was written as two words. It was not until the 1920s that it first appeared in the press as one word. Clark and Halbouty, *Spindletop*, 67; *Beaumont Enterprise*, Oct. 30, 1901 (quotation), cited in House, "Spindletop," 4; W. T. Block, "Spindle Top Once Isolated Plague Victims," *Beaumont Enterprise*, Jan. 9, 1999.

Chapter Eight

1. A. Hamill interview with Owens, Sept. 2, 1952, Tulsa, Okla., tape #85, p. 5.

2. Caldwell Diary, Apr. 14–27, 1901.

3. U.S. Census for 1900; *Beaumont Enterprise*, Apr. 4, 10, 1901, Clark and Halbouty, *Spindletop*, 81; *Houston Daily Post*, Apr. 28, 1901 (quotation), Lucas Scrapbook.

4. *Houston Daily Post*, Apr. 28, 1901, Lucas Scrapbook.

5. "William Perry Herring McFaddin of Beaumont," *Beaumont Enterprise*, Feb. 20, 1927.

6. Clark and Halbouty, *Spindletop*, 90.

7. Unattributed article, probably Birmingham newspaper, May 30, 1901 (1st quotation), Lucas Scrapbook; *Galveston Daily News*, Feb. 3, 1901 (2nd and 3rd quotations); "Impressions in Oil," *Houston Daily Post*, May 5, 1901 (4th quotation).

8. Clark and Halbouty, *Spindletop*, 86.

9. Boatright and Owens, *Tales from the Derrick Floor*, 21 (quotations), 22–23.

10. Parker, *Oil Field Medico*, 1.

11. Ibid.

12. Parker, *Oil Field Medico*, 2 (quotations); Clark and Halbouty, *Spindletop*, 83.

13. Parker, *Oil Field Medico*, 3 (quotation), 4–6.

14. Clark and Halbouty, *Spindletop*, 75; Caldwell Diary, Apr. 15, 1901.

15. Clark and Halbouty, *Spindletop*, 82–83, 89; *Galveston Daily News*, Feb. 3, 1901 (quotations).

16. Clark and Halbouty, *Spindletop*, 87, 89; *Beaumont Enterprise*, May 16, 1901. Oil historian C. A. Warner comments that 400 companies with a total authorized capital of over $200,000,000 were organized at Spindletop during the first year of the field's development. Warner, *Texas Oil and Gas Since 1543*, 45.

17. Clark and Halbouty, *Spindletop*, 90.

18. *Beaumont Enterprise*, May 16, 1901; McBeth, *Pioneering the Gulf Coast*, 41; *Beaumont Age*, June 28, 1901. The *Age* reported that Lucas had sued the Lucas Oil Company to enjoin them from using the name, but the directors of the company succeeded in convincing the Captain, "a reasonable man," that they had no desire to profit from his name. He dropped the suit.

19. Clark and Halbouty, *Spindletop*, 87–90; John O. King, *Joseph Stephen Cullinan: A Study of Leadership in the Texas Petroleum Industry, 1897–1937* (Nashville: Vanderbilt University Press, 1970), 91.

20. *Beaumont Journal*, Jan. 16, 1901.

21. Ibid., Jan. 18, 1901.

22. *Beaumont Enterprise*, Jan. 30, 1901; *Beaumont Journal*, Jan. 26, 1901.

23. *Beaumont Journal*, May 15, 1901 (1st quotation); *New Orleans Times-Democrat*, reprinted in the *Beaumont Enterprise*, Apr. 19, 1901 (2nd quotation).

24. *Beaumont Age*, Mar. 15, 1901; *DuPont Magazine*, 1959; *Houston Post*, Oct. 4, 1901; *Beaumont Journal*, Jan. 18, 1901 (quotation); *Beaumont Age*, Feb. 8, 1901.

25. Rosine McFaddin Wilson, interview with Ellen Rienstra, Sept. 24, 2000; John J. Wheat, untranscribed interview by unidentified interviewer, Mar. 7, 1977 (quotation), Beaumont, Tex. (TEM); *Beaumont Journal*, Jan. 16, 1901; Linsley and Rienstra, *Beaumont*, 80; *Beaumont Journal*, July 2, 1901.

26. Bud Simmons, interview with Suzy Wilson, Aug. 5, 1981, material in possession of Jo Ann Stiles; Clark and Halbouty, *Spindletop*, 81; *Galveston Daily News*, Jan. 21, 1901.

27. Boatright and Owens, *Tales from the Derrick Floor*, 66.

28. Linsley and Rienstra, *Beaumont*, 174; *Beaumont Journal*, Mar. 21, July 2, 1901; *Beaumont Enterprise*, May 31, 1936, 14-F; Parker, *Oil Field Medico*, 13; Marilyn Dianne Stodghill Trevey, "The Social and Economic Impact of the Spindletop Oil Boom on Beaumont in 1901" (unpub. Master's thesis, Lamar University, 1974), 131.

29. *Beaumont Enterprise*, Jan. 12, 1915, Aug. 7, 1971, Oct. 28, 1973; Vivian Yvetta Simons, "The Prohibition Movement in Beaumont, Texas, 1835–1919" (unpub. Master's thesis, Lamar University, Beaumont, Tex., 1963), 21; Linsley and Rienstra, *Beaumont*, 83–84; Trevey, "The Social and Economic Impact of the Spindletop Oil Boom," 101; Clark and Halbouty, *Spindletop*, 83.

30. Simons, "The Prohibition Movement in Beaumont," 22; *Beaumont Enterprise*, Jan. 1, 1901; Linsley and Rienstra, *Beaumont*, 80–81.

31. *Beaumont Age*, Feb. 15, 1901 (1st quotation); *Beaumont Journal*, Mar. 19, 1901 (2nd quotation).

32. *Beaumont Age*, Mar. 15, 1901.

33. *Beaumont Journal*, Mar. 14, 18, 1901 (quotation); *Beaumont Age*, Mar. 15, 1901.

34. The Rev. V. A. Godbey, "Christian Citizenship," Sermon, May 22, 1904 (Church Records of the First Methodist Church of Beaumont, Tex.).

35. Boatright and Owens, *Tales from the Derrick Floor*, 85 (quotation); Linsley and Rienstra, *Beaumont*, 83.

36. *Beaumont Daily Journal*, Sept. 27, 1901.

37. Boatright and Owens, *Tales from the Derrick Floor*, 87, 88 (quotation).

38. Rioux, "Biographical Sketch of George Washington Carroll," 13; Clark and Halbouty, *Spindletop*, 189, 190 (quotation), 191; *Advantages and Conditions of Port Arthur Today* (Beaumont: Oil Exchange and Board of Trade, 1901), 68. Ennis also served as boss of the crew that built the Texas Company pipeline from Spindletop to Port Arthur, and was recognized as having "no superior" at that job, "[al]though he could not sign his name." Marquis James, *The Texaco Story: The First Fifty Years* (New York: The Texas Co., 1953), 19.

39. Rioux, "Biographical Sketch of George Washington Carroll," 14–16.

40. Boatright and Owens, *Tales from the Derrick Floor*, 86 (1st quotation); Beaumont City Council Minutes, 1898 (THL) (2nd and 3rd quotations).

41. Boatright and Owens, *Tales from the Derrick Floor*, 86; Ethel Alice Slausen, interview with Jo Ann Stiles, June 14, 1989, tape #60, and July 20, 1989, tape #61 (MWH).

42. *Beaumont Enterprise*, Apr. 27, 1901 (1st quotation); "Beaumont was dirtiest, noisiest, busiest town on the continent," Penny Clark, *Beaumont Journal*, Mar. 15, 2001 (2nd–4th quotations), quoting undated *Harper's Weekly* article, probably about May 1901.

43. Boatright and Owens, *Tales from the Derrick Floor*, 84 (1st and 3rd quotations), 85 (2nd quotation). It is possible that the bodies in the river numbered only six, and were actually found in 1902, as the January 1, 1903, *Beaumont Journal* mentioned six men "taken from the river" the past year, noting that 1902 was "a black [year] in crime so far as Jefferson County is concerned."

44. *Beaumont Journal*, May 7, 1901.

45. *New York Journal*, Aug. 18, 1901 (quotations); Linsley and Rienstra, *Beaumont*, 83.

46. *Cleveland Press*, May 14, 1901, Lucas Scrapbook.

47. Bruffey, "Captain Lucas, Oil King of the World" (1st and 2nd quotations) "The Lucas Gusher and Its Romance," unidentified newspaper, May 14, 1901 (3rd quotation), Lucas Scrapbook; *Nashville Banner*, July 1901 (4th quotation), Lucas Scrapbook.

48. *Atlanta Constitution*, May 31, 1901 (1st and 3rd quotations), and Bruffey "Captain Lucas, Oil King of the World" (2nd quotation); Clark and Halbouty, *Spindletop*, 121–122.

49. McBeth, *Pioneering the Gulf Coast*, 42.

50. *Oil Investors' Journal*, 1 (May 24, 1902)), 7.

51. Sealy, Tex., newspaper, Oct. 11, 1901, Lucas Scrapbook.

52. McDaniel and Dethloff, *Pattillo Higgins*, 78; Clark and Halbouty, *Spindletop*, 125–126, 127 (quotation).

53. McDaniel and Dethloff, *Pattillo Higgins*, 75–76; Clark and Halbouty, *Spindletop*, 123–125; Higgins, *The True History of the Beaumont Field*.

54. Rioux, "Biographical Sketch of George Washington Carroll," 82–83, citing Carroll vs. Higgins, No. 2747, filed Apr. 18, 1901, Jefferson County, Tex., Original Instrument, Jefferson County Collection (Sam Houston Regional Library); Higgins v. Carroll, No. 2907, filed June 14, 1901, Jefferson County, Texas, Plaintiff's Original Petition, Original Instrument, Higgins Collection (TEM); G. W. Carroll, answer, Higgins v. Carroll to No. 2907, courtesy of Jonathan Gerland (THL); McDaniel and Dethloff, *Pattillo Higgins*, 74–75; Clark and Halbouty, *Spindletop*, 76–77.

55. Clark and Halbouty, *Spindletop*, 112–113.

56. *Beaumont Journal*, Jan. 21, 1901; *Beaumont Age*, Feb. 1, 8, 1901; *Beaumont Enterprise*, Apr. 12, 1901. The deepwater channel became a reality in 1908, when, with the help of Congressman Samuel Bronson Cooper, a canal with a depth of nine feet was dug in the Neches from Beaumont to the Port Arthur Ship Channel. Linsley and Rienstra, *Beaumont*, 86.

57. *Beaumont Enterprise*, Jan. 16, 1902; *Beaumont Journal*, May 18, 1901 (quotation).

58. *Beaumont Journal*, Nov. 27, 1901.

59. *Beaumont Enterprise*, Nov. 12, 1901.

60. *Beaumont Journal*, Nov. 11, 1901; Rundell, *Early Texas Oil*, 65–66; *Galveston Daily News*, May 29, June 21, 1901, cited in W. T. Block, *Sour Lake, Texas: From Mud Baths to Millionaires* (Liberty, Tex.: Atascosito Historical Society, 1995), 66–67.

61. *Beaumont Enterprise*, Oct. 12, 1901 (quotation); Henrietta M. Larson and Kenneth Wiggins Porter, *A History of the Humble Oil and Refining Company* (New York: Harper and Brothers, 1959), 15.

Chapter Nine

1. James Donahoe, interview with William A. Owens, Aug. 1, 1952, Batson, Tex., tape #24, p. 12, Pioneers in Texas Oil Collection (CAH).

2. *Galveston Daily News*, Feb. 19, 1901.

3. Clark and Halbouty, *Spindletop*, 100.

4. Clark and Halbouty, *Spindletop*, 99; Sam Webb, interview with William A. Owens, Sept. 1952, Fort Worth, Tex., tape #76, p. 5, Pioneers in Texas Oil Collection (CAH); Boatright and Owens, *Tales from the Derrick Floor*, 67; Slausen interview with Stiles, June 14, 1989, Beaumont, Tex., tape #60, p. 12.

5. Slausen interview with Stiles, June 14, 1989, Beaumont, Tex., tape #60, pp. 3–4 (quotation), 12.

6. Slausen interview with Stiles, June 14, 1989, Beaumont, Tex., tape #60, p. 12 (1st quotation); *Galveston Daily News*, Feb. 21, 1901 (2nd quotation); Boatright and Owens, *Tales from the Derrick Floor*, 64 (3rd quotation).

7. Boatright and Owens, *Tales from the Derrick Floor*, 63 (1st quotation); Claude Deer, interview with William A. Owens, July 7, 1952, Spindletop, Tex., tape #8, pp. 4–5, Pioneers in Texas Oil Collection (CAH); Harry R. Paramore, interview with William A. Owens, July 7, 1952, Beaumont, Tex., tape #7, pp. 4 (2nd quotation), 5, Pioneers in Texas Oil Collection (CAH).

8. Clark and Halbouty, *Spindletop*, 96–99. At one time the postmaster at Guffey was Walter Wherry, a favorite of Alice Slausen's.

9. Clark and Halbouty, *Spindletop*, 97–99. The name was originally written "Spindle Top." For the sake of uniformity, the modern spelling of "Spindletop" will be used throughout.

10. Clark and Halbouty, *Spindletop*, 98–99.

11. Parker, *Oil Field Medico*, 4 (1st quotation), 5 (2nd quotation), 6.

12. Ibid., 5–6, 7 (quotation), 8.

13. Ibid., 11–24, 25 (quotation).

14. Deer interview with Owens, July 7, 1952, Spindletop, Tex., tape #8, p. 4; C. B. Hice, *Spindle Top Guide and Directory* (Beaumont, undated, probably 1903); Boatright and Owens, *Tales from the Derrick Floor*, 62.

15. W. T. Block, *Sour Lake, Texas: From Mud Baths to Millionaires* (Liberty: Atascocito Historical Society, 1995), 90 (1st quotation); V. B. Daniels, interview with William A. Owens, July 3, 1952, Sour Lake, Tex., tape #22, pp. 12 (2nd quotation), 13, 29, Pioneers in Texas Oil Collection (CAH).

16. Daniels interview with Owens, July 3, 1952, Sour Lake, Tex., tape #22, p. 29.

17. Parker, *Oil Field Medico*, 25 (1st quotation), 34, 35 (2nd quotation).

18. Block, *Sour Lake, Texas*, 114, 123, citing *Houston Daily Post*, June 6, 1903; Parker, *Oil Field Medico*, 35–36, 37 (quotation).

19. Donahoe interview with Owens, Aug. 1, 1952, Batson, Tex., tape #23, pp. 5 (quotations), 6–7.

20. Ibid., 5 (2nd quotation), 6–7, 8 (1st quotation), 9.

21. Boatright and Owens, *Tales from the Derrick Floor*, 118 (1st quotation); W. H. "Bill" Bryant, interview with William A. Owens, July 3, 1952, Sour Lake, Tex., tape #27, p. 15, Pioneers in Texas Oil Collection (CAH); Parker, *Oil Field Medico*, 48, 73; Donahoe interview with Owens, Aug. 1, 1952, Batson, Tex., tape #23, p. 15 (2nd quotation).

22. Donahoe interview with Owens, Aug. 1, 1952, Batson, Tex., tape #23, p. 14 (quotations); Simons, "The Prohibition Movement in Beaumont," 36, 46–47; *Beaumont Journal*, Apr. 27, 1903 .

23. Alice Cashen, "Boom-Town Tales," in *Tales from the Big Thicket*, ed. Francis E. Abernethy (Austin: University of Texas Press, 1966), 143–144.

24. *Beaumont Age*, Feb. 15, 1901.

25. W. M. Hudson, interview with William A. Owens, Sept. 18, 1952, Austin, Tex., tape #80, pp. 23 (1st and 2nd quotations), 24 (3rd quotation), Pioneers in Texas Oil Collection (CAH).

26. Paramore interview with Owens, July 7, 1952, Beaumont, Tex., tape #7, pp. 24 (quotation), 25.

27. Boatright and Owens, *Tales from the Derrick Floor*, 108 (1st and 2nd quotations), 109. Donahoe interview with Owens, Aug. 1, 1952, Batson, Tex., tape #23, p. 9 (3rd quotation).

28. Terry Lee Rioux, *G. W. Carroll: Southern Capitalist and Dedicated Beaumont Baptist* (Austin: Eakin Press, 2001), 54; *Beaumont Enterprise*, Oct. 12, 1901.

29. Charlie Jeffries, "Reminiscences of Sour Lake," *Southwestern Historical Quarterly*, 50 (July, 1946), 32–33.

30. Donahoe interview with Owens, Aug. 1, 1952, Batson, Tex., tape #24, p. 7 (1st quotation); S. Webb interview with Owens, , Sept. 1952, Fort Worth, Tex., tape #76, p. 12 (2nd and 3rd quotations).

31. Lucas, "The Great Oil Well near Beaumont, Texas," 362–374.

32. Clark and Halbouty, *Spindletop*, 94–95; A. Hamill interview with Owens, Sept. 2, 1952, Tulsa, Okla., tape #84, pp. 31–33.

33. Lucas, "The Great Oil Well near Beaumont, Texas," 374 (2nd quotation); A. Hamill interview with Owens, Sept. 2, 1952, Tulsa, Okla., tape #84, pp. 31–33; Clark and Halbouty, *Spindletop*, 95 (1st and 3rd quotations).

34. Clark and Halbouty, *Spindletop*, 95–96.

35. Clark and Halbouty, *Spindletop*, 118–119.

36. Ibid.

37. S. Webb interview with Owens, Sept. 1952, Fort Worth, Tex., tape #76, p. 32.

38. Parker, *Oil Field Medico*, 83.

39. Jeffries, "Reminiscences of Sour Lake," *Southwestern Historical Quarterly*, 50 (July, 1946), 25–35, quoted in Block, Sour Lake, Texas, 100.

40. Donahoe interview with Owens, Aug. 1, 1952, Batson, Tex., tape #24, pp. 2 (1st quotation), 3; Bryant interview with Owens, July 3, 1952, Sour Lake, Tex., tape #27, p. 12 (2nd quotation).

41. S. Webb interview with Owens, , Sept. 1952, Fort Worth, Tex., tape #76, p. 10 (1st and 2nd quotations); Parker, *Oil Field Medico*, 92 (3rd quotation), 94–95 (4th quotation), 95 (5th quotation).

42. Clark and Halbouty, *Spindletop*, 103.

43. Jonathan Gerland, Director, Temple Archives, Diboll, Tex., May 23, 2000, telephone interview with Judith Linsley; Vernon Jenson, *Lumber and Labor* (New York and Toronto: Farrar and Rinehart, 1945), 76–77, 89.

44. Slausen interview with Stiles, July 20, 1989, Beaumont, Tex., tape #61, pp. 4, 5 (quotation).

45. Boatright and Owens, *Tales from the Derrick Floor*, 69.

46. Slausen interview with Stiles, July 20, 1989, Beaumont, Tex., tape #61, p. 2.

47. LeVert Mollett, telephone interviews with Judith Linsley, Feb. 23, 2000, and July 21, 2000, Beaumont, Tex.

48. *Beaumont Enterprise*, Nov. 11, 1902. The reporter also interviewed black workers at Little Africa, as well as J. L. Black, of the firm of Black and Laid, and the wounded man. According to him, all corroborated Callahan's story.

49. Ibid.

50. *Beaumont Enterprise*, Nov. 12, 1902.

51. Boatright and Owens, *Tales from the Derrick Floor*, 68–69 (2nd quotation), 69 (1st quotation).

52. "Budget from Beaumont," *Houston Daily Post*, Feb. 6, 1903 (1st quotation), quoted in Block, *Sour Lake, Texas*, 99; Daniels interview with Owens, July 3, 1952, Sour Lake, Tex., tape #22, 30–31 (2nd quotation).

53. Donahoe interview with Owens, Aug. 1, 1952, Batson, Tex., tape #24, pp. 19.

54. Ibid., 19–20.

55. Deer interview with Owens, July 7, 1952, Spindletop, Tex., tape #8, p. 8; Boatright and Owens, *Tales from the Derrick Floor*, 64 (quotation).

56. Daniels, interview with William A. Owens, July 3, 1952, Sour Lake, Tex., tape #22, p. 9; Parker, *Oil Field Medico*, 42 (quotation), 61; Paramore interview with Owens, July 7, 1952, Beaumont, Tex., tape #7, p. 23.

57. Boatright and Owens, *Tales from the Derrick Floor*, 64.

58. Clark and Halbouty, *Spindletop*, 113.

59. Boatright and Owens, *Tales from the Derrick Floor*, 70 (quotations).

60. Bryant interview with Owens, July 3, 1952, Sour Lake, Tex., tape #27, p. 11. The fight probably took place in Sour Lake, because Crosby House hotels operated not only in Beaumont, but also Sour Lake and Batson.

61. Boatright and Owens, *Tales from the Derrick Floor*, 70.

62. Clark and Halbouty, *Spindletop*, 98 (quotation); Marilyn Dianne Stodghill Trevey, "The Social and Economic Impact of the Spindletop Oil Boom on Beaumont in 1901" (unpub. Master's thesis, Lamar University, 1974), 103.

63. Paramore interview with Owens, July 7, 1952, Beaumont, Tex., tape #7, p. 23;

Cashen, "Boom-Town Tales," 144.

64. Block, *Sour Lake, Texas,* 127; Boatright and Owens, *Tales from the Derrick Floor,* 69 (quotation), 70.

65. Parker, *Oil Field Medico,* 62 (1st quotation); Donahoe interview with Owens, Aug. 1, 1952, Batson, Tex., tape #23, pp. 12, 16 (2nd quotation).

66. Parker, *Oil Field Medico,* 135–136, 137 (quotation).

67. Ibid., 125, 126 (quotations), 127–130.

68. Donahoe interview with Owens, Aug. 1, 1952, Batson, Tex., tape #23, p. 17.

69. James S. Hogg to J. S. Cullinan, Beaumont, Jan. 22, 1903 or Jan. 20, 1904 (both dates appear on the letter), 3K9, folder 5, Miscellaneous Manuscript Letters (CAH).

70. Boatright and Owens, *Tales from the Derrick Floor,* 71.

71. Ibid., 69, 70 (quotation).

72. Ibid., 75.

73. Ibid., 76.

74. Parker, *Oil Field Medico,* 25, (1st quotation), 26 (3rd quotation), 34 (2nd quotation).

75. Ibid., 27 (1st quotation), 28, 29 (2nd quotation), 30–31.

76. Boatright and Owens, *Tales from the Derrick Floor,* 111.

77. Ibid., 67, 68 (quotations).

78. Slausen interview with Stiles, July 20, 1989, Beaumont, Tex., tape #61, p. 13.

79. Parker, *Oil Field Medico,* 28.

80. Boatright and Owens, *Tales from the Derrick Floor,* 67; C. Hamill, *We Drilled Spindletop!,* 35; C. Hamill interview with Owens, July 17, 1952, Kerrville, Tex., tape #17, pp. 11–12.

81. Slausen interview with Stiles, July 20, 1989, Beaumont, Tex., tape #61, p. 4.

82. Slausen interview with Stiles, June 14, 1989, Beaumont, Tex., tape #60, p. 16; ibid., July 20, 1989, tape #61, p. 8 (quotation).

83. Ibid., June 14, 1989, tape # 60, p. 14.

84. Ibid., July 20, 1989, tape #61, p. 12.

85. Ibid., July 20, 1989, tape #61, p. 15 (quotations). If the crew wanted to stir the mud for any reason, or to move it from one slush pit to another, they would shoot steam through a nozzle to mix it well. This made the slush pit hot. Other times the contents were cool, depending on what the crew was doing with it. "Blowing the boiler" to release steam also created a pool of very hot water. Arnold Pelt, Petroleum Well Services, telephone interview with Judith Walker Linsley, Sept. 7, 2000, Sour Lake, Tex.; B. A. Coe, interview with Judith Walker Linsley, Sept. 7, 2000, Kountze, Tex.

86. S. Webb interview with Owens, Sept. 1952, Fort Worth, Tex., tape #76, p. 36 (2nd quotation), 37, 38 (1st quotation); Boatright and Owens, *Tales from the Derrick Floor,* 109–111.

87. Slausen interview with Stiles, July 20, 1989, Beaumont, Tex., tape #60, p. 7 (quotation); Clark and Halbouty, *Spindletop,* 99; Estep, *And God Gave the Increase,* 73.

88. Minutes of First Baptist Church, Beaumont, Dec. 1902 (quotation); Deer in-

terview with Owens, July 7, 1952, Spindletop, Tex., tape #8, pp. 17–18.

89. Ray Asbury, *The South Park Story 1891–1971 and the Founding of Lamar University 1923–1941* (Fort Worth: Evans Press, 1972), 6.

90. Donahoe interview with Owens, Aug. 1, 1952, Batson, Tex., tape #23, pp. 5, 6 (2nd quotation), 7 (1st quotation).

91. Parker, *Oil Field Medico*, 38 (1st quotation); Mrs. Sam W. Webb, interview with William A. Owens, Sept., 1952, Fort Worth, Tex., tape #76, p. 40 (2nd quotation), Pioneers in Texas Oil Collection (CAH).

92. Pratt, *The Growth of a Refining Region*, 42.

Chapter Ten

1. Clark and Halbouty, *Spindletop*, 122–123, 135.

2. McDaniel and Dethloff, *Pattillo Higgins*, 74–75.

3. Clark and Halbouty, *Spindletop*, 134–140; Mellon and Sparkes, *Judge Mellon's Sons*, 153; Pratt, *The Growth of a Refining Region*, 37. Galey received $366,000 and some of Guffey's mining stock as his proceeds.

4. Clark and Halbouty, *Spindletop*, 139–140.

5. Ibid., 138–139.

6. Letter from George M. Craig to L. A. Leovy, Vice Chairman Gulf Oil Corporation, Apr. 13, 1937, and untitled typescript of the life of George M. Craig, written for his daughters, Apr. 1939 (Port Arthur Library).

7. Ibid.

8. Pratt, *The Growth of a Refining Region*, 44–45.

9. Mellon and Sparkes, *Judge Mellon's Sons*, 153; Clark and Halbouty, *Spindletop*, 134–135, 140, 142; James, *The Texaco Story*, 15; Pratt, *The Growth of a Refining Region*, 38, 44.

10. Clark and Halbouty, *Spindletop*, 143; James, *The Texaco Story*, 12.

11. A. Hamill, "The Lucas Gusher," 4.

12. Ibid.; King, *Joseph Stephen Cullinan*, 40; Clark and Halbouty, *Spindletop*, 144; James, *The Texaco Story*, 6.

13. King, *Joseph Stephen Cullinan*, 96.

14. James, *The Texaco Story*, 15; King, *Joseph Stephen Cullinan*, 95–96.

15. Pratt, *The Growth of a Refining Region*, 38; Clark and Halbouty, *Spindletop*, 145; Deer interview with Owens, July 7, 1952, Spindletop, Tex., tape #8, p. 4 (quotation).

16. Clark and Halbouty, *Spindletop*, 145; *Oil Investors' Journal*, 1 (May 24, 1901), 10.

17. Boatright and Owens, *Tales from the Derrick Floor*, 129.

18. Clark and Halbouty, *Spindletop*, 108; Deed Records of Jefferson County, vol. 5, May 23, 1901, pp. 245–246; King, *Joseph Stephen Cullinan*, 97–98; *Beaumont Age*, June 28, 1901 (quotation).

19. Clark and Halbouty, *Spindletop*, 108; Deed Records of Jefferson County, vol. 53, July 5, 1901, pp. 140–141.

20. King, *Joseph Stephen Cullinan*, 98–100; Clark and Halbouty, *Spindletop*, 108–109; Pratt, *The Growth of a Refining Region*, 43.

21. King, *Joseph Stephen Cullinan*, 92, 98, 99 (quotation).

22. Ibid., 92 (quotation); Clark and Halbouty, *Spindletop*, 110.

23. King, *Joseph Stephen Cullinan*, 100.

24. Ibid., 104–105; Clark and Halbouty, *Spindletop*, 143 (quotation), 150–151; letter from Craig to Donoghue, Apr. 10, 1937.

25. Clark and Halbouty, *Spindletop*, 143–154; James, *The Texaco Story*, 15–16; King, *Joseph Stephen Cullinan*, 100–101.

26. Pratt, *The Growth of a Refining Region*, 38, 40; James, *The Texaco Story*, 16–17; Clark and Halbouty, *Spindletop*, 148–149; King, *Joseph Stephen Cullinan*, 103–104.

27. *Port Arthur*, Work Projects Administration in the State of Texas, Federal Writers Project, American Guide Series (Houston: Anson Jones Press, 1940), 49–52, 144; King, *Joseph Stephen Cullinan*, 104–105; Pratt, *The Growth of a Refining Region*, 24, 48.

28. James, *The Texaco Story*, 12–13; King, *Joseph Stephen Cullinan*, 104; WPA, *Port Arthur*, 49 (quotation), 50–51.

29. James, *The Texaco Story*, 20–23; King, *Joseph Stephen Cullinan*, 133, 137; Clark and Halbouty, *Spindletop*, 154–156.

30. King, *Joseph Stephen Cullinan*, 18, 106–108.

31. Ibid., 111 (1st quotation); James, *The Texaco Story*, 18 (2nd quotation).

32. *Beaumont Enterprise*, Jan. 9, 1902; Clark and Halbouty, *Spindletop*, 161–163.

33. Clark and Halbouty, *Spindletop*, 160–164.

34. Ibid., 163–167.

35. W. J. McKie to Matthew Cartwright of Terrell, Tex., Apr. 2, 1901 (1st quotation), copy in possession of Jo Ann Stiles and the Cartwright Collection (CAH); 46. Larson and Porter, *A History of the Humble Oil and Refining Company*, 19 (2nd quotation).

36. *History of Magnolia Operating Division*, 22–25 (copy at TEM); *Beaumont Enterprise*, Jan. 4, 1902.

37. *History of Magnolia Operating Division*, 23 (1st quotation), 24–25; Clark and Halbouty, *Spindletop*, 175 (2nd quotation), 176; *Beaumont Enterprise*, Jan. 4, 1902.

38. *History of Magnolia Operating Division*, 23–25; Clark and Halbouty, *Spindletop*, 175–176; *Beaumont Enterprise*, Jan. 4, 1902 (quotation).

39. *History of Magnolia Operating Division*, 26 *(quotation)*; Pratt, *The Growth of a Refining Region*, 46–47.

40. Clark and Halbouty, *Spindletop*, 177–178; *History of Magnolia Operating Division*, 25–27, 29.

41. *History of Magnolia Operating Division*, 30–31; Clark and Halbouty, *Spindletop*, 178.

42. *Beaumont Daily Journal*, Dec. 30, 1902 (1st and 2nd quotations); Clark and Halbouty, *Spindletop*, 179 (3rd quotation).

43. *History of Magnolia Operating Division*, 37–38; Pratt, *The Growth of a Refining Region*, 47; Clark and Halbouty, *Spindletop*, 180–181.

44. Clark and Halbouty, *Spindletop*, 136; King, *Joseph Stephen Cullinan*, 152; James, *The Texaco Story*, 25.

45. King, *Joseph Stephen Cullinan*, 93; Yergin, *The Prize*, 54.

46. *Beaumont Enterprise*, Oct. 14, 1901 (quotation); *Oil Investors' Journal*, 1 (May 24, 1902), 6.

47. Clark and Halbouty, *Spindletop*, 183–185; Larson and Porter, *A History of the Humble Oil and Refining Company*, 24–28.

48. Clark and Halbouty, *Spindletop*, 185–186; Larson and Porter, *A History of the Humble Oil and Refining Company*, 24–28; Linsley and Rienstra, *Beaumont*, 34, 49.

49. Clark and Halbouty, *Spindletop*, 183–186; Larson and Porter, *A History of the Humble Oil and Refining Company*, 24–28; *Beaumont Journal*, Aug. 14, 1908 (1st quotation); *Beaumont Enterprise*, Aug. 16, 1908 (2nd quotation).

50. Clark and Halbouty, *Spindletop*, 183–184, 185 (2nd quotation), 186 (1st quotation); Larson and Porter, *A History of the Humble Oil and Refining Company*, 24–28; *Beaumont Journal*, Aug. 14, 1908; *Beaumont Enterprise*, Aug. 16, 1908. One Ervin house boarder, while not technically an oil man, nevertheless came to wield huge influence in the oil industry. Holland Reavis came to Beaumont to cover Spindletop for a St. Louis newspaper and stayed to found the *Oil Investors' Journal*. With the motto, "The Truth and Nothing but the Truth Concerning the Beaumont Field and Other Southwestern Oil fields," Reavis's publication focused on "legitimate journalism" and promised "a strict policy of honesty and accuracy in its news reports." The *Oil Investors' Journal* hoped to become a "permanent institution," and it did, eventually evolving into the highly respected *Oil and Gas Journal*. Clark and Halbouty, 186; *Oil Investors' Journal*, 1 (May 24, 1902), 1 (footnote quotations).

51. Larson and Porter, *A History of the Humble Oil and Refining Company*, 55; Clark and Halbouty, *Spindletop*, 199–200.

52. Daniels interview with Owens, July 3, 1952, Sour Lake, Tex., tape # 22, p. 18.

53. Clark and Halbouty, *Spindletop*, 148 (quotation); Clark and Halbouty, *Spindletop*, 154–155, 188; King, *Joseph Stephen Cullinan*, 115.

54. Bryant interview with Owens, July 29, 1952, Sour Lake, Tex., tape #27, pp. 16 (quotation), 17.

55. S. Webb interview with Owens, Sept. 1952, Fort Worth, Tex., tape #76, pp. 6 (quotation), 24.

56. Boatright and Owens, *Tales from the Derrick Floor*, 121, 124; S. Webb interview with Owens, Sept. 1952, Fort Worth, Tex., tape #76, p. 14, 15, 19–20.

57. S. Webb interview with Owens, Sept. 1952, Fort Worth, Tex., tape #76, p. 23.

58. King, *Joseph Stephen Cullinan*, 115–118; Clark and Halbouty, *Spindletop*, 188, 196–197.

59. Boatright and Owens, *Tales from the Derrick Floor*, 125 (quotation), 126–127.

60. A. Hamill interview with Owens, Sept. 2, 1952, Tulsa, Okla., tape #85, p. 18 (1st quotation); C. Hamill interview with Owens, July 17, 1952, Kerrville, Tex., tape #18, pp. 3 (2nd quotation), 4 (3rd quotation), 5–6.

61. King, *Joseph Stephen Cullinan*, 117–118; C. Hamill interview with Owens, July 17, 1952, Kerrville, Tex., tape #18, p. 4 (quotation).

62. King, *Joseph Stephen Cullinan*, 92, 98–99; Clark and Halbouty, *Spindletop*, 108–110; A. Hamill interview with Owens, Sept. 2, 1952, Tulsa, Okla., tape #85, pp. 2, 33–34.

63. H. P. Nichols, interview with Mody Boatright, Oct. 11, 1952, Tyler, Tex., tape #82, p. 3.

64. A. Hamill interview with Owens, Sept. 2, 1952, Tulsa, Okla., tape #85, pp. 18, 19–20 (quotation).

65. Ibid., 18–20, 29; C. Hamill interview with Owens, July 17, 1952, Kerrville, Tex., tape #18, pp. 10, 16 (1st quotation), 21–22. An advertisement for Mission Petroleum, a company apparently founded by Walter Sharp and counting among its executive officers two of his sons and oil pioneer Ed Prather, stated that Walter Sharp was the first driller to use mud instead of water for a rotary rig, and that the occasion was before Spindletop, when the Hamills were drilling for him in Corsicana. *Oil and Gas Journal*, Golden Anniversary Issue (May, 1951). This, of course, contradicts Curt Hamill's 1952 interview. C. Hamill interview with Owens, July 17, 1952, Kerrville, Tex., tape #16, 21 (2nd quotation), 22.

66. C. Hamill interview with Owens, July 17, 1952, Kerrville, Tex., tape #18, p. 10 (1st quotation); A. Hamill interview with Owens, Sept. 2, 1952, Tulsa, Okla., tape #85, p. 29 (2nd quotation); Owen, *Trek of the Oil Finders*, 135 (3rd quotation).

67. Deer interview with Owens, July 7, 1952, Spindletop, Tex., tape #8, p. 24 (1st–3rd quotations); C. Hamill interview with Owens, July 17, 1952, Kerrville, Tex., tape #18, p. 9 (4th quotation).

68. C. Hamill interview with Owens, July 17, 1952, Kerrville, Tex., tape #18, pp. 9–10.

69. *History of Magnolia Operating Division*, 30 (1st quotation); Clark and Halbouty, *Spindletop*, 178 (2nd quotation).

70. *Beaumont Enterprise*, June 21, 1901; C. Hamill interview with Owens, July 17, 1952, Kerrville, Tex., tape #18, pp. 18, 19 (quotations); James, *The Texaco Story*, 21, 24–25; Clark and Halbouty, *Spindletop*, 112.

Chapter Eleven

1. Jack Donahue, *Wildcatter: The Story of Michel T. Halbouty and the Search for Oil* (New York: McGraw-Hill, 1979), 92.

2. *New York Journal*, Aug. 18, 1901 (quotation); Chernow, *Titan*, 431.

3. Rundell, *Early Texas Oil*, 135ff; Clark and Halbouty, *Spindletop*, 269.

4. Pratt, *The Growth of a Refining Region*, 54.

5. Ibid., 16–17, 29, 54–56.

6. Larson and Porter, *A History of the Humble Oil and Refining Company*, 19, 47 (quotation), citing Rister, *Oil!*, 70, 74, 78 ff.

7. Asbury, *The South Park Story*, 14–16.

8. Clark and Halbouty, *Spindletop*, 224–225.

9. Linsley and Rienstra, *Beaumont*, 92–93.

10. Because of sulphur mining on the hill and the resulting subsidence, the monument was moved in the mid-1950s by the Texas Gulf Sulphur Company to a site on Sulphur Drive, near the field, then again in 1978 to its present location at the Spindletop/Gladys City Boomtown Museum. Boyce House Papers folder, in Pioneers in Texas Oil Collection (CAH).

11. D. Ryan Smith, "Spindletop's 50th Anniversary Celebration," *The Texas Gulf*

Historical and Biographical Record, 32 (Nov., 1996), 62.

12. Ibid., 65–66.

13. Ibid., 67.

14. Ibid., 68–70.

15. Ibid.; Clark and Halbouty, *Spindletop*, 268–273.

16. Linsley and Rienstra, *Beaumont, 110*.

17. Sanders, *Captain George Washington O'Brien*, 31; Judith Linsley and Ellen Rienstra, "George Washington O'Brien," *The New Handbook of Texas*, IV, 1098–1099.

18. Rioux, "Biographical Sketch of George Washington Carroll," 18–19; Linsley and Rienstra, "George Washington Carroll," 990.

19. Jessica Foy and Judith Linsley, *The McFaddin-Ward House* (Austin: Texas State Historical Association, 1992), 38 (quotation), 39–40.

20. King, *Joseph Stephen Cullinan*, 184–193, 214.

21. John H. Galey II, Neosho, Missouri, to Jo Ann Stiles, Mar. 25, 2000; Clark and Halbouty, *Spindletop*, 131–142.

22. Clark and Halbouty, *Spindletop*, 63 (1st quotation); Mellon and Sparkes, *"Judge Mellon's Sons*, 159 (2nd quotation).

23. Galey to Stiles, Mar. 25, 2000.

24. Clark and Halbouty, *Spindletop*, 142.

25. Mellon and Sparkes, *"Judge Mellon's Sons*, 149, 261 (quotation).

26. A. Hamill interview with Owens, Sept. 2, 1952, Tulsa, Okla., tape #85, pp. 2, 12–15.

27. Ibid., 3.

28. C. Hamill interview with Owens, July 17, 1952, Kerrville, Tex., tape 16, p. 1 (quotation), tape #17, pp. 11–12.

29. A. Hamill interview with Owens, Sept. 2, 1952, Tulsa, Okla., tape #85, p. 35 (quotation).

30. McDaniel and Dethloff, *Pattillo Higgins*, 75–76, 83–90, 99–119.

31. At the time of the Spindletop Centennial Celebration, Gladys Higgins Forrester still lived in San Antonio. For other Higgins family information, see Etienne-Gray, "Pattillo Higgins," 594–595.

32. McDaniel and Dethloff, *Pattillo Higgins*, 155.

33. McBeth, *Pioneering the Gulf Coast*, 51.

34. Rickard, "Anthony F. Lucas, and the Beaumont Gusher," 894.

35. DeGolyer, "Anthony F. Lucas and Spindletop," 86.

36. McBeth, *Pioneering the Gulf Coast*, 51.

37. Anthony Lucas, Washington D.C., to Allen W. Hamill, Tulsa, Okla., July 18, 1918; AFL to AWH, Dec. 28, 1919; AWH to AFL, Jan. 10, 1920 (quotation); letters in possession of Al's son, Allen W. Hamill Jr. of Houston, Tex.

38. Copy of will in Tyrrell Historical Library, Beaumont. Section V (1st quotation), Section VIII, # 3 (2nd quotation).

39. "A Biography of Captain Anthony Francis Lucas, 1855–1921," no author given, dateline Washington, D.C., Dec. 14, 1944, typescript (CAH).

40. Wooster, "Anthony F. Lucas," 326; DeGolyer, "Anthony F. Lucas and Spindletop," 87.

41. C. Hamill interview with Owens, July 17, 1952, Kerrville, Tex., tape #18, p. 2.

42. DeGolyer, "Anthony F. Lucas and Spindletop," 85.

43. Clark and Halbouty, *Spindletop*, 270.

44. *Kansas City Star,* Apr. 21, 1901, Lucas Scrapbook.

45. Parker, *Oil Field Medico*, 139.

46. Rioux, "George Washington Carroll: A Biography," 63.

47. Clark and Halbouty, *Spindletop*, 249.

48. Joseph A. Pratt, "Spindletop: Fueling the Nation," paper given at Beaumont History Conference, Jan. 8, 2000, Beaumont, Tex.

49. Warner, *Texas Oil and Gas Since 1543*, 40.

50. Yergin, *The Prize*, 781.

51. Roger M. Olien, "The Oil and Gas Industry," *The New Handbook of Texas*, IV, 1128.

52. Yergin, *The Prize*, 781.

53. Morris Albert Adelman, *The Genie Out of the Bottle: World Oil Since 1970* (Cambridge: MIT Press, 1995), 11.

54. James C. Gentry, president of Gentry Petroleum Corporation, and Alan Balser, president of Palaura Exploration Company, two of the Four Horsemen, telephone and personal interviews with Jo Ann Stiles, Jan. 2001; Herbert Hunt and other officials of Petro-Hunt, interviews with John Burnett and Wayne Bell of National Public Radio, Dec., 2000; Joe Lucas, project manager for Centennial Oil Company, interview with Jo Ann Stiles and Ellen Rienstra, Mar. 6, 2001.

INDEX

Illustrations are indicated by boldfaced page numbers.

A

A. Broussard, Undertaker, Livery and Boarding Stable: **120**

Adams, Lige: land at Spindletop, 129, 130

Adelman, M. A.: 232

African American(s): P. Higgins harasses, 28; W. Henry, 97, 260n; reaction to Lucas Gusher, 111; laborers at Spindletop, 156; in early oil industry, 168–173; in lumber industry, 168–169; mule drovers, **169**, 172; in oil industry, 169–173; at Spindletop, 169–172, 273n; O. Blanchette and U. Hebert, **170**, 170-171; in the Big Thicket, 172; in Sour Lake, 172, 176; in Batson, 172, 176; "Negro quarters" in Batson, 172; in Saratoga, 172–173; bordellos in Sour Lake, Batson, 176; pulling skiff in Beaumont, 190

Alabama: 148; Lucas in, 55

Alaska: 153; gold in, 130

alcohol: in Beaumont, 27, 142–144, 178; A. Lucas and, 117, 265n, 266n; at Gladys City, 156; at Spindletop, 158; in oil fields, 173; in Saratoga, 173, 176–177; drunken fights, 176–177; workers drinking, 178. *See also* prohibition; saloons; temperance; Women's Christian Temperance Union

Algeria: A. Lucas in, 226

alligators: in Big Thicket boomtowns, 163

America: 76, 185

American Institute of Mining (and Metallurgical) Engineers: 258n, 262n, 263n; A. Lucas's membership in, 227

American Lumberman: on Lucas Gusher, 117

American Salt Company: 59

Anahuac, Texas: 204

Angelina County, Texas: early oil leasing in, 17

Angelina River: conjunction with Neches, **27**

"Ann's Place": Batson bordello, 176

Anse la Butte, Louisiana: salt mining at, 59; A. Lucas finds petroleum at, 59, 60

anticline(s): 48, 49, 64; arch of tilted rock strata, 40; theory developed by P. Higgins, 40, 60, 64

antitrust laws: 72, 130, 186, 202. *See also* Waters-Pierce Oil Company

Appomattox: cease-fire at, 15, 26

Armageddon: 165

Armstrong, Will: Beaumont during oil boom, 144

Ashley, Grace: fighting, 175

asphalt: used in Ur, Mesopotamia, 5

assumed names: *See* nicknames

Atlanta Constitution: erroneous story on A. Lucas, 147

Aubey, Victor: A. F.G. Lucas's teacher, 264n

Austin, Texas: 50

Austria: petroleum in, 6; A. Lucas's birthplace, 53

automobile industry: Spindletop oil used as fuel for, 3–4

automobiles: racing, 204; Winton, 207

Avery Island (Petit Anse), Louisiana: salt domes at, 56– 57; salt mining at, 57

B

back-pressure (check) valve: invention of, 94–95, 221. *See also* technology, oil field

bailer: 101, 261n. *See also* technology, oil field

Baku, Russian fields at: 3; export of oil from, 5; source of foreign crude at turn of century, 22; Drooja "fountain," gusher at, 266n

Balser, Alan: Dallas oilman, one of "Four Horsemen," 232

Bank of Bacchus Saloon: D. Dowling's Houston headquarters for oil activities, 17

Baptist church: 156; mission at Spindletop and Riverside, 182–183

Barbers Hill, Texas: oil field at, 211

Barfield, Plummer: remembers Lucas Gusher, 111; undertaker work in Batson, 177–178

Barrett, Lynis Taliaferro: drills Texas's first producing oil well, 17

Barton, Clara: relief after Galveston Storm, 91

Batson (Prairie), Texas: 174, 175, 184, 173n; oil in, 152; oil boom, 159–160; boomtown life, 160–163, 182–183; Thanksgiving in, **161**; saloons, 162, 173; poisonous gas, 167–168; race relations, 172; law enforcement in, 175–176, 177; prostitution in, 176; barbecue, **179**; childbirth in, 179; entertainment, 182; "sawmill marriages," 183; oil field, 211, 221; Crosby House Hotel branch in, 273n. *See also* Big Thicket

Baumé gravity: degree of oil density, 72, 255n